Breaking Japanese Diplomatic Codes

David Sissons and D Special Section during the Second World War

Breaking Japanese Diplomatic Codes

David Sissons and D Special Section
during the Second World War

Edited by Desmond Ball
and Keiko Tamura

ASIAN STUDIES SERIES MONOGRAPH 4

E PRESS

Published by ANU E Press
The Australian National University
Canberra ACT 0200, Australia
Email: anuepress@anu.edu.au
This title is also available online at http://epress.anu.edu.au

National Library of Australia Cataloguing-in-Publication entry

Title: Breaking Japanese diplomatic codes : David Sissons and D Special Section during the Second World War / edited by Desmond Ball and Keiko Tamura.

ISBN: 9781925021073 (paperback) 9781925021080 (ebook)

Subjects: Sissons, D. C. S. (David Carlisle Stanley), 1925-2006.
Allied Forces. Southwest Pacific Area. Allied Intelligence Bureau
World War, 1939-1945--Cryptography.
World War, 1939-1945--Secret service--Australia.
World War, 1939-1945--Electronic intelligence--Australia.
World War, 1939-1945--Military intelligence--Australia.
World War, 1939-1945--Japan.
Cryptography--Australia--History.
Military intelligence--Australia--History--20th century.

Other Authors/Contributors:
Ball, Desmond, 1947- editor.
Tamura, Keiko, editor.

Dewey Number: 940.548694

All rights reserved. No part of this publication may be reproduced, stored in a retrieval system or transmitted in any form or by any means, electronic, mechanical, photocopying or otherwise, without the prior permission of the publisher.

Cover design and layout by ANU E Press

Cover image: David Sissons about 18 years old before joining the Army in 1944. Photo courtesy of Mrs Bronwen Sissons.

This edition © 2013 ANU E Press

Contents

Preface ix
Acknowledgements. xi
Acronyms and Abbreviations xiii
Chapter 1. David Sissons and D Special Section 1
    Desmond Ball

Chapter 2. The Diplomatic Special Intelligence Section:
    Its Origins and History 15
    D.C.S. Sissons

Chapter 3. Japanese Diplomatic Cyphers: Cryptographic
    Survey Report Of Special Intelligence Section HQ
    Australian Military Forces Melbourne 1946 53

Annexes: Interviews, Correspondence and Notes

Annex 1. David Sissons to Alan Stripp, 9 November 1988. 105
Annex 2. Notes from an Interview with with Professor Arthur
    Dale Trendall by Desmond Ball on 10 May 1990. 115
Annex 3. David Sissons to Ian Smith, 3 August 1990 119
Annex 4. Ian Smith to David Sissons, 8 August 1990 125
Annex 5. Interview of Dr A. P. Treweek by David Sissons,
    11 October 1990 131
Annex 6. Ronald Bond, Notes on Sissons (3 August 1990),
    Smith (8 August 1990) and Treweek (11 October 1990),
    undated but probably late 1990.. 135
Annex 7. David Sissons to Desmond Ball, 11 October 1993. 143
Annex 8. Steve Mason to David Sissons, 26 June 1994 145
Annex 9. Steve Mason to Desmond Ball, 7 July 1995 149
Annex 10. Ronald Bond to Desmond Ball, 29 September 1994. 153
Annex 11. David Sissons to Desmond Ball, 22 May 1996 157
Annex 12. David Sissons to Desmond Ball, 9 September 1996. 163
Annex 13. David Sissons to Desmond Ball, 16 October 1996. 165
Annex 14. David Sissons to Desmond Ball, 23 March 1998 167
Annex 15. David Sissons to Kenneth McKay, 9 November 2004. 169
Annex 16. Notes on the Breaking of GEAM Using the
    'Winds – Set-Up' Message. 175
Annex 17. David Sissons to Kenneth McKay, 28 November 2004. 185
Annex 18. David Sissons to Kenneth McKay, 19 December 2004. 189

David Sissons at his graduation with BA from Melbourne University in 1950

Source: Photo courtesy of Mrs Bronwen Sissons

Preface

This volume is part of a larger project intended to make available to a broader readership the research activities and lesser known publications of David C.S. Sissons, a Fellow in the Department of International Relations at The Australian National University from 1961 until his retirement in 1990. This project was instigated by Professor Arthur Stockwin, Emeritus Fellow at St Antony's College at Oxford University, who was Sissons's first PhD student (1961–64) and Keiko Tamura who co-edited this volume.

Sissons was productive throughout his academic career, but much of his work was either never completed or failed to find its way into major journals or hard covers. He left numerous unpublished, but almost publishable, papers, not counting others that were published only in relatively obscure places. He was an extreme perfectionist, too often prepared to sacrifice an important article for want of the last detail, which was sometimes untraceable anyway. He expended great effort in composing correspondence, memos and notes, extensively recapitulating his research findings while articulating areas where he sought further information, and which amount essentially to brief research notes in their own right.

Sissons's research, over 40 years, was concerned with various aspects of Australian–Japanese relations. The greater part was devoted to the history of Australian–Japanese diplomatic relations, but he retained a strong particular interest in the Australian war crimes investigations and trials that ran between 1942–51. He served as a court interpreter in the Australian trials at Morotai in early 1946, and as an interpreter with the British Commonwealth Occupation Forces (BCOF) in Yamaguchi in 1946–47. His research covered a myriad of matters, including such diverse topics as Japanese immigration to Australia; Japanese pearl divers in northern Australia; 'Japanese acrobatic troupes touring Australasia, 1867–1900'; 'Japanese prostitutes in Australia, 1887–1916'; Japanese military intentions towards Australia at the outset of the Pacific dimension of the Second World War in 1941–42; and, the breakout of Japanese prisoners of war at Cowra in 1944. His work on the Diplomatic Special Section (D Special Section) during the Second World War, the subject of this volume, highlights a critically important aspect of the relationship between Japan and Australia at its most adversarial. It is anticipated that his work in these other areas will be collected and edited for subsequent publication by this press.

Sissons had planned to publish an account of the role of the D Special Section, together with a top-secret report on its cryptanalytical activities that was written after the end of the war, and which he managed to obtain after immense perseverance. This project was not quite finalised when he died in October 2006.

He continued to explore particular aspects of the Special Section's activities until his incapacitation, having planned to publish further work on the subject. This material had lain dormant since 2006, until resuscitated by Stockwin and Tamura in 2011.

D Special Section was the most secret of the Allied code-breaking organisations in Australia during the Second World War. Its primary role was breaking the codes and cyphers that were used in Japanese diplomatic communications. The British and Australian governments sought to maintain the secrecy concerning the Section's activities and, indeed, its very existence, for half a century after the war ended.

By the 1980s, 40 years after the war, Sissons, on the other hand, was persuaded that it was time for the story of the Special Section to be told. The US authorities had already broken ranks with their counterparts in London and Canberra, and had declassified large quantities of documents concerning the subject, including actual decrypts of Japanese diplomatic traffic, which during the war had been called *Magic*. This book is the product of his quest.

It consists of four parts. First, an essay by Desmond Ball describes Sissons's quest and outlines its historical importance. Second is the unpublished account of 'the origins and history' of D Special Section, which Sissons wrote in 2006. Third is the postwar *Report of Special Intelligence Section, HQ Australian Military Forces, Melbourne [on] Japanese Diplomatic Cyphers: Cryptographic Survey*, as lightly edited by Sissons in 2006. The fourth part is an Annex consisting of notes, interviews, and correspondence concerning D Special Section and its activities, either written by Sissons, or his colleagues in response to his entreaties, or otherwise directly related to his endeavours. It is an invaluable record, contributing immensely to appreciation of the critically important role that interception and decryption of Japanese diplomatic communications played during the war.

Acknowledgements

The editors are grateful to Professor Arthur Stockwin, who encouraged us to produce a separate volume devoted to the story of David Sissons and his research and writings concerning Diplomatic Special Section (D Special Section).

We are indebted to Mrs Bronwen Sissons, David's widow. She has been supportive of this project from the outset. She provided us with details of David's matriculation and first-year university subjects and results, personal papers relevant to his recruitment and service during the Second World War, and the photographs of him reproduced on the front cover and frontispiece of this volume.

David Horner, Professor of Australian Defence History in the Strategic and Defence Studies Centre at The Australian National University, provided us with advice and material throughout this project. We are grateful to Professor John Mack, Honorary Associate Professor in the School of Mathematics and Statistics at the University of Sydney, for his assistance with respect to technical aspects of D Special Section's cryptographic activities.

We would like to thank Ms Meredith Thatcher, formerly a research assistant in the Strategic and Defence Studies Centre, who assisted Sissons with editorial matters in 2006 during the preparation of his essay on 'The Origins and History' of D Special Section and the postwar report on the Section for eventual publication. We also wish to thank Ms Oanh Collins, who word processed several handwritten pieces of correspondence and notes for inclusion in the Annex; Mr James Ball, who scanned most of the materials in the Annexes; and Ms Jenny Sheehan, Ms Kay Dancey, Ms Alyx Russell and Mr Tyrone Mason of the Multimedia Services Unit, College of Asia and the Pacific at The Australian National University.

We acknowledge the assistance of the Australian War Memorial, specifically with respect to the reproduction of extracts from the war diaries of the 52nd Special Wireless Section for March 1943 (AWM52 AIF and Militia Unit War Diaries, 1939–45, Item:7/39/3 March 1943) and May 1944 (AWM52 AIF and Militia Unit War Diaries, 1939–1945, Item: 7/39/19 January – June 1944).

We are also grateful to Dr Craig Reynolds, Chair of the Asian Studies Committee of ANU E Press, for shepherding us through the publication process.

Desmond Ball and Keiko Tamura
The Australian National University
Canberra
September 2013

Acronyms and Abbreviations

ADMI	Assistant Director of Military Intelligence
AIC	Australian [Army] Intelligence Corps
AIF	Australian Imperial Force
AMF	Australian Military Forces
ANU	Australian National University
ASWG	Australian Special Wireless Group
ASWS	Australian Special Wireless Section
AWAS	Australian Women's Army Service
CAS	Chief of the Air Staff
CGS	Chief of the General Staff
CNS	Chief of Naval Staff
CO	Commanding Officer
CQMS	Company Quarter Master Sergeant
CSM	Company Sergeant Major
FECB	Far East Combined Bureau
DMI	Directorate of Military Intelligence
DMO&I	Director of Military Operations & Intelligence
DNI	Director of Naval Intelligence
D/R	Dispatch Rider
DSD	Defence Signals Directorate
FRUMEL	Fleet Radio Unit, Melbourne
GC&CS	Government Code & Cypher School
GEAM	Greater East Asia Ministry
GHQ	General Headquarters
GSO	General Staff Officer
HF DF	High-frequency direction-finding
IJN	Imperial Japanese Navy
Ix	Intelligence, Branch x
JAA	HINOKI Machine Cypher [also known as PURPLE]
JBC	Foreign Office Cypher Book No. 1
JIB	Joint Intelligence Bureau
LAA	Light Anti-aircraft Regiment
LHQ	Land Headquarters
MI	Military Intelligence

MIS	Military Intelligence Service
NAA	National Archives of Australia
NSA	National Security Agency
OC	Officer Commanding
POW	Prisoner of War
PMG	Postmaster General
RAN	Royal Australian Navy
SIB	Special Intelligence Bureau
SIGINT	Signals intelligence
SWPA	South West Pacific Area
UKUSA	United Kingdom, United States of America (Communication Intelligence) Agreement
USN	United States Navy

Chapter 1. David Sissons and D Special Section

Desmond Ball

During the Second World War, Australia hosted three organisations concerned with the cryptanalysis of intercepted Japanese radio communications. The activities of two of these, respectively concerned with Imperial Japanese Navy (IJN) signals and Japanese army and air force signals, have been widely described and discussed by historians and veterans since the 1970s.[1]

This volume, which has been produced primarily as a result of painstaking efforts by David Sissons, provides a comprehensive and authoritative account of the third, Diplomatic Special Section (D Special Section) of the Australian Military Forces HQ in Melbourne, which was responsible for cryptographic activities concerning Japanese diplomatic communications. D Special Section and its activities remained a closely guarded secret for 20 years after the navy and army stories became public. The Australian Government consistently refused to admit that it ever intercepted diplomatic communications, even in wartime. After all, it was and still is a signatory to Vienna and Geneva conventions on diplomatic relations under which 'the host country must permit and protect free communication between the diplomats of the mission and their home country'. Fortunately, the US cryptological authorities have been much less sanctimonious.

The Royal Australian Navy's (RAN) involvement in signals intelligence (SIGINT) activities began in 1940 when two high frequency (HF) radio interception and direction-finding (HF DF) stations became operational, located at HMAS *Coonawarra* near Darwin and HMAS *Harman* outside Canberra. These stations operated as part of the Royal Navy (RN) component of the Far East Combined Bureau (FECB), then based in Singapore and itself a component of Britain's SIGINT organisation, the Government Code & Cypher School (GC&CS). Paymaster-Commander Eric Nave, RN, set up a small cryptanalytic organisation in Melbourne, which analysed Japanese naval traffic from the Mandated Islands and Japanese commercial shipping traffic that was collected at *Coonawarra* and *Harman*, as well as some Japanese diplomatic traffic. In early 1942, the US navy's SIGINT unit, codenamed Cast, was evacuated in three tranches from the Philippines to Melbourne. It was established there on the middle floor of the

---

1   Desmond Ball and David Horner, *Breaking the Codes: Australia's KGB Network, 1944–1950* (Sydney: Allen & Unwin, 1998), chapter 4.

heavily guarded Monterey flats in Queens Road, South Yarra, near Albert Park. Soon formally known as FRUMEL (Fleet Radio Unit, Melbourne), it effectively subsumed the RAN's SIGINT organisation.

The Australian army's SIGINT organisation was the Australian Special Wireless Group (ASWG), which established intercept stations at Coomalie Creek, about 80 kilometres south of Darwin and initially maintained by the 51st Special Wireless Section; Kalinga near Brisbane, maintained by the 53rd Special Wireless Section and, from May 1943, the HQ of the ASWG; and, Mornington, south of Melbourne, maintained by the 52nd Special Wireless Section. Elements of the 55th Section moved to New Guinea in July 1942. Soon after General Douglas MacArthur arrived in Melbourne, it had been agreed to form a combined Allied organisation called Central Bureau. It was established on 15 April 1942 in a large house, Cranleigh, at 225 Domain Road in South Yarra and moved to Brisbane in September 1942. The bureau was responsible for cryptanalysis of Japanese army and Japanese army air force signals, with material collected by both US army and ASWG stations.

Both the RAN and the army began fledgling activities with respect to Japanese diplomatic communications before Japan attacked Pearl Harbor in December 1941. In the case of the navy, Nave's Special Intelligence Bureau (SIB) had worked on diplomatic cyphers through 1940–41. In the case of the army, in early 1940 the Military Intelligence staff at Eastern Command in Sydney formed a small group of mathematicians and classicists from Sydney University to practise code-breaking on Japanese consular traffic. In 1941 the group succeeded in breaking the Japanese LA code, a low-grade consular code. In early 1940 a Diplomatic and Press Section was formed in Melbourne, with an intercept station at Park Orchards that was maintained by the army's 5th Special Wireless Section. In mid-1941 several members of the Sydney University group were called up and posted to Nave's SIB; the first of these was Dr Athanasius P. Treweek. Others, including Professor Arthur Dale Trendall, joined it soon after the outbreak of the Pacific war.[2] When FRUMEL began operations, the SIB joined it in the Monterey Building. The uniformed members went to the middle floor to work on Japanese naval traffic and the civilian members moved to a one-bedroom flat on the top floor to concentrate on diplomatic traffic.

In November 1942, the diplomatic group was transferred from RAN control to the army, moved to the second floor of 'A' Block in Victoria Barracks, and named D Special Section. From January 1942, until his return to Sydney in June 1944,

---

2   Peter Donovan and John Mack, 'Sydney University, T.G. Room and Codebreaking in WWII', part 1, *Australian Mathematical Society Gazette*, vol. 29, no. 2, 2002; and Peter Donovan and John Mack, 'Sydney University, T.G. Room and Codebreaking in WWII', part 2, *Australian Mathematical Society Gazette*, vol. 29, no. 3, 2002.

the section was headed by Trendall, Professor of Greek at Sydney University.[3] Intercepts were initially obtained by the station at Park Orchards. In April 1942 a station was established at Ferny Creek, in the Dandenong Ranges, specifically to intercept Japanese diplomatic traffic for Trendall's section. In August the station was moved to Bonegilla, near Albury-Wodonga, where the 52nd Special Wireless Section was formed. It was staffed mainly by women of the Australian Women's Army Service (AWAS). It moved to Mornington in November 1943.

David Sissons

Sissons matriculated in 1942 from Scotch College in Melbourne, where he was dux in Latin and also received high marks in mathematics. He entered Melbourne University, where he planned to major in Classics, at the beginning of 1943. At the end of his first year, however, following his 18th birthday on 21 December 1943, he was called up for active service and 'marched in' for full-time duty on 27 June 1944. He spent eight weeks at a recruit training camp at Cowra in western New South Wales, not far from a Japanese prisoner of war camp near the town. Sissons was there on 5 August when the Japanese prisoners attempted a mass breakout; during the escape and subsequent recapture of the POWs, four Australian soldiers and 231 Japanese soldiers died and 108 prisoners were wounded. Sissons was among the young recruits who were employed in rounding up the escapees and he went on to receive seven months Japanese language training. He was posted to D Special Section as a linguist/translator in April 1945, where he worked until September 1945.

In 1978, my colleague David Horner and I published articles on Australia and Allied SIGINT during the Second World War in which we noted the existence of a unit concerned with cryptanalysis of Japanese diplomatic traffic.[4] I had found a reference in US Congressional testimony on the Pearl Harbor attack in December 1941, published in 1946, which stated that: 'The Australians had a small Communications Intelligence Organization and in December 1941 they were intercepting Japanese diplomatic radio traffic and reading messages in the J-19 system'.[5] It also noted that the interception stations in Australia often picked up transmissions that 'skipped over' other US and British intercept stations in Southeast Asia, 'particularly if the Japanese were using frequencies optimised for communications with their Embassies in Washington, Rio and

---

3 R.S. Merrillees, 'Professor A.D. Trendall and his Band of Classical Cryptographers', Working Paper No. 355, Strategic and Defence Studies Centre, The Australian National University, Canberra, January 2001.
4 Desmond J. Ball, 'Allied Intelligence Cooperation Involving Australia During World War II', *Australian Outlook*, vol. 32, no. 3, December 1978, pp. 299–309; and, D.M. Horner, 'Special Intelligence in the South-West Pacific Area in World War II', *Australian Outlook*, vol. 32, no. 3, December 1978, pp. 310–27.
5 US Congress, Hearings before the Joint Committee on the Investigation of the Pearl Harbor Attack, *Pearl Harbor Attack* (Washington, D.C.: US Government Printing Office, 1946), part 8, p. 3614.

Buenos Aires'.[6] Sissons was excited about our revelation, and was energised to compile as much information as he could about the history and activities of his former unit.

He assembled everything he could find on the public record, including relevant records held by the National Archives of Australia and the Australian War Memorial (AWM) in Canberra. Somewhat disappointed with his scant and fragmented findings, he decided to enlist the assistance of others who had been involved in one way or another with D Special Section, and Japanese diplomatic traffic more generally.

Fittingly, he began with Alan Stripp, a famous wartime cryptanalyst who had worked on Japanese cyphers at both the GC&CS HQ at Bletchley Park and one of its major 'outstations' in Delhi in India. He published a detailed account of 'breaking Japanese codes' in October 1987 and, in late 1988, had just completed a book on this subject which included a survey of the codes and cyphers used by the Japanese, including several systems used for diplomatic traffic (such as J-19, PURPLE and Greater East Asian Ministry (GEAM)).[7] In a long letter to Stripp in 1988, Sissons explained what he knew at that time about the interception of Japanese diplomatic traffic in Australia. He attached to this letter a page from the war diary of the 52nd Special Wireless Section categorising the 4,457 Japanese diplomatic messages that had been intercepted at Bonegilla in March 1943, and five pages from the war diary summarising the 3,348 intercepts taken at Mornington from 1 to 31 May 1944, which he had found in the AWM. This letter and the attachments are reproduced as the beginning entry in the Annexes to this volume. (See Annex 1)

In the early 1990s Sissons initiated correspondence with several of his former colleagues from D Special Section. His letters were extremely detailed and meticulous, sometimes amounting to several thousand words, often with annexes. In his inimitable way, he usually followed up with further questions to clarify names, events, dates or other details. His principal interlocutors were Ronald Bond, Ian Smith, Eric Barnes, Kenneth McKay, and Mary Stewart, a member of the office staff from November 1942 to September 1943. He also interviewed Treweek in 1990.[8] Some of that correspondence, together with the interview with Treweek, contains information of immense use to historians and cryptanalysts, and is also reproduced later in this volume.

---

6   Ibid., p. 3615.
7   Alan Stripp, 'Breaking Japanese Codes', *Intelligence and National Security*, vol. 2, no. 4, October 1987, pp. 135–50; and, Alan Stripp, *Codebreaker in the Far East* (London: Frank Cass & Co, 1989), chapter 7.
8   It should be noted that, along with his unique insights, Treweek was surprisingly disparaging about two of his colleagues, mathematicians T.G. Room and R.J. Lyons. They were the two initial members of the army's Sydney University group, who had joined Nave's SIB in August 1941. Lyons returned to Sydney University in late 1942, but Room transferred to MacArthur's Central Bureau, where he headed the unit working on Japanese meteorological codes, which alerted the Allies to the targets of forthcoming Japanese air raids in

In addition to those who had worked in the Special Section, Sissons corresponded with Steve Mason, a former sergeant who spent the war with the ASWG and who worked at the Mornington station from December 1945 until his discharge in October 1946. His accounts of the ASWG activities at Park Orchards, Bonegilla and Mornington, in letters to Sissons and me comprise a unique historical record (Annexes 8, 9).

He also began a systematic search in the US National Archives, where most of the Japanese diplomatic messages, known as *Magic*, that were intercepted throughout the war had been released for public access. In early 1986 he engaged a research assistant, Emma Craswell, to scour this archival material. He was excited to find a file entitled 'Copies of Messages Supplied by Australia with Clarifying Notes', dated 6 April 1943. He concluded to his absolute satisfaction that many of the *Magic* intercepts had originated at the Mornington station and been processed by D Special Section. Selections of his correspondence concerning his *Magic* searches in the United States are also reproduced later in this volume.

I joined Sissons in aspects of this quest in the mid-1980s. I interviewed Trendall in 1990 and Bond in 1994, and subsequently engaged in correspondence with them both. A letter from Bond to me is reproduced herein (Annex 10). It contains sketches of the layout of the Monterey Building in Queens Road and 'A' Block in Victoria Barracks, together with the names of the occupants of the particular rooms. (Note that Bond uses the British terminology of Ground Floor, First Floor and Second Floor in his diagrams, while most other accounts refer to the First, Second and Third floors).

In 1986 Sissons learned from Bond and Smith that, after the war and before the Section was disbanded, they together with Barnes had compiled a report on the Japanese diplomatic cyphers with which the unit had been engaged. (Over the next two decades, Sissons sometimes referred to this as 'the Barnes Report' or 'the Bond Report'). He immediately sought to locate a copy and request its declassification, as well as that of related material concerning the unit. At first, his efforts through the Defence Signals Directorate (DSD), the successor SIGINT organisation, were consistently stymied on the grounds that the material he wanted contained information that 'reveals details of an arrangement between Australian and foreign governments' and that 'the foreign governments concerned have not agreed to the public release of such information'. This was

---

the south-west Pacific area. The US secretary of the army stated in a letter to the vice-chancellor of Sydney University in September 1945 that Room had made 'a very valuable contribution … to the Allied War Effort'. See Donovan and Mack, 'Sydney University, T.G. Room and Codebreaking in WWII', part 1; and, Donovan and Mack, 'Sydney University, T.G. Room and Codebreaking in WWII', part 2.

a reference to the UKUSA Agreement, the postwar arrangements for SIGINT cooperation and exchange between the United States, the United Kingdom, Australia, Canada and New Zealand, and finally declassified in June 2010.[9]

Sissons, however, persisted with his efforts. Finally, after a decade of perseverance, in 1997, DSD released the 45-page report, entitled *Report of Special Intelligence Section, HQ Australian Military Forces, Melbourne [on] Japanese Diplomatic Cyphers: Cryptographic Survey*, produced in 1946 (NAA Series A6923/2, Item 1). The report was lightly edited by Sissons in 2006 with a view to publication. He wrote a 13,000-word introduction (not counting three pages of tables), covering the section's origins and history, and also appended a brief note on 'Sources'. He died before publication was secured, however, and his plan lapsed. The 1946 report, together with Sissons's introduction, comprises the main body of this volume.

Sissons continued to pursue aspects of the subject up until his death in October 2006. His later efforts were less concerned with reconstructing the organisation's history and more focussed on its cryptanalytic activities. As exemplified in his correspondence with McKay in late 2004, and with Bond in early 2005, he was particularly interested in the techniques and processes used by Trendall, Bond, Barnes, Smith and McKay to break specific Japanese diplomatic codes and cyphers, especially the FUJI and GEAM transposition cyphers. Three of his letters to McKay in November–December 2004 are reproduced herein (annexes 15, 17, 18). Sissons attached to his letter of 9 November 2004 an 11-page note describing his ongoing attempt to re-create the techniques that Trendall had used to break GEAM by encoding the famous Japanese 'Winds – Set-up' messsage sent from Tokyo to the Japanese embassy in Washington on 19 November 1941 (Annex 16). He was stymied at the point where Trendall had invariably determined the correct sequence of the ten possible bigram columns used in the transposition blocks, and sought McKay's assistance.

Sadly, towards the end of his last letter in this collection, on 19 December 2004, he expresses his disappointment that he had been unable to uncover everything he had wanted about the Special Section's activities, and admits his eventual defeat in re-creating the techniques that Trendall had used with GEAM (Annex 18). He should not have been too distraught at his failure to match Trendall who, himself, was unable to explain how he did it. He told me in May 1990 that, although he was no mathematician, he had an inexplicable ability to see the patterns in the encoded text underneath the jumbled bigrams: 'You get a feeling for it. Your eye lights up on something, and … bang' (Annex 2).

---

9   National Security Agency (NSA), 'Declassified UKUSA Signals Intelligence Agreement Documents Available', 24 June 2010, at http://www.nsa.gov/public_info/press_room/2010/ukusa.shtml

D Special Section

D Special Section was a small but select organisation. A total of only 33 people worked in the section during the entire period from January 1942 to the end of the war. These consisted of eight 'technical' personnel, or 'code-breakers', plus another five lent by Central Bureau 'during heavy periods'; 11 'language and translation' personnel, plus two others 'lent by Central Bureau for short periods of heavy pressure'; and seven women typists and clerical assistants. In June 1943, it had ten members, comprised of three 'technical' personnel, four linguists/translators, and three typists and clerks. In July 1944, it had 17, comprised of six 'technical' personnel, five linguists/translators, and six typists and clerks. In August 1945, it had 18 members, comprised of six 'technical' personnel, plus one on loan, four linguists/translators plus two on loan, and five typists/clerks.

They were an illustrious group. The 'technical' members came from the worlds of Classics and Mathematics. They included Trendall, Professor of Greek and Archeology at Sydney University from 1939 to 1954, and then Deputy Vice-Chancellor and Master of University House at The Australian National University (ANU) until 1969;[10] Treweek, later Professor of Classics at Sydney University; Ronald Bond, another Classics scholar who was later Vice-Principal of Scotch College for 18 years; McKay, who later became Reader in Classics at the ANU; Barnes, who later became Professor of Pure Mathematics and then Deputy Vice-Chancellor of the University of Adelaide; and Ian Smith, who was later Professor of Modern Languages at the University of Tasmania.

The linguists/translators included C. H. Archer and Hubert A. Graves from the British Consular Service, and Arthur R. V. Cooper from the FECB of the British Government GC&CS. Archer had been the British Consul-General in Harbin, Manchuria. Cooper, brilliant and erratic, had worked at the FECB station in Hong Kong until late 1939 when, following Japan's invasion of China, the main body of the station was moved to Singapore. He was evacuated from Singapore by ship and submarine, together with his pet gibbon Tertius, and arrived at Monterey in March 1942. The gibbon was given to the Melbourne Zoo when Cooper returned to the United Kingdom in December 1942. Trendall said in May

---

10 Sissons lived in University House from when he arrived at ANU in 1961 until mid-1966. He was a fellow of the Governing Board and steward in 1964–66. From August 1965, when he and Bronwen were married, they lived in an apartment directly below Trendall's. They frequently dined with Trendall, on both formal and social occasions. Sissons later told me, however, that on no occasion did he and Trendall ever discuss their wartime service in D Special Section, nor even intimate that they were aware of the other's role. Trendall, of course, may not have known Sissons during the war, as he only returned to the section infrequently after June 1944, whereas Sissons only joined it in April 1945. Sissons would not have broached the subject. His natural shyness was a factor, but so was their age difference; Sissons thought himself too junior to the famous professor to share confidences. In any case, they were both men of discretion and respect for official secrecy.

1990 that Cooper 'had a very fine brain' and that 'for intelligence purposes, [he] was very much at the top of the tree'. Sissons was one of the linguists/translators who was officially 'on loan' from Central Bureau.

D Special Section's role was to conduct crypanalytical activities with respect to intercepted Japanese diplomatic communications. The intercepts were obtained by monitoring Japan's worldwide network of HF radio stations used by the Foreign Ministry, including stations in Japan and stations in the Soviet Union, Germany, occupied China, French Indo-China, the Netherlands East Indies, and Thailand. The 52nd Australian Special Wireless Section was dedicated to intercepting this traffic, at Bonegilla until November 1943 and then Mornington until it was demobilised in late 1945. When reception of particular frequencies of interest was poor at Mornington, these were monitored by the ASWG stations at Darwin and Kalinga in Brisbane.

In addition, the Section received intercepts of Japanese diplomatic messages from the New Zealand army's Special Section located at Nairnville Park, Wellington, which extended coverage another 2,500 kilometres further east.[11] Messages intercepted by the Special Section, as well as by the New Zealand navy's SIGINT organisation, were sent to FRUMEL on the daily commercial flights from Wellington. Much of the Nairnville Park material was forwarded to Central Bureau in Brisbane. Intercepted diplomatic traffic, such as FUJI and Type B Machine (PURPLE) material, was dispatched to D Special Section, where it was sorted according to whether it should be analysed by the Section or sent on to the Government Communications Bureau at Berkeley Street in London, the Diplomatic Section of GC&CS.

The most lucrative source was the radio telegraphy circuit between Kuibyshev and Tokyo, via Irkutsk, which had the call sign RTZ. From October 1941 to around August 1943, from the German offensive intended to capture Moscow to the withdrawal of the German forces, much of the Soviet governmental apparatus, as well as the foreign legations, moved from Moscow to Kuibyshev, about 870 kilometres southeast of Moscow. It was also the primary circuit for communications between Moscow and Tokyo, relayed from Kuibyshev.

The Bonegilla station had begun 'highly successful' coverage of RTZ before February 1943. In early 1943 Bond instructed the station to watch the circuit carefully. In the six-month period from February to July 1943, the station intercepted 1,421 messages from Kuibyshev to Tokyo and 1,212 messages from Tokyo to Kuibyshev. RTZ accounted for 27 per cent of the messages from stations outside Japan intercepted at Mornington in May 1944. The New Zealand army's

---

11 Desmond Ball, Cliff Lord and Meredith Thatcher, *Invaluable Service: The Secret History of New Zealand's Signals Intelligence During Two World Wars* (Waimauku, New Zealand: Resource Books, 2011), pp. 202–04, 213.

Special Section at Nairnville Park in Wellington maintained a special 24-hour watch for Japanese diplomatic communications on the RTZ link between Irkutsk and Tokyo.[12]

The cyphers analysed by the Section are the subject of the *Cryptographic Survey* produced in 1946. From its inception until July 1943, the Section's principal task was to decypher and process diplomatic messages sent in the high-grade FUJI transposition cypher, which was changed daily. The 1946 report notes that, by May 1942, 'virtually all traffic in the FUJI cypher [was] being read locally'. Trendall evidently 'devised an ingenious way of breaking the daily cypher so quickly and routinely that he could usually send the solution to London before work began there the next morning.[13] The Section was the first Allied unit to break a transposition cypher introduced by the GEAM in July 1943. Soon afterwards, it broke the Foreign Ministry's BA transposition cypher.

The highest grade diplomatic encypherment system involved the HINOKI Machine Cypher (JAA, Type B, or PURPLE). The GC&CS obtained a replica machine in early 1941, but none was available to D Special Section. It sorted the PURPLE intercepts from Mornington and Nairnville Park for forwarding to the Diplomatic Section of GC&CS in London for decypherment. It also forwarded to London intercepts of messages from the Japanese military and naval attaches located with their overseas legations. By the end of 1943, the Section was sending about 800–900 attache messages to London per month.

Intercepting Soviet radio traffic

In 1994 Sissons told Horner that he believed D Special Section had had some involvement in cryptanalytical activities concerning Soviet radio traffic during the war. He explained this further in a letter to me in 1996 (Annex 11). He specifically recalled that Bond, who had succeeded Trendall as head of the Section in June 1944, had had a Russian intercept in his safe, which Sissons thought had probably predated his arrival in April 1945; and that members of the ASWG at the station near Darwin were intercepting Soviet diplomatic traffic around December 1945 and had been intercepting it 'during hostilities'.[14]

One former AWAS member, Margaret McBrien (later Griffin, as described by Steve Mason in Annex 8), told members of her family that she was engaged in interception of Russian traffic while she was at Mornington from September

---

12   Ball, Lord and Thatcher, *Invaluable Service*, pp. 202–13.
13   Merrillees, 'Professor A. D. Trendall and His Band of Classical Cryptographers', p. 14.
14   Ball and Horner, *Breaking the Codes*, p. 165.

1944 to January 1946. She recalled traffic concerning Russian troop movements prior to their invasion of Manchuria and the northern Japanese islands during 9–20 August 1945.

By December 1945 the Mornington station was devoted almost entirely to Russian transmissions. Sergeant Steve Mason, who arrived at Mornington that month, has stated that: 'We took mostly Russian high speed traffic. On occasions, with the use of incentives, full logs were produced — I can remember one night's work which yielded more than 1000 messages'. The Russian intercepts were taken on Edison wax cylinders and transcribed later. They were taken each Wednesday to Victoria Barracks by a warrant officer, who passed them to the Diplomatic Section, now headed by Lieutenant Colonel Alastair ('Mic') Sandford, who occupied the same room as had Trendall and Bond (Annex 8).

D Special Section was only interested in the Japanese diplomatic traffic, at least until after Japan's surrender in August. It is likely, however, that at some point before December 1945, when the Mornington station was intercepting mostly Russian traffic, and prior to the ending of the war in August, it was intercepting both Japanese and Russian traffic, with D Special Section presumably passing the latter directly to London, along with some of the Japanese traffic.

Detection of the Soviet espionage network in Australia

It is likely that around this juncture the Mornington station and, incidentally, D Special Section, became involved in the beginnings of Australia's most serious espionage episode. On 6 January 1945, in a 'Top Secret and Personal' letter to the Acting Minister for the Army, General Sir Thomas Blamey, Commander-in-Chief of the Australian Military Forces (AMF) reported that, in the course of Allied intelligence operations, 'it has been definitely proved that there are leakages of information from Australia which have their origin apparently in Canberra'. Blamey gave four examples of intercepts of Japanese signals which contained details of Allied 'plans for certain operations in the Philippines' and details of recent Australian army intelligence estimates of Japanese strength there. The information came from Department of Information 'news background sheets' and AMF *Weekly Intelligence Reviews* prepared for War Cabinet and Advisory War Council meetings. The contents of an AMF *Weekly Intelligence Summary* issued on 4 November 1944 'were known in full' in Tokyo on 11 November. A file of material on which Blamey had based his letter was released in Canberra in July 1997. It contained details of eight instances of similar leaked information, sourced to the Soviet embassy in Canberra, during November–December 1944. For example, the details of Australian army deployments in New Guinea that were prepared for a meeting of the Advisory War Council on 16 November 1944, and circulated to members a few days beforehand, were in Japanese hands by 19 November.[15]

Neither Blamey's letter nor the supporting file identified the Allied agency that had discovered the leakages and thence informed Blamey about them. Neither does the material in the file specify the Japanese circuits monitored, or the relevant cypher used, or the station responsible for the intercepts.

Declassified files in the UK National Archives, however, indicate that the Allied agency which decyphered the Japanese traffic and alerted Blamey was the Diplomatic Section of GC&CS in London. It is very likely that at least some of the messages were intercepted by the Mornington and Nairnville Park stations. Several of the messages originated in Harbin in Japanese-occupied Manchuria, and were sent to Tokyo by the Japanese Consulate in Harbin. Sissons thought it was possible that Mornington had intercepted these, which would then have been forwarded by D Special Section to London for decypherment. In addition, monitoring the RTZ circuit would have yielded important pieces of information about the leakages. For example, a telegram from Tokyo to Moscow on 13 May 1944, which said that the Japanese Consul-General in Harbin was receiving information from the Soviet Consul-General, was presumably transmitted on RTZ. In 1996, Sissons asked Craswell to search a series of recently released intercepts of telegrams between Harbin and Tokyo in the US National Archives for copies of either three particular messages mentioned by Blamey or any similar intercepts, but she found that intercepts for the dates of interest were still withheld from public access.

There is also the intriguing possibility that in early 1945 the Mornington station was tasked with monitoring Soviet traffic in the Far East in an attempt to discover any clues as to the process through which the leaked Australian secrets were being passed from Soviet to Japanese hands. Did the Japanese obtain them only in Harbin or also in Moscow or Kuibyshev, and in the case of Harbin, how were they transmitted from Moscow to Harbin for the handover? The stations at Mornington, Nairnville Park, Darwin and Kalinga were best suited for this search as they already monitored the airwaves across the relevant geographical area for GC&CS's Diplomatic Section either on a dedicated basis or as radio reception conditions required. Sandford, the deputy head of Central Bureau, who was fully apprised of the matter from the beginning, took over D Special Section in late 1945 and was the personal recipient of the Soviet intercepts taken at Mornington. In February 1945 he noted, in connection with the investigation

---

15 Ibid., chapter 6; and, Desmond Ball, 'The Moles at the Very Heart of Government', *Australian*, 16 April 2011.

of the leakages, that 'the Russian Diplomatic traffic will still be required by the United Kingdom' and had asked that all such traffic should be sent to him at Central Bureau.

The subsequent US–UK cryptological operation known as *Venona*, in which large portions of Soviet intelligence communications between Moscow centre and its major overseas posts (such as London, Washington, New York and Canberra) for selected periods from 1943 to 1948 were decrypted, revealed the existence of a Soviet espionage network active in Australia, with at least ten members. It seems now clear that the office of Dr H. V. Evatt, the Attorney General and the Minister for External Affairs, in Martin Place in Sydney, was the source of the leakages concerning Allied war plans in 1944–45. The specific culprits were almost certainly Allan Dalziel, Evatt's private security (who was codenamed DENIS by the Soviet foreign intelligence service), and Ric Throssell (later codenamed FERRO). For example, it is most likely that Dalziel gave a Department of Information 'news background sheet' in November 1944 to Feodor Nosov (TEKHNIK), the Soviet Press Agency (TASS) representative (and senior Soviet intelligence officer) in Sydney. The information in this sheet was later found 'in practically identical terms' in an intercept of a Japanese message from Harbin to Tokyo. Nosov had immediately sent it to Moscow, from whence it was quickly sent to Harbin, somehow passed to the Japanese Consulate and then sent to Tokyo. Stalin was engaged in the higher statecraft of prolonging the fighting in the southwest Pacific theatre for as long as possible, or at least until Soviet forces could be moved from the western front to enter the war against Japan and enable Moscow to join in the peace negotiations, for which the eventual prize was Sakhalin Island and the Japanese 'Northern Territories'.[16]

There remain important unanswered questions concerning this opening phase of the espionage case. Some answers could well be derived from the files of GC&CS's Diplomatic Section and US *Magic* records that are still classified. Sissons's painstaking research and analysis of the activities of the Mornington station and the possible role of D Special Section in the handling of Soviet intercepts, however, uncovered enough to keep the door slightly ajar for eventual discoveries.

The *Kormoran* cryptogram and the sinking of HMAS *Sydney*

In his essay in 2006 on D Special Section's origins and history, Sissons revealed that the Section had successfully decyphered a German account of the sinking

---

16   Ball and Horner, *Breaking the Codes*, pp. xx, 343; and, Ball, 'The Moles'.

of HMAS *Sydney* by the *Kormoran*, a German auxiliary cruiser or 'raider', off the coast of Western Australia near Carnarvon, on 19 November 1941. How a modified merchant ship could sink a *Leander*-class cruiser, with the loss of all 645 men aboard, has never been satisfactorily explained. Sissons's essay, however, casts new light on this controversial incident.

Sissons recalls that on 11 January 1945, a group of about 20 survivors from the *Kormoran*, including Commander Theodor Detmers, the ship's captain, attempted to escape from a POW camp in Victoria. While a prisoner, Detmers wrote an encoded account of the battle, which was found on him when he was recaptured a week after the breakout. The cryptogram, which consisted of about 6,250 characters, was given to D Special Section to decypher. Smith, who was fluent in German, played the main role in its solution, assisted by Barnes on the mathematical side. (It should be noted, however, that Treweek told Sissons in October 1990 that it had been solved by Keith Miller, who is not listed as a member of D Special Section in the 1946 account, but had previously worked under Nave in the Special Intelligence Bureau). It involved a relatively simple form of 'polyalphabetic substitution' cypher; Sissons shows, through a six-page reconstruction, how it was soon decyphered. It evidently consisted of the deck and engine room logs from the sighting of the *Sydney* until the scuttling of the *Kormoran* some eight and a half hours later and, Sissons notes, provides 'the most reliable account of how *Sydney* met her fate'. It shows that, 'before verifying the raider's identity, *Sydney* approached to within point blank range and was crippled by fire from *Kormoran*'s main and secondary armament before she could bring fire to bear'.

The Sissons legacy

Sissons served in D Special Section for only five months. It is only because of his extraordinary efforts, however, that the Section's story could be reconstructed and published. It is very likely that the 1946 cryptographic report would have remained unreleased and unknown, were it not for his persistence, fuelled by his knowledge of its existence. He initiated and pursued most of the correspondence with former members of the Section, and arranged key interviews, putting together a detailed account of its origins and history that would otherwise have not been recorded. He was assiduous and indefatigable. He is owed a great debt by scholars and practitioners concerned with the science of cryptography as well as historians of the cryptological aspects of the war in the Pacific.

Withdrawal of the 1946 report

In late 2012, when we were checking the archival sources cited by Sissons, we learned that the *Report of Special Intelligence Section, HQ Australian Military Forces, Melbourne [on] Japanese Diplomatic Cyphers: Cryptographic Survey (1946)* had been withdrawn from public access on 2 June 2011. After 14 years of public viewing and copying as NAA Series A6923/3, Item 1, the report is now officially 'withheld pending access advice from an agency/agencies'. Sissons would not have been surprised at the redaction; he would have smiled, commented wryly on the ludicrousness of the decision, and continued doggedly with his efforts to secure public appreciation of the activities of the Special Section.

We also found that the associated items in Series A6923/3 had recently been either recatalogued or removed from access. (We have retained Sissons's NAA references in his footnotes, however; they were undoubtedly correct during his last visits to the NAA in 2004–06). Sissons would have regarded all this as just another tiresome challenge for investigative scholars.

Chapter 2. The Diplomatic Special Intelligence Section: Its Origins and History[1]

D.C.S. Sissons

Three months after the outbreak of war, the Chief of the Naval Staff (CNS) on 12 December 1939 wrote to his colleagues, the Chief of the General Staff (CGS) and Chief of the Air Staff (CAS) that it had 'been suggested' that it might be desirable to set up in Australia 'a cryptographic organisation on the lines of the Government Code and Cypher School (GC&CS) in London, with a view to breaking down enemy codes and cyphers'. He sought their views. The source of the 'suggestion' he did not state. Presumably it had come as an informal feeler from the GC&CS through the Admiralty.

The CNS was lukewarm to the suggestion:

> As far as European nations are concerned it is doubtful whether we can do much at this distance, either on our own account or to help the UK Organisation. As far as Asiatic nations are concerned, any local organisation would appear to be a duplication of the UK Organisation in the East ... .

The CGS was a little more enthusiastic:

> I consider that we should have at least a nucleus organisation in Australia against the contingencies of operations in and about Australia and her territories. The work is clearly of a highly skilled nature and much practice is necessary, and the sooner a commencement can be made the better.
>
> I agree that the aid of the British authorities should be involved ... .

---

1 As a result of the wholesale and unsystematic destruction of the records of the Naval Intelligence Division and the Directorate of Military Intelligence and their subsidiaries, the source material for this study has been limited to the occasional file that has survived and to the recollections of some of the participants.

The only surviving records of the Section's activities appear to be: (i) the 30-page report (stripped of its appendices) tendered by the Section at the time of its disbandment in 1946 (National Archives of Australia (NAA): A6923/2, 1); (ii) the Department of the Army, Central Registry file on the Section (NAA: A6923/3, 37/401/425); unregistered box files from the office of the Captain Ix at Land Headquarters of outwards signals dispatched by the Section through the Assistant Director of Military Intelligence for the period 28 November 1942 – 23 April 1943 (consisting principally of summaries of translations of selected intercepts) and 5 August 1943 – 27 May 1944 (consisting principally of daily traffic lists and newly solved code groups, cypher keys and additives) (NAA: A6923/3, [DMI Diplomatic Message Traffic]).

The chiefs considered the matter at the meeting of the Defence Committee on 15 February 1940, at which it was resolved that 'as a preliminary to any further action, the advice and assistance of the United Kingdom authorities should be sought'.[2] At the measured pace of officialdom, the views of the chiefs and this request for advice were conveyed to the British Government in a letter over the signature of the Prime Minister dated 11 April.

In the army, the General Staff took prompt preparatory steps for setting up this 'nucleus organization'. By the end of January 1940 the GSO II (Intelligence) at Eastern Command, Sydney had gathered together a group of four academics at Sydney University — two mathematicians (Professor T. G. Room FRS and Mr R. J. Lyons) and two classicists (Professor A. D. Trendall and Mr A. P. Treweek) — to teach each other cryptography in their leisure hours, using as their raw material copies of the past traffic of the Japanese Consul-General provided by the cable and wireless company.

By October the GSO II was able to report that:

> Work has been concentrated on an attempt to break down the Japanese commercial and diplomatic codes … . Three definite codes have been identified in use and in the case of one of these it has become apparent that a new code was brought into operation on 1 October 1940. As the general principles underlying this are assumed to be identical, it is believed that if the code upon which work is being done is broken, it will be an easy matter to apply the results to the new code … .[3]

He also reported that for variety he had sent the group coded portions of overseas mail that had been detected by the District Censor and that, in a single sitting, they had broken the dot code in which, through a forwarding address in Sydney, an English knight residing in China was exchanging most torrid and explicit love letters with a married woman in Melbourne. (It is not stated whether the District Censor adopted the academics' suggestion that, prior to delivery, they annotate the originals in the same dot code with 'Careful! — The Censor').

Similar preparatory steps were taken by the Royal Australian Navy (RAN) in mid-1940 when Commander T. E. Nave RN, an experienced cryptographer and Japanese linguist at the Far Eastern Combined Bureau (FECB), Singapore, returned to his home in Australia on sick leave. When a medical survey found him unfit for tropical service, the Admiralty approved his temporary attachment to the RAN to work on Japanese signals intelligence.[4]

---

2   NAA: A816, 43/302/18, Cryptographic Organization in Australia.
3   NAA: A6923/3, 37/401/425, [Special Intelligence Section].
4   Captain J. Foley to Secretary Defence Committee, 12 November 1941, 'Special Intelligence Organisation' (NAA: A816, 43/302/18).

Chapter 2. The Diplomatic Special Intelligence Section

In response to the Australian request for advice, the British Government replied on 15 October to the following effect: (i) It agreed that it would be inadvisable to establish any large-scale organization which would duplicate the work done by the GC&CS and suggested that the RAN's small section under Nave, which was working in close cooperation with the FECB, be expanded; (ii) It was prepared to assist with the training of cryptographers; (iii) It would welcome Australian assistance in the interception of Japanese fixed commercial stations.

The British reply was considered by the Defence Committee at its meeting of 28 November where it was decided that the CNS should further examine the matter and take up with the CGS and CAS the question of appropriate training.[5]

In the months immediately following, the role of Nave's organisation appears to have been to assist FECB by traffic analysis and decryption of Japanese naval traffic in the Japanese Mandated Islands. Incidental to discharging this function, it provided the Dutch signals intelligence department at Bandoeng with Japanese diplomatic and consular intercepts in exchange for Mandated Islands traffic. Nave requested that FECB provide him with 'copies of the Consular and Diplomatic codes, and of any other codes regularly intercepted in Australia'. As late as March 1941, however, FECB were refusing to do this, on the grounds that 'the Consular and Diplomatic codes are now so complicated that a large staff of experts is required to obtain results, and that anything of interest read from this or other codes or cyphers would be forwarded to the [Australian] Naval Board'.[6]

The engagement of the Sydney University group for full-time duty

On 2 May 1941 a conference was convened at Victoria Barracks, Melbourne, to consider the future employment of the Sydney University group. Those attending were: for the navy — the Director of Naval Intelligence (DNI) and Nave; for the army — the Director of Military Operations & Intelligence (DMO&I), the Signals Officer in Chief, a GSO II (Military Intelligence) and a Captain (Military Intelligence, Cypher Security); for the Sydney University group —Room and Treweek. The conference reported that:

> (a) The breaking of Japanese diplomatic codes could be regarded as a feasible proposition.
>
> (b) It was desirable that a section for this purpose should be organised — it being considered that existing facilities at Singapore may not always be available.

---

5 NAA: A816, 43/302/18.
6 Minute by Director of Signals Communications, RAN, 19 March 1941 (NAA: MP1185/8, 1937/2/415).

(c) The present strength of this section should be four officers and three clerks additional to the existing Naval nucleus organization. One officer to be a competent Japanese linguist.

(d) The section should be of a Combined Service nature, for the benefit of all Services although initially the work would mainly be concerned with naval codes.

In the course of the discussion Room and Treweek indicated that, if required, the university would probably be prepared to release them (and Lyons also) for full-time service in Melbourne after the end of first term.

Following the conference the Acting CNS on 15 May addressed the CGS as follows:

1. Consequent upon the interception by Army personnel of Japanese consular and diplomatic messages, it becomes necessary to consider the means of dealing with these messages. It is desirable that they should be handled in Australia if possible, in order to obtain intelligence and also in order to avoid relying permanently on Singapore for this work. This additional task would be beyond the capacity of the small naval section and would throw an additional strain on the Bureau at Singapore.

2. At the request of the DMO&I, Paymaster Commander Nave has examined the work performed by the Army Cypher Group from Sydney University, and reports that some of the members would be most useful in dealing with the Japanese diplomatic messages and other similar work.

3. Before embarking on this work, it would be necessary to secure the services of a competent interpreter for translation ... .

4. If [the latter] can be obtained, it is recommended that three members of the Sydney University Cypher Section be sent to Melbourne to work with Paymaster Commander Nave. It is considered that each should be provided with a suitable clerical assistant.

5. Before commencing Consular work in Australia, it would probably be necessary to send two of the staff to Singapore for a short time to study the latest methods.

6. Would be glad to know your views on these proposals.

On 3 June the CGS tendered to the Minister for the Army (P. C. Spender) the letter from the CNS together with a request for 'authority to call up for full-time duty with pay and allowances of Major' up to three of the Sydney University group. This, Spender approved the same day.

Treweek, who was already a Major in the Citizen Military Forces commanding a field battery in the Sydney University Regiment, duly reported at the Navy Office, Melbourne for full-time duty on 19 June. Engaging other members of the group, however, proved more difficult. The university argued that, for the professors, appointment to a rank of less than full colonel was inappropriate. This the DMO&I would not countenance. The Vice-Chancellor accordingly took the matter up directly with the Minister, representing that: (i) the rank of Major did not accord with the professional expertise and attainments of a Professor; (ii) that the practice of the university with regard to members of its staff on war service was to make up the gap between their pay in the services and their former university salaries and that the difference between a Major's and a Professor's income was so great that this would impose a considerable burden on the university.

It was agreed that the professors and Lyons would be engaged as civilian experts at their existing salaries and that the university would undertake their superannuation contributions. Room and Lyons took up duty in Melbourne on 18 August.[7] On 1 September, Room and another newly enlisted member of Nave's organisation, Pay Lieutenant A. B. Jamieson were flown to Singapore for training at FECB[8] (Jamieson had resided in Japan since taking up Melbourne University's Mollison Travelling Scholarship in Japanese in 1934). They arrived back in Melbourne in November.

Attempts to find the 'competent interpreter' were not immediately successful. In April 1941, however, the British Foreign Office, at the request of the Australian Government, had despatched a member of the Consular Service on a tour of inspection to Portuguese Timor and to report on Japanese activities there. The Foreign Office chose for this assignment C. H. Archer, a senior officer who had served in a succession of consular posts in Japan and its territories since 1922 and who was proficient in both spoken and written Japanese. By direction, on the completion of his tour he flew on to Australia in May to pass on his impressions to the relevant departments in Australia.[9] During his meeting with the DNI in Melbourne the latter asked him whether, if the Foreign Office agreed, he would be prepared to join Nave's organisation. Archer was on leave between postings. On completion of his tour of duty as Consul at Tamsui in February he had been appointed Consul-General at Mukden to take up his duties there on the expiration of his accumulated leave. Recently, however, he had been informed that his posting to Mukden was likely to be deferred indefinitely in line with the Foreign Office's policy of ensuring that, if war broke out, a nucleus

---

7   NAA: A6923/3, 37/401/425.
8   Australian Commonwealth Naval Board to Chief of Intelligence Staff [Far East] 25 August 1941 (NAA: MP1074/8/1 'Outward Signals (B Category)', 3B, Serial 155).
9   For Archer's 40-page report on Portuguese Timor and visit to Australia in April–May 1941, see NAA: A981, TIM P9 & TIM P23.

of senior Japanese-speaking experts would continue to be available instead of their being interned by the Japanese for the duration. Archer welcomed the DNI's proposal and on 15 May both he and the CNS cabled the Foreign Office recommending it.[10] The Foreign Office agreed, in principle; but first it had a task for him in Tahiti. It was not until 21 January 1942 that he joined Nave's organisation.[11]

On 19 September the Secretary, Department of the Army, addressed a minute to the Secretary, Military Board that:

> The Minister notes ... that on the 15 May, the Acting Chief of the Naval Staff in a minute addressed to the Chief of the General Staff stated that 'consequent upon the interception by Army personnel of Japanese Consular and diplomatic messages it became necessary to consider the means of dealing with them'.
>
> In view of the fact that such diplomatic messages are generally immune from interference, the Minister desires to have a report as to the extent to which such action is being taken to intercept such messages and whether this action is in contravention of any international agreement, and in accordance with action similarly taken by the UK authorities or by Japan.

The Minister was promptly assured that:

> In general, the position is that diplomatic messages in secret cypher are sighted in Cable Companies' offices. Copies of these messages are secured and placed before the Special Section. Similarly, British or Allied messages sent from and received in foreign countries would be available to the foreign governments concerned. In any case, telegraphic or radio communications are not subject to diplomatic privileges ... .[12]

Interception of the 'Winds' message

The implications of two circular telegrams despatched by the Japanese Foreign Ministry to overseas posts on 19 November were of such gravity, indicating the imminence of hostilities, that the intercepts were taken to the Secretary to War Cabinet (F. G. Shedden) to be shown to the Prime Minister. In the first of these the recipient was instructed urgently to nominate the mission best qualified 'in the event of the development of an emergency situation' to assume

---

10 NAA: MP1074/8/1, 2B, Serial 102 & 103.
11 Foreign Office List, 1947.
12 NAA: A9293/3, 37/401/425.

Japan's responsibilities of locally representing Italian interests. The second was the famous 'Winds – Set-Up' message instructing that the severance of communications with enemy countries would be indicated by inserting certain bogus weather reports in news broadcasts, e.g. 'West wind, clear' would signal 'Japanese–British crisis (including the invasion of Thailand or an attack on Malaya or the Netherlands East Indies)'. These two intercepts were delivered, on 28 November, by the Second Naval Member to Shedden, who immediately showed them to the Prime Minister.

On 2 December, in a circular telegram, the Japanese Ministry of Foreign Affairs instructed Melbourne and certain other posts to burn their telegram files and all codes except 'O' and 'TSU' and to signal the word 'HARUNA' to signify completion. This intercept, together with the intercept of Melbourne's 'HARUNA', was delivered to Shedden on 4 December.[13]

The code words 'West wind, clear' were not transmitted until four hours after the bombing of Pearl Harbor. They were picked up by one of Nave's linguists on listening watch, Lieutenant I. L. Lloyd (Australian Intelligence Corps) and phoned to Shedden at 8.15 am on 8 December EST (2215 hours on 7 December GMT) — $1\frac{3}{4}$ hours before similar messages were intercepted in the United States.

Trendall's diplomatic section under RAN control (December 1941 – November 1942)

On Japan's entering the war, Nave's organisation was promptly reinforced. The last of the Sydney group, Trendall, arrived for full-time duty on 12 January 1942.[14] Archer and another senior officer from the British Consular Service, H. A. Graves, were seconded to the organisation from 21 January and 1 February respectively.[15] On 28 February, Private R. S. Bond, who had just graduated with First Class Honours in Greek and Latin in Trendall's Classics Department in December, was marched in from the ranks of the Sydney University Regiment. He had just turned 19. He was promptly promoted to Corporal so that he could afford to lodge at the same boarding house as Trendall in St Kilda Road and continue their work after hours.

By the end of March, when the entire organisation moved to its new site, the Monterey block of flats in Arthur Street, they had been formed into a discrete sub-unit within Nave's organisation, headed by Trendall, working exclusively

---

13   NAA: A5954, 558.
14   NAA: A6293/3, 37/401/425.
15   Foreign Office List, 1947.

on Japanese diplomatic traffic. (Room, Treweek and Lyons, however, remained directly under Nave, working on naval traffic). At Monterey they were soon joined by one of GC&CS's cryptographers and linguists, A. R. V. Cooper, who had been with FECB since 1938. Cooper and Lieutenant Norman Webb's small Special Wireless section had volunteered to remain in Singapore to monitor the Japanese air attacks. They, together with Cooper's pet gibbon, Tertius, were evacuated to Australia (via Java) on one of the last escape ships, leaving Singapore on 11 February.[16] In later years Trendall had this to say of Cooper: 'There was a somebody — a really good linguist ... . For intelligence purposes he was very much at the top of the tree — a very fine brain'.[17]

Two trainee cryptographers were recruited during 1942. Gunner J. C. Davies[18] was plucked from the Artillery Training Depot in June. Like Bond, he had secured First Class Honours in Trendall's Latin III class at the 1941 annual examinations. Dr Elizabeth Sheppard, a resident tutor at the University Women's College, whose specialty was English Language and Literature, arrived in August.[19]

A single-bedroom top-floor flat on Monterey's north staircase overlooking Arthur Street was the Section's home throughout 1942, the cryptographers (Trendall, Cooper and Bond) installed in the bedroom; the linguists (Archer and Graves) and the three clerks/typists, in the lounge.

Trendall's Section operated under RAN control until transferred to the army in November 1942. The only high-grade cyphers in use by the Japanese Foreign Ministry at that time were FUJI and JAA (i.e. PURPLE). The Section's principal tasks throughout this period were, therefore, the solution of FUJI intercepts and the forwarding of PURPLE intercepts to GC&CS for solution (GC&CS had been operating a replica of the PURPLE machine since early 1941).

The transfer from the RAN to the Australian Army

In October 1942, Archer, Graves and Trendall were informed that: (i) It had been decided that Nave's organisation was to be absorbed into the US navy

---

16   M. Smith, *The Emperor's Codes* (London: Bantam, 2001), pp. 102–03.
17   Cooper and Tertius at Hong Kong in early 1941 figure prominently in Emily Hahn's, *China to Me: A Partial Autobiography* (New York: Doubleday, 1944).
18   He was professor of French, University of Adelaide, 1971–87.
19   Sheppard's field was Old English and 15th century Scottish. The biographical chapter of her PhD thesis 'Studies in the Language of Bellenden's Boece' had recently been published in *The Chronicles of Scotland Compiled by Hector Boece*, vol. 1, Scottish Text Society, 3rd series, no. 15 (1941), pp. 411–61. She had also recently been awarded a Reinhardt Fellowship to pursue postdoctoral research in the United States. She was associate professor, English language, University of Auckland, 1963–72.

cryptographic unit operating alongside it at Monterey (FRUMEL — Fleet Radio Unit, Melbourne); (ii) Nave was being reposted elsewhere and all civilian personnel would no longer be required; (iii) The Diplomatic Section would be disbanded and the solution of diplomatic traffic concentrated at Washington and London, who would pass on to Australia any messages of concern.[20]

On 22 October, Archer and Graves visited the General Staff Officer Intelligence (GSOI) in the Directorate of Military Intelligence (DMI) at Land Headquarters, Lieutenant Colonel Robert A. Little, and apprised him of these decisions. They urged on him that, rather than the disbandment of the Diplomatic Section, Military Intelligence should take it over. According to their experience, the prompt and effective decryption at London or Washington of messages intercepted in Australia would be quite impossible — principally because of garbling and delays resulting from retransmission. In addition, Archer was most critical of the process by which the decision had been reached: 'When this new proposal came up, the working out of its practical applications was entrusted to a Committee consisting of two Commanders in our Naval Service and one Lieutenant Commander in US Navy. The future of the diplomatic traffic was summarily decided over the heads alike of Foreign Office officials of superior rank, and of the Director of Naval Intelligence himself.'[21]

Trendall and Cooper visited Little the following day and made similar representations.

Little addressed a memorandum to the Director of Military Intelligence supporting their proposal:

> My feeling is that since the advent of the USN Crypto Section under Lieutenant Commander Fabian, Army have not been treated fairly as, although Army provided about 1/3 of the staff and all the intercepts, all Army was allowed to have was a précis of the diplomatic material. More recently we have been permitted to read through in the presence of a N[aval?] O[fficer?] some of the diplomatic messages that Commander Nave was good enough to pass us. These were taken away as soon as read.

---

20 FRUMEL's decision not to cover diplomatic traffic would have followed naturally from the interdepartmental agreement reached in Washington between the army and navy departments on 30 June 1942 regarding the rationalisation of cryptographic activities between the two departments. Previously, both departments had covered diplomatic traffic on a cooperative basis. Under the agreement it was allocated exclusively to the army (US National Archives, 457, SRH-200, 'OP-20-G File on Army/Navy Collaboration 1931–45', pp. 44–46). The disbandment of Nave's section and FRUMEL's decision not to cover diplomatic traffic were included in the terms of the bilateral UK–US 'Holden Agreement' negotiated at that time (R. Erskine, 'The Holden Agreement on Naval Sigint: The First BRUSA', *Intelligence and National Security*, vol. 14, no. 2, Summer 1999).
21 Archer to Little, 24 October 1942 (NAA: A6293/3, 37/401/425).

> I am of the opinion that this diplomatic group should be continued for the benefit of the Commonwealth Government and the Forces but think it would be best to keep it under Army away from Central Bureau as, if under Central Bureau, it would again be under GHQ, SWPA [South West Pacific Area] control who might act similarly to USN.

(In explanation of the preceding, it should be noted that MacArthur's General Headquarters (GHQ) was, essentially, an American organisation responsible to the US Chiefs of Staff, while 'Army' despite its temporary and misleading title, 'HQ Allied Land Forces SWPA (LHQ)', was none other than HQ, Commander-in-Chief Australian Military Forces — the Australian equivalent of the War Office).

The CGS concurred and, on 30 October, wrote to the CNS informing him that Military Intelligence would take over the Diplomatic Section:

> From information received, it would appear that it is intended to discontinue the Special Intelligence Section dealing with Diplomatic traffic, which is at present operating at 'Monterey', and that the civil and army personnel which the Army has provided for the purpose will not be required thereafter.
>
> It is understood that in your view the information obtained from this source is of minor value, nevertheless it has been in the past of great interest to the Army on the broad strategic plane and it is considered that it may well prove of even greater interest in the future.
>
> For this reason, it is my intention that the Section should continue to function because —
>
> (i) intercepts obtained here are frequently not obtained elsewhere;
>
> (ii) delay would occur if intercepts were re-transmitted to London or Washington as they would be inclined to deal with intercept traffic from areas that would concern them intimately before attending to material from more distant fields which delay might, occasionally, be dangerous;
>
> (iii) the danger of corruptions occurring during transmission to London or Washington would make successful treatment still more difficult.
>
> It is therefore desired to continue the work, and it is proposed to return the personnel to MI at LHQ.

On the same day, Archer, with Little's concurrence, despatched the following cable to the Foreign Office:

> Presumably you will have been informed that under a new arrangement reached between London and Washington American Navy is absorbing

Chapter 2. The Diplomatic Special Intelligence Section

naval section of Australian Special Intelligence Unit. No civilian personnel will be used and our services with Naval board are therefore redundant.

Australian Army which already supplies much of personnel and whole of traffic is most unwilling that diplomatic section in which Graves and I have been concerned should be abandoned and General MacArthur concurs. If therefore our services remain available Army will take over and improve diplomatic section.

Following points are submitted for your consideration:

(a) For several months series of enquiries from London mainly on economic subjects as well as India has seemed to prove that much material was collected here which London did not receive from elsewhere.

(b) Alternative system of relaying all texts to London has so far proved dismal failure since additional corruption acquired en route impairs and frequently destroys value of material.

(c) Statistics show that thanks to services of extremely skilful local expert we have during past three months supplied to London and Washington nearly twice as many solutions of recurrent technical problems as we have received from both countries combined. This presumably has enabled them to handle some material which otherwise would have been useless.

On evidence available here therefore it seems that unit is serving imperial as well as Australian interest and since improved Army machinery has enormously increased volume of traffic received since mid-September we hope usefulness may substantially increase. In particular we feel that improved local organisation should give us chance of making useful contribution to breaking of new Great East Asia system shortly coming into force ... .

If you concur we suggest that formal application for our services to be made shortly by Australian Army be approved ... .[22]

The Diplomatic Section moved from Monterey to Land Headquarters at Victoria Barracks on 27 November 1942 and, from that date, was responsible to the CGS through Little (whose appointment was renamed Assistant Director of Military Intelligence — ADMI — in March 1943). There it was housed in its own secluded and secure area — the small, top floor of 'A' Block overlooking St Kilda Road, where it remained for the rest of the war. At the time of the move it acquired

---

22 NAA: A6923/3, 37/401/425.

three more clerical staff and two additional translators — Miss Mavis Tilley (one of Nave's translators) and L. R. Oates (a civilian, aged 17, who had just completed the 12-month, full-time language course at the Military Intelligence Japanese language school at the District Censor's Office). Oates remained with the Section until November 1943 when, on reaching military age, he enlisted in the AIF (Australian Imperial Force).

On 3 January 1943, one month after the move, Archer tendered to Little a report on the work of the Section. He noted that during the previous half year the number of messages in high-grade cyphers received by the Section had increased as follows: June, 178; July, 211; August, 155; September, 254; October, 466; November, 408; and, December, 445; i.e. from a daily average of 6 to one of 15.[23] As a consequence of Cooper's recent return to England, the Section now had only two accomplished cryptographers to exploit this increasing volume of traffic — Trendall and Bond. Trendall was a cryptographer of outstanding quality and he had recently reported that Bond (now a Sergeant) was now no less expert than himself. These two were under intense pressure, working seven days a week, often until 11 pm. It was therefore essential that Trendall be authorised without delay to seek out another member with Bond's potential 'from that small circle of bright young men of whom he has personal experience'. It was also essential that Bond be promoted to commissioned rank — not only in recognition of his skills but also to enable him to deputise for Trendall during his absences.

Archer's recommendations were adopted. For the new member, Trendall's choice fell on E. S. Barnes who, some weeks before at the age of 18, had graduated at Sydney University, carrying off the prizes in Mathematics and French. He had been brought to Trendall's notice by Room (his Professor) and by Bond (his senior by one year at Canterbury Boys High School). Corporal Barnes duly joined the Section (and Trendall and Bond at their boarding house) in February. It immediately became apparent that he did, indeed, possess the cryptographic flair and, in mid-March, Trendall was able to return to Sydney University for what was expected to be 'an extended period', leaving Lieutenant Bond (commissioned on 11 March 1943) in charge. Barnes was promoted to commissioned rank on 10 July 1944.

---

23 Cf the considerably higher figures reported in 52 Section's Monthly Traffic Records for November and December 1942 — 1,763 and 1,654 respectively. Perhaps Archer's figures exclude not only low-grade traffic (such as LA) but also the traffic in those high-grade cyphers on which his Section was not working, but merely forwarded to GC&CS for solution, i.e. PURPLE and Attaché traffic. By the end of 1943 Trendall was forwarding to GC&CS about 800–900 military and naval attaché messages per month (NAA: A6923/3, SI/2, Military Intelligence file, 16 June 1942, 'Y Organization in Australia', folio 158).

Chapter 2. The Diplomatic Special Intelligence Section

London's anxieties

While the Section was under Naval control its communications with GC&CS had passed through RAN channels, its outwards messages being despatched on a Typex machine at Monterey using the appropriate secret settings/drums provided by GC&CS. On the Section's transfer to LHQ, its outwards signals to GC&CS were despatched by the most secure means available to the army, the LHQ (LANDFORCES) — War Office (TROOPERS) circuit, using the one-time recyphering pads provided by the War Office for that circuit. This did not meet GC&CS's security standards; it meant that, between despatch and delivery, the plaintext of the signals could be read by the general cypher sections at both LANDFORCES and TROOPERS. The reaction of GC&CS was that it could have no dealings with strangers — Military Intelligence at LHQ — who were unindoctrinated and had not subscribed to GC&CS's rigorous and elaborate directions regarding the secrecy, transmission and distribution of intercepts and intelligence derived from them. On 3 January 1943, Archer informed Little that no signals had been received from GC&CS since 26 November and that requests for the resumption of communications had not been acknowledged.[24] Eventually, on 10 March, the following message from the Director GC&CS was conveyed to the CGS through the Commanding Officer of the British Army Liaison Mission in Australia:

> He [the Director] is greatly concerned about the handling by the Australian Military of ULTRA diplomatic material and, as he is receiving requests for assistance, asks me to ascertain the working arrangements of the Diplomatic Section under the Australian Military authorities. His anxiety particularly concerns the control of distribution of material and the number of individuals who have access to it.
>
> Provided he can receive the assurances for which he asks me, that the proper security is fully assured, he will co-operate fully.

This was followed the next day by a list of the specific undertakings required — chiefly acceptance of the regulations regarding ULTRA telegrams and Special Intelligence in force throughout British theatres of war and the US navy and an assurance that there would be no 'political interference' in handling such material. To this the CGS gave a prompt reply, accepting each of the undertakings.[25]

Later in the month the Army's most senior Signals Intelligence officer, Lieutenant Colonel A. W. Sandford (Officer Commanding, Australian Army

---

24 Ibid.
25 NAA, A6923/3, SI/10.

Section, Central Bureau, GHQ SWPA), whose relations with GC&CS were already firmly established, was flown to England to confer with GC&CS on this and other matters. At a meeting with A. G. Denniston, Head of its Diplomatic and Commercial Section, and his officers on 30 April, it was agreed that:

(i) GC&CS would pass to Australia all relevant cryptographic information on Japanese diplomatic codes (including microfilms of complete information on FUJI and X) and translations of London intercepts thought to be of interest to Australia — with special reference to Timor, the Greater East Asia area, and general Pacific strategy;

(ii) Australia would cease sending summaries, would send cypher texts of messages of interest to GC&CS (reserving the right to send translations where preferable), and would continue to send *at once* all B [i.e., PURPLE] machine traffic and any other unidentified diplomatic traffic intercepted by them (e.g. NE);

(iii) On receipt by the Australian Army of special Typex settings, communications would be transferred from the Navy to the Army and passed from LANDFORCES to TROOPERS (MI8);

(iv) Sandford would arrange with GC&CS a revised allocation of intercept coverage (with particular reference to traffic between Berlin and Tokyo, where UK stations experienced considerable difficulty).[26]

The very scattered and fragmentary records that survive suggest that the extensive daily exchange of raw material that this envisaged continued and expanded. For example, on 3 April 1944, Sandford relayed to Little the following signal from GC&CS: 'Reference Little's WWW78. Japanese texts or summaries about Portuguese Timor in JBC (the Foreign Office Cypher Book) or other systems, but excluding JAA, will henceforth be sent to you for your limited circulation in the north. Series JAA will be sent in ABC series just begun'.[27] In April 1944 the Section was sending GC&CS, in addition to Attaché traffic, between 4,000 and 5,000 groups of diplomatic traffic daily, consisting of selections from the daily lists of intercepted messages, all Moscow to Tokyo traffic and all Greater East Asia Ministry (GEAM) commercial traffic.[28] Apparently, reception conditions for traffic between Tokyo and its Embassy in Russia were better in Australia than at GC&CS and its overseas outstations. For example, Bond, on 25 May 1943, signalled 52 Section as follows: 'Both quantity and quality of traffic to and from RTZ [i.e. Kuibyshev] during the last fortnight has been most pleasing. Hope flow

---

26 Interception of Berlin–Tokyo traffic was also difficult in the United States: 'We eventually found we could get best coverage of the Berlin–Tokyo circuit at Corregidor' (L.F. Safford, 'Brief History of Communications Intelligence in the United States', US National Archives: 457, SRH–149).
27 NAA: A6923/3, Military Intelligence file 16/6/289, 'Central Bureau — Administration of', folio 75.
28 NAA: A6923/3, SI/10 Military Intelligence file 16/6/328, folio 88.

will continue from this source as we seem to intercept more of it than anyone else'.[29] For a period in early 1944, when reception conditions at Mornington were unfavourable, the watch on RTZ was delegated to a section of Australian Special Wireless Group located elsewhere, with 'considerable success'.[30]

July 1943 — The Japanese Foreign Ministry changes its codes

Since its inception, the principal function of the Section was to decrypt and process the telegrams sent in the code FUJI that were intercepted in Australia and New Zealand. In February 1943 the Section consisted of: on the cryptographic side, Trendall, Bond, Barnes and an assistant cryptographer; on the language side, the two British Consular officers (Archer and Graves) and two locally engaged translators, and a clerical staff of about five. After the recruitment of Barnes to fill the gap caused by the recall of Cooper, Trendall was able, in March, to take leave to return to Sydney University. On 1 July, however, the Japanese Foreign Ministry replaced FUJI with three new recyphered codes. Next, on 21 July a new transposition cypher was introduced for communications between Asian posts and the GEAM. Then, on 20 August another high-grade cypher, BA, was introduced by the Ministry for Foreign Affairs. Thus, the Allies were suddenly deprived of a considerable proportion of Japanese diplomatic traffic — until such time as their cryptographic organisations managed to break the new systems and laboriously establish their constituent code groups. In this vital task GC&CS urgently sought the Section's assistance. The immediate response was to recall Trendall to full-time duty on 9 July and to postpone for some weeks Graves's transfer to the Department of External Affairs (to become Adviser on Political Warfare to the Minister) and his replacement by another Consular officer (H. R. Sawbridge).

The role of the Section in breaking these new systems and establishing the new code groups is described in the report on Japanese Diplomatic Cyphers reproduced in Chapter 3. It was not until 13 June 1944 that Trendall could again be released to the university. He was back with the Section again from 4 August until 5 September, on which date he returned to the university for good.[31]

During 1944 Trendall was able to recruit and train three additional cryptographers. Private A. C. Eastway from the 2/3 Machine Gun Company at Merauke joined the Section in February. He had probably been brought to Trendall's attention

---

29 Australian War Memorial (AWM): 52, 7/39/19.
30 Little to CO Aust. Special Wireless Group 2 March 1945 (NAA: A6923/3, [DMI Message Traffic]).
31 University Archivist, University of Sydney to D.C.S. Sissons, 10 June 1998.

by J. W. Gibbes, his Classics master in his final year at North Sydney Boys High School in 1940. Private I. H. Smith (who had taken the exhibition at final honours in French language and literature at Melbourne University in December 1943) arrived in May. He also had been recommended to Trendall by Gibbes. In July, Trendall secured the transfer of Sergeant K. L. McKay from a LAA Regiment at Darwin. He had taken high distinctions in Classics in his second year at Sydney University when he enlisted in December 1941. The cryptographic section had now reached it maximum size and continued at this strength for the rest of the war.

Another translator, Warrant Officer II C. A. James (an Oxford classics undergraduate who had just completed the British army's Japanese language course at Bedford) arrived in May 1944. Later in the year Sawbridge and Archer were recalled to the United Kingdom and replaced by other Consular offices, E. T. Biggs in July and R. L. Cowley in December.

The raw material

In April 1942 a small W/T [Wireless/Telegraphy] Section of the Australian Corps of Signals was set up at Ferny Creek in the Dandenongs to intercept Japanese diplomatic circuits. In July it received reinforcements from 2nd Company GHQ Signals to bring it up to strength as a Special Wireless Section (Type B) and was named 52 Australian Wireless Section. It operated successively at Ferny Creek between April and August 1942, Bonegilla between August 1942 and November 1943 and Mornington between November 1943 and February 1946. Its sole task was intercepting Japanese diplomatic traffic for delivery to Trendall's Section (about 20 per cent by hand Morse by a direct landline, the remainder by a daily bag delivery). From the time of its move to Bonegilla it was the principal source of the Diplomatic Section's raw material and, after the latter's transfer to the army it was, with certain exceptions, its sole source of raw material.[32] 52 Section's all-ranks strength was 85, comprising one Captain, one Lieutenant, one Lieutenant (Australian Women's Army Service), one Company Quarter Master Sergeant/Company Sergeant Major, two Sergeants, seven Corporals, 72 Signalwomen/Signalmen (including seven Lance Corporals). Of the rank and

---

32 The principal exceptions were diplomatic traffic intercepted by the New Zealand cryptographic organisation and specific intercepts provided to the Diplomatic Section by GC&CS at the former's request. For a period from December 1942 the US army's 126 Signal Company in Brisbane were providing Trendall with copies of their intercepts of Japanese diplomatic traffic (Sandford to DDMI, 14 December 1942, NAA: A6923/3, 16/6/289). On occasion, when reception conditions at Mornington for a particular station or circuit were poor, the task of covering Japanese diplomatic traffic was undertaken by other Sections of the Australian Special Wireless Group — e.g. the Russian station RTZ in early 1944 and the low-power Far Eastern network R75 in February 1945 (ADMI to CO Aust. Special Wireless Group, 2 March 1945, NAA: A6923/3, [DMI Diplomatic Message Traffic]).

file, 52 were operators.[33] The unit operated 24 hours a day in four shifts using communications receivers of various makes (Kingsley, Hallicrafters, AWA and Philips) and an elaborate system of rhombic aerials set up on the Bonegilla racecourse. The operators kept watch on designated call signs and frequencies and were able to identify Japanese diplomatic traffic from the sending station's output by the originator and addressee designated in the preamble of each message (which, of necessity, was transmitted *en clair* and at hand speed). The text of the message was usually transmitted at machine speed. The operator recorded this on Edison wax cylinders and later replayed it at manageable speed and transcribed it.[34]

The Monthly Traffic Records that occasionally appear in 52 Section's war diary indicate the quantity and extent of the intercepts received by the Special Intelligence Section. An example is their record for May 1944 (see Annex 1, herein). It includes a listing of the stations from which traffic was received.

In the table that follows, I have shown the earliest and latest monthly totals available and those of two intermediate months. These figures, of course, include much material that the Special Intelligence Section did not read, e.g. naval and military attaché and JAA (i.e. PURPLE) traffic (all of which was forwarded to GC&CS) and messages in the low grade cypher LA (which were read only if specifically referred to in a high grade message).

Japanese diplomatic traffic intercepted by 52 Aust Wrls Sect:[35]

Originators and addressees

Country	Nov 1942	Feb 1943		May 1943		May 1944	
	From	From	To	From	To	From	To
Japan	1,000	828	817	1,351	1,318	1,108	1,621
Germany		1	195	101	421	817	315
Russia	2	125	79	293	243	623	266
Netherlands East Indies						424	602
French Indo-China	126	272	126	232	115	173	288
Thailand	231	218	186	88	60	84	50
Afghanistan	16	20	26	48	41	53	25
China (Occupied)		2	8		26	29	10

---

33 War Establishment III/38B/4, issued 31 May 1944 (NAA: A10908/1, 2, 'Report on Special Wireless Units (Signals) 1940–45').

34 ASWG Association to D.C.S. Sissons, 26 September 1994.

35 These figures are taken from Monthly Traffic Records occasionally appearing in the war diaries of HQ Australian Special Wireless Group (AWM: 52, 7/39/3) and 52 Australian Wireless Section (AWM: 52, 7/39/19), November 1942 and March 1943 and May 1943 and May 1944, respectively.

Country	Nov 1942	Feb 1943		May 1943		May 1944	
	From	From	To	From	To	From	To
Sweden	3	3	32	94	61	27	49
Philippines						9	2
Spain						1	9
Switzerland	122	83	23	85	81		45
France		6	44	22	16		26
Burma							16
Portugal				3	8		9
Vatican City							9
Italy	129	153	71	415	186		3
Hungary							3
South America	134	4	106	3	153		
Other (Call Sign YOM)					5		
Unaccounted for			2		1		
Total: Messages	1,763	1,715	1,715	2,735	2,735	3,348	3,348
Total: 5-Figure Groups	145,101	126,645		212,723		268,219	

The product and its dissemination

From the time of the transfer to the army, Archer produced a weekly Special Intelligence Précis of Japanese diplomatic intercepts, which the ADMI distributed to the following recipients: Commander-in-Chief Australian Military Forces, CGS, Director of Military Intelligence, Director of Naval Intelligence, Director of Intelligence (RAAF), Director of Military Intelligence (New Zealand), Director of Naval Intelligence (New Zealand), Central Bureau Brisbane, G2 GHQ SWPA, and Commander SWP Force (US navy).[36] All recipients were required to burn the précis after perusal and to sign a receipt stating that this had been done. It was distributed to the New Zealand recipients because there was close cooperation with the New Zealand signals intelligence organisation, which provided Australia with the cypher texts of any Japanese diplomatic telegrams that it intercepted.[37]

36　Northcott to Dewing 16 June 1943 (NAA: A6293/3, 37/401/425).
37　Undated note, Archer to Little (NAA: A6293/3, 37/401/425).

Initially, the Australian Department of External Affairs was not a recipient. This is surprising; in the United Kingdom it was the practice of GC&CS to pass on an intercept, under the strictest conditions of secrecy, to those civil departments that it might concern.[38] And, in this manner, some intercepts reached External Affairs in Canberra via the Dominions Office, introduced on each occasion by the well understood formula 'Information available from a secret but entirely trustworthy source'.[39] In June 1943 the content of a telegram despatched by the Japanese Ambassador at Kuibyshev on 14 April reached External Affairs by this route. In it, the Ambassador reported that he had heard from a diplomatic colleague that William Slater, the Australian Ambassador at Kyibyshev, was returning to Australia for good the following day because he had found that he was making no headway against Russian officialdom. The Domions Office passed this on to the External Affairs Officer in London, together with the information that the message had been intercepted at Melbourne.

When this became known to the Secretary of the Department of External Affairs, W. R. Hodgson, he immediately called on Little and enquired why the information had not been passed to him direct. In replying, Little laid stress on the danger to the source should it become known, as it might be if it came to the notice of a Minister. For this reason, he said, it was not possible to provide Hodgson with the information. Hodgson then intimated that if such information were not made available he would have no alternative but to take the matter up officially. Little thereupon promised to refer the matter to the CGS.

In a letter to Hodgson dated 14 June the CGS proposed the following solution, which Hodgson accepted:

> You will be sent a copy of the Special Intelligence Précis issued weekly on the understanding that the précis is regarded as being for your own personal information and is to be destroyed by fire immediately after perusal.
>
> The contents are to be used as background information only. Where you consider any information contained in the précis vitally affects Australia

---

38 For example, among the 41 GC&CS intercepts of Japanese diplomatic telegrams for the period 21 November 1941 – 22 December 1941 that were later tendered to the Clausen Investigation (US 79th Congress, *Joint Committee on the Investigation of the Pearl Harbor Attack*, Hearings, part 35, exhibit 8) a typical distribution had been: Director GC&CS (3 copies), Foreign Office (3 copies), Political Intelligence Division, Admiralty, War Office (3 copies), India Office (2 copies), Colonial Office, Air Ministry, Ministry of Economic Warfare (2 copies), Sir Edward Bridges, and Dominions Office.

39 For example, in this manner the Australian External Affairs Officer in London was able, on 9 January 1940, to cable to the Department in Canberra summaries of telegrams from the Japanese Minister at Lisbon dated 24 November, 4 and 22 December and his Foreign Minister's replies of 21 and 30 December regarding Japanese plans to apply pressure on Portugal in order to secure oil concessions in Timor (NAA: A981, TIM P20).

and should be disclosed to the Minister, I would be glad if you could get in touch with me so that the paraphrased edition of that particular portion of the document might be made available.

I will instruct the Intelligence Branch to bring under my notice specially any matters of this nature which should be brought officially to the notice of your Department so that by this means we will endeavour to keep you informed officially apart from our present arrangements.[40]

Eight months later, on 3 February 1944, Sandford, from Central Bureau, Brisbane, informed Little that arrangements had been made for Hodgson to receive texts or summaries of telegrams of interest to Australia intercepted by other partners in the cryptographic network:

I have just received a personal signal passed by the DMI, War Office from the Director GC&CS. He states that the Foreign Office have consulted the American authorities and have agreed to send to me texts or summaries of Japanese highest grade messages for showing to the Australian Department of External Affairs when the interests of that Department are directly concerned.

The messages are to contain the phrase 'Pass to Archer', and Archer is to be made responsible for passing this material to Colonel Hodgson. London insist that Hodgson should be reminded of the conditions of security which were enjoined on him last July. They state that no further distribution, not even to Central Bureau, should be given to these messages which are only intended for Hodgson.

They suggest in a final paragraph that Archer should make it clear if necessary that he is not in a position to discuss the political implications of the messages.

I shall therefore send the messages when they arrive by safe hand means 'Most Secret and Personal' to Archer care of you, so that he will be the only people [sic] at LHQ to whom they are available. I should think this should meet London's requirements.[41]

Surprisingly, distribution of the précis to US recipients ceased in April 1944. On 29 March Sandford informed Little that:

---

40 Northcott to Hodgson, 14 June 1943 (ibid.).
41 Presumably after May 1944, when the Melbourne Section acquired its own cypher section and Typex machines, for which GC&CS provided its designated settings, such intercepts were dispatched by GC&CS to Archer direct and not through Sandford.

(a) London has requested that we no longer supply diplomatic Special Intelligence to United States authorities in the South-West Pacific Area and they state that this request emanates from G2 (Special Branch) Washington.

(b) They also specially request that political intelligence contained in these and the UKBJs be not discussed by Australian recipients with their United States counterparts.

As a result, G2 GHQ SWPA and Commander SWP Force (USN) were promptly excised from the distribution list of the Special Intelligence Précis.[42]

The content of the intercepts

This is dealt with in the section of the report entitled 'Intelligence Derived from the Messages' (see below). On this, one is little able to elaborate; for the records of the Section systematically and painstakingly maintained in its own office appear to have been destroyed in their entirety. These included: (i) the leather-bound foolscap register (dubbed by Trendall 'The Koran') into which the particulars of every intercept was entered; (ii) the file of every intercept received (including the message form filled in by the telegraphist, and, where decrypted, the cryptographer's work sheets and the typed translation); (iii) a file of the weekly précis; (iv) a person and subject card index of the contents of all intercepts translated; (v) files of the Section's inwards and outwards correspondence and signals.

The Department of External Affairs appear scrupulously to have fulfilled their obligation to burn on perusal each document received from the Section.

The recipients of the précis appear to have done the same. Of the copies received by G2 HQ SWPA, only one, No. 4, for the week ending 21 December 1942, escaped destruction. It has found its way into the MacArthur Archives at Norfolk, Virginia (Box 60, Typescript 5 pp). We have, however some indication of the contents of No. 13 (22 February 1943) to No. 45 (22 November 1943) of the précis; G2 SWPA, when tendering these to the Chief of Staff SWPA for his perusal, attached to each a one-page 'brief' of its contents, and these have survived among the wartime records of the US National Security Agency.[43] Two typical examples are reproduced in the following pages.

---

42   NAA: A6293, 37/401/425.
43   US National Archives: 457, SRH-307.

G.H.Q. South-west Pacific area, Checksheet
From: G-2   To: C. of S.   Date: July 9/43
Brief of Special Intell. Precis No.32, July 8, 1943

Note the following items:

Russo-Japanese Negotiations: The question of American air bases in Russia is still alive; Sato fears Russia will demand Tokyo's assurances that Germany will not be granted submarine bases in Far Eastern waters, and he discusses the dangers of such grants: German subs would surely attack Soviet shipping in order to bring Japan into war against Russia.

Prime Minister Tojo: Extraordinary secrecy surrounding itinerary and schedule of Tojo's tour of occupied territories suggests Japanese suspicion concerning Admiral Yamamoto's death. (Comment: Central Bureau's reports since 1 July indicate the Japanese have introduced new W/T security measures).

Shipping: A Bangkok message indicates no shipping available for shipping of cereals from Siam to S. China.

Europe: Jap Minister in Budapest does not expect much action on Eastern front this year, nor a European Second Front. He admits that grounds for optimism are few, but expects a stalemate rather than a German defeat. He also argues that England is playing a deep game by seeing the exhaustion of Russia as well as the destruction of Germany.

Japan's Outlook on the War: [About 17 characters expunged by NSA] furnish a most interesting insight into past and future Japanese aims. It is recommended that this section of the Precis be read in detail. Significant items: original Tokyo war aims; attitude toward Russia; food and shipping situation; a/c and pilot losses; damage from Tokyo raid; policy on treatment of captured airmen; strained Army–Navy relations after war reverses.

V.S.M-S [presumably Colonel Van S Merle-Smith]

Chapter 2. The Diplomatic Special Intelligence Section

G.H.Q. SOUTH-WEST PACIFIC AREA, CHECK-SHEET
From: G-2   To: C. of S.   Date: 23 Oct '43
Brief of Special Intell. Precis No.41, 14 October, 1943

Note the following items:

Italy: The Italian diplomats in Greater East Asia have failed to rally to the establishment of the Fascist Party, resulting in the Japanese Ambassador [sic] having no dealings with them. Japan's decision is still to hand over all Italian extra-territorial rights in China to the Nanking Puppet Government.

Philippines: Raul Jose P. Laurel, President Designate, and Bargas Jorge Vargas, head of prospective Administration, have been summoned to Tokyo; also, they have been notified of Japan's decision to grant independence. Shozo Murata has been appointed Japanese Ambassador to the Philippines and will conduct negotiations for a formal treaty.

French Indo-China: Allied air raids cause considerable damage on port of Haiphong. Japan is trying to purchase the newspaper 'La Depeche' for propaganda; the French appear reluctant on the matter.

Siam: Pi-bun claims that his health will prevent him from attending the Greater East Asia Conference as Chief Siamese delegate. Pi-bun has proposed to send a deputy, likely Vichit, who was lately Foreign Minister, and is now Ambassador Designate to Japan. The transfer of 'new territories' to Siam has been fixed for 18 October. In anticipation of air raids on Bangkok, the Japanese Ambassador asks that arrangements be made for insurance of Japanese property.

Inter-Axis Trade: Bangkok message, 6 October, states a German vessel will call at this place to purchase tin. The Germans want 1,000 tons; Japan's tin holdings total 1,747 tons. Purchase of Siamese rubber for October have been fixed at 250 tons for Germans, 750 for Japan.

Shipping: Hanoi, 13 October, of the two ships being constructed under naval contract, one was laid down 15 April and launched 9 October. the engines do not appear ready. Both vessels are the 20 ton class.

C.A.W. [presumably Maj.Gen C.A.Willoughby]

The report alludes, very briefly, to the high intelligence value of the intercepts of the telegrams exchanged between the Japanese Foreign Ministry and its Ambassador in Russia, Sato Naotake.

It seems that in its coverage of the Kuibyshev–Tokyo–Kuibyshev circuit, the Section was able to provide strategic intelligence of value. In this connection two preliminary points should be made. The first point is that, as we have already noted, thanks partly to its location, 52 Section's coverage of this circuit was successful. Several signals from Bond to 52 Section during the period February to May 1943 indicate that 52 Section were instructed to watch this circuit carefully, and that they were more successful in this than were GC&CS and its various outstations.[44] Indeed, it seems that GC&CS were in fact relying heavily on 52 Section for its coverage of this circuit. The figures in 52 Section's Monthly Traffic Records attest to this success.

Kuibyshev–Tokyo–Kuibyshev circuit
Messages intercepted by 52 Section February–July 1943

	Feb	Mar	Apr	May	Jun	Jul
Kuibyshev–Tokyo	125	114	152	293	374	363
Tokyo–Kuibyshev	79	163	192	243	273	262

The second point is that all the communications on this circuit appear to have been sent in cyphers that the Section could read — Kahn's statement that the Embassy at Kuibyshev was not equipped with a PURPLE machine appears to be correct.[45]

We know the content of some of these messages; some of them (intercepted by Washington and its outstations) are quoted in Washington's daily *Magic Summary*. It is likely that most, if not all, of those quoted there were also intercepted and solved by Melbourne. An example of this traffic is the Ambassador's long telegram of 26 February 1943, the full text of which is reproduced in Washington's *Magic Summary* No. 344 issued on 5 March. One can be confident that 52 Section also intercepted this. Their traffic log indicates that, for messages from Kuibyshev, 26 February was one of their good days — they intercepted 12 messages from Kuibyshev on the 26 February, followed by one on 27 February.[46] The telegram would have been sent in FUJI and, according to the report, by May 1942 the Section was able to read virtually all the FUJI traffic it received. Below is the telegram in full, as reproduced in the *Magic Summary*.

---

44 AWM: 52, 7/39/3, Trendall to Walker, 10 February 1943, 12 February 1943, 6 March 1943; Bond to Walker, 16 March 1943. AWM: 52, 7/39/19, Bond to Walker, 20 April 1943, 21 April 1943, 25 May 1943, 28 May 1943.
45 D. Kahn, *The Codebreakers* (New York: Macmillan, 1967), p. 446.
46 In light of the time difference between Kuibyshev and Melbourne, the message intercepted on 27 February could also have been sent on the previous day.

Kuibyshev to Tokyo 26 February 1943

What the Russians have done to the Germans this winter has astonished everyone. Whether the Russians can continue their headlong advance for three or four weeks more until the middle of March defies conjecture, but everything up until February 20, about which I have already wired you, indicates that this is a possibility. The course of the war between Germany and Russia naturally has great bearing on the battle of Greater East Asia. That is why I venture to express to you my very frankest feelings, and I hope that my Government will not fail to consider them.

1. It is problematical whether the Germans will stop in the Ukraine at the Dnieper line, or whether they will flee beyond the border, form a line and come back this summer as they did last. Some say they can and some say they can't, but I will tell you my frank opinions. I personally am pessimistic. The Germans have to think about the war in North Africa and I don't think they can afford to waste too much of their strength in this dim battle of the East. I think that they will, rather, get out of the Soviet Union and then make a truce. Germany lacks men, materials, and oil, so I believe that she will concentrate on Western Europe and will strive to save North Africa, all the while continuing her aerial and U-boat campaign against British and American ships.

2. The fall of Stalingrad caused Germany to propagandize the danger of the Bolshevization of Europe. That was, of course, to frighten England and the United States, and this prospect, to tell the truth, is a real danger. I think it may be quite true that in their hearts England and America have both begun to fear the dread strength of the Soviet. But I do not think they will let up on the Reich, nor do I believe that they will forsake the Soviet, refusing her aid. Nevertheless, facing what they consider the peril of Bolshevism, they must be in quite a dilemma.

Of course, I do not know, but I think it hardly likely that after the Soviet forces chase the Germans beyond the borders they will pursue them far into the Reich. Stalin's various statements indicate that they will not. I do not mean to say that we can take every word that falls from Joseph Stalin's mouth as the gospel truth, and we have to make allowance for the possibility of his changing his mind, if it is to his advantage. Nevertheless, under the present circumstances in Europe, I doubt if Stalin considers it to his own advantage to see Germany exterminated. So rather than cooperate further with England and the United States, he might, quite possibly, let Germany turn on them and fight it out to the destruction of both sides. It would seem to me that after driving

Germany completely out of her borders, after retaking her cities, and being faced with the problem of reconstruction, the Soviet Union would be loath to have the Red Army go on and on.

In other words, I believe that when she gets back all the land she has lost, she will not try to annihilate the Reich. I think that she will let it go at that and turn to the task of rebuilding her nation.

3. That is how it seems to me the German–Soviet situation is shaping up. As soon as it becomes apparent that a German–Soviet peace or truce is imminent, England and the United States will, of course, do their level best to prevent it. However, I think there is every likelihood that the Russians will stop at the border. I already seem to perceive a lack of interest throughout the land of the Soviets as to what happens in Western Europe, and I doubt if Russia will continue her blows against Germany for the sake of the Anglo-Saxons. Thus, if the Kremlin adopts an entirely new policy, there will be no point for England and America to try to sway her. As soon as Russia decides just what to do with respect to Germany, it will have a tremendous effect.

4. And again I must point out to you that these sudden changes in the European picture will certainly have a big effect on our own Empire. I tell you that the time has already come when we must reconsider our policy, which has been one of friendliness towards Germany, neutrality towards Russia and war on England and the United States. I know that in Japan there are those who agree that we must save Germany, because if we don't the Soviet will get so great that she will forever be a tremendous threat against us. They say that, while Germany is recouping, we ought to strike the Soviet immediately, breaking her suddenly, and make our Empire safe and stable.[47] But as for me, I tell you that the only course to follow is to do our level best to avoid a clash with Russia. As man to man, that is how I see it.

We Japanese can be expecting harder blows from America and England, so we ought to try to wean the Russians from them. I earnestly pray that we will not attack Russia, because, if we do, don't you know that she will join hands with the United States, establish a new front and ruin

---

47 As the Military Intelligence Service (MIS) analyst editing that number of the *Magic Summary* noted, this is probably a reference to the repeated advice from Oshima, the ambassador at Berlin, that Japan should come to Germany's aid by launching an attack on Siberia. Oshima again urged this on the foreign minister in a telegram dispatched on 26 January (see C. Boyd, *Hitler's Japanese Confidant: General Oshima Hiroshi and MAGIC Intelligence, 1941–45*, University of Kansas Press, 1993, pp. 62–65, 79–80).

us? That is a thought from which I recoil instantly. In spite of all the vicissitudes to which our Empire has been exposed, have we not, thus far, managed to keep level-headed in our policy toward Russia?

5. Let us consider our own Empire's relations with Germany and with Russia. Germany has already fought twenty months in Russia and in the end she has lost much and gained nothing. In the meantime, we got into war with America and England, but we still maintained good relations with the Soviet. Of course, if Germany had been able to whip the Russians, everything would have been better for Germany and for us, but that is like crying over spilt milk. Now Germany herself is so thoroughly demoralized that I personally do not believe that she can keep up her fight against the Soviet. So let us forget Russia for a moment.

We Japanese have one thing in common with the Germans: It is to our mutual interest to increase our prowess against the Anglo-Saxons, and, at the same time, wean Russia from their camp. Let Russia and Germany make peace if they will — because if Germany didn't have to waste so much of her strength on the Eastern front, she could help us out more against America and England. I don't need to tell you that.

As a matter of fact, since it has already been demonstrated that it would be futile for Germany again to try to shatter Russia and take her resources, I think we should take it upon ourselves to try to mediate for peace between those two powers, at the same time making clear to Germany that our Empire expects her to help us out even in Greater East Asia in our struggle against America and England.

Let me repeat again, this time more clearly, that I think the time has come for us to become even more friendly with Russia and to convince Germany that the time has come to desist, and for us to try to mediate for peace between the two combatants.

6. If Germany is headstrong, and says she is going back for more, let her go. But as for me, I still say that, insofar as the battle of Greater East Asia will permit, we should remain on the best of relations with Russia and do nothing that would harm those good relations. I tell you that this is of the utmost importance, because, even if Germany is not now ready to stop, sooner or later she is going to find it necessary. Let us, in the meantime, do our best to wean Russia from the United States, and when Germany has had a belly full, mediate for peace.

7. In trying to settle the question of border lines, the question of interests in northern Sakhalin comes up most frequently. Judging from my experience, since I arrived here a year ago, the question of those

interests is the most important obstacle to amity between our two nations. In the spring of 1941 Molotov and Matsuoka talked this over. If war hadn't broken out, I think we would have already settled this trouble, and, if so, we wouldn't have this facing us now in the midst of fireworks.

Right after I took office here last April, I expressed this feeling in an interview with Molotov and we both agreed that the present was no time to worry about it and that we had better wait, leaving the status as of 1941. However, it is true that this status is very shaky, a status in name only. The fact is that, after the Communist regime was established, it took over many of the rights of other countries which held over from the Imperial regime, and the only instance where foreigners are still allowed to manage and control any of these interests is in the case of our rights in northern Sakhalin and our fishing rights.

We can easily imagine that Russia is worried considerably about this, because it is a question of a great nation saving face. The fishing question is a little different and they have not yet called us to task about it, but the question of our interests in northern Sakhalin is a source of great dissatisfaction to them. I think, therefore, that, for the time being, we should withstand their pressure as much as possible, and, if we come to mediate between Germany and Russia, or when we independently begin to improve our relations with Russia, we should certainly do our very best at the outset to settle these provoking questions once and for all.

[The parts numbered 8 and 9 were so badly garbled in transmission that they cannot be read]

10. The best policy would be for us Japanese to get together with the Germans and help them to make peace and ourselves to establish better relations with Russia. I would like to see a truce between those two nations, but, if Germany won't listen, we must remember that we are waging a terrible battle in Greater East Asia and we will have to make up our own mind. What Germany says need not matter! Our country is free to make her own diplomatic decisions, isn't she? Please bear that in mind when you negotiate with Berlin.

11. Of course, it may be said that, if Russia gets out of the war and we keep fighting America and England for a long time, as soon as we are exhausted there is the great danger that the Far East will be Bolshevized. This is the same problem that confronts Europe. But is it a real problem? I doubt it. If we are exhausted, the Soviet will still be so busy reconstructing her nation that she would be no great menace to us.

However, the settlement of borders and interests is something for the future. Right now we are forced to fight the United States and England, and until we have whipped them, it is very necessary to keep on the good side of the Soviet Union. So I say that we should continue to strike at the Anglo-Saxons and, in the meantime, endeavour to establish firmly what we call Greater East Asia. That is enough for our present objective. After we have established this Greater East Asia, then it will be time enough to make it a bulwark against Bolshevism.

12. What I have told you here has direct bearing on our war effort in Greater East Asia, so will you please follow my advice? Please get in touch with the military, and as soon as you can possibly get a chance bring about a Cabinet decision along these lines. Also please listen to what Morishima* has to say and see that his views are given due consideration.

I have confidentially given the Army and Navy Attachés here a copy of this message.

[* Minister Morishima, second in charge at the Japanese Embassy in Russia, recently returned to Tokyo to submit a first-hand report to the Foreign Office.]

From the telegrams quoted in successive issues of the *Magic Summary*, it becomes apparent that Sato's policy of accommodation with Russia at all costs was adopted and pursued. In early May, Morishima telegraphed to Sato that he was returning on 15 May and that: 'As for the big thing ... I have reached a degree of understanding with the quarters concerned here which makes me think there is no longer any question of there being a disaster after I leave'. Shigemitsu, the Foreign Minister, telegraphed to Sato on 26 May: 'We are agreed that the fundamental principle of Japan–Soviet relations must be adjusted. Therefore we are glad to say that we are able to concur with the message you sent us by Morishima .... We want to get down to business now, and in all subsequent talks you are to make our primary object the ironing out of all political difficulties between Japan and Russia'. Shigemitsu's telegraphed to Sato again on 28 June: ' ... These negotiations are designed to settle gradually all problems pending between Japan and Russia and to compose relations between the two nations. ... As you say, we are going to conduct these negotiations in order to keep the Soviet neutral.' The daily totals of 52 Section's Kuibyshev–Tokyo–Kuibyshev intercepts shown in its Monthly Traffic Records for the period February to July indicate that Melbourne was intercepting at least as much of these exchanges as was Washington.

The talkative signalman

About 20 per cent of Mornington's intercepts were delivered to the Section in hand Morse by a direct landline. The telegraphist on duty would bring each message into the cryptographers' room as soon as he had taken it down. One evening late in 1944, one of these telegraphists, an Australian Corps of Signals corporal, was relaxing in the servicemen's recreation hut beside St Paul's Cathedral. He was an outgoing, helpful chap by nature, and the few drinks that he had had at Young & Jackson's across the road had made him more so. He got into conversation with a young soldier at the same table who had just completed his recruit training and was awaiting allocation. The corporal urged him to apply to join the Section and explained to him in some detail the work that it was doing. By way of illustration he sketched out the transposition block of the GEAM cypher (JBB) and showed him how each row was read off from it. He told him to go to Victoria Barracks and ask for Little. The following day the recruit did so. He was directed to the office of Little's Captain I(x). There he stated his business and the Corporal was placed under arrest. There were several courses open. One was to charge him with the unlawful communication of secret information under Section 79 of the *Crimes Act* (Penalty: seven years imprisonment). This, however, could be tried only by a civilian court and this would entail the secrets being further disseminated. An alternative was to charge him under Section 73A of the *Defence Act* with communicating naval, military or air force information otherwise than in the course of his official duty (the charge commonly preferred against soldiers who mentioned troop movements in their letters to their families). This was tryable by court martial, which could impose a penalty up to £10. Instead, the matter appears to have been disposed of extra-judicially: he was posted forthwith to a remote and insalubrious part of New Guinea and remained there for the duration of the war.

The *Kormoran* — HMAS *Sydney* Vigenère

Early in 1945 a small cryptographic task, quite unrelated to signals intelligence or Japanese cyphers, was assigned to the Section. On 11 January, 20 German prisoners of war (POW), including Commander Detmers, the Captain of the raider *Kormoran* that had sunk HMAS *Sydney* off the coast of Western Australia in 1941, tunnelled their way out of the Dhurringile POW camp in northern Victoria. When, a week later, Detmers was recaptured, there was found in his possession an exercise book of the type on sale in the camp canteen (the local 'VANA' brand), the contents of which were in code. This was seized by Military

Intelligence and sent to the Section for decryption.[48] The text, amounting to about 6,250 characters (the 26 letters of the alphabet plus an additional four: A̲, B̲, C̲, D̲), consisted of 25 sections (or entries) of unequal lengths varying from 39 to 525 characters. To give an example, the largest section read as follows:

```
L X C̲ F U R Y I B̲ Y B D̲ U V E J M K B̲ H Z A O Y J A R O I
H K J̲ X A̲ H Z I J̲ E M V N V X K T U K S P M C̲ H V J F B̲ G
Q Y M J A̲ J U T E V J Q W R W C̲ D N A̲ U S G M C T I L F N
J I J P R Y H K Z U J D J B V R B̲ E Y J T W D C C̲ J P Y W
A̲ G Z K J P B Z Q M B B G S A R V A̲ B H S M B H Q B B̲ P I
W A̲ E M I J M G I L O J X P K W D̲ H Z B V X I M O M C̲ I W
S Y M H Z X Y Z I P V W Z D T Y K N J N C̲ M Q K N Q A̲ I B
G G W W Y Q Y Y K A̲ S I M C̲ C U B̲ S L K U U Z H N N Q Q I
I O J D̲ M H B C B̲ S J Q L K B W G R C̲ X P U U U I G S W M
D T W K V N U J H B H Q J C̲ C̲ X B G X W A̲ C M C̲ A L O S J
M D W K J A X W W H L S J Z U K B̲ D O I H K H N C̲ L M R Y
C̲ C L X T X I L K M D D J̲ T N J A̲ J X P X W R Q M D T T Z
T̲ U A C̲ X F J F T O I H C Z H J N W C B G S S U O M L L W
Y Z F P̲ Y B̲ P I W W P I I J M O S H V H T W R W R Q D K K
W O S J M D̲ L C W W W H Z Z V Q M Q R A̲ Y B P X K V X J Y
Y R O Y W M B I G G W O H P B R R J Y W M B X H T B R V K
B̲ C T T Q H K A O G S H A̲ D T Y H S R Y L U C T U H Z U H
Q J̲ Z Y G S G T D B G Q V̲ N W M P B̲ W A̲ H N L U H N G W O
H P B
```

As Smith was fluent in German, he was given first shot at the material. With some help from Barnes and from one of the clerical staff whose native language was German, he soon broke it. The method, Smith tells me, was simple. First the cryptogram was examined for its constituent symbols. This showed an alphabet of 30 characters — the standard 26-letter alphabet plus the additional A̲, B̲, C̲, and D̲ — each of the 30 symbols appearing frequently. Next, a sample portion was tested for periodicity — the recurrence of the same interval between repeated polygrams. This revealed numerous examples of intervals of 15 and its multiples between repetitions — e.g. in the sample above, between: the HZs in rows 1 and 2, the OIHs in rows 2 and 12, the OSJMDs in rows 11 and 16, and the GWOHPBs in rows 17 and 20.

Taken together, these phenomena strongly suggested polyalphabetic substitution in which a cycle of 15 encyphering alphabets was employed. Working on this hypothesis, they then sought to identify in each of the 15 encyphering alphabets the most frequently occurring symbol. These should each represent the most frequently occurring letter in the plaintext message, which if the message was

---

48 A copy of Detmers' GEFECHTSBERICHT cryptogram and the solution of it by GC&CS in England is available from NAA: B5823, 'Folder of documents titled Dietmars' Diary — account of action between Kormoran and Sydney — decode and translations'. Treweek, when interviewed in 1990, had a clear recollection of what he termed the GEFECHTSBERICHT cryptogram and its speedy solution by his colleague at FRUMEL, Miller, at the time of its capture.

Breaking Japanese Diplomatic Codes

in the German language, must be E, which constitutes about 16.7 per cent of normal German text (The runners-up are N and I with 9.9 per cent and 7.8 per cent respectively).

If we apply this method to our sample section, ordering it into the 15 columns representing the encyphering alphabets produces the following:

```
0                     1
1  2  3  4  5  6  7  8  9  0  1  2  3  4  5

L  X  C  F  U  R  Y  I  B  Y  B  D  U  V  E
J  M  K  B  H  Z  A  O  Y  J  A  R  O  I  H
K  J  X  A  H  Z  I  J  E  M  V  N  V  X  K
T  U  K  S  P  M  C  H  V  J  F  B  G  Q  Y
M  J  A  J  U  T  E  V  J  Q  W  R  W  C  D
N  A  U  S  G  M  C  T  I  L  F  N  J  I  J
P  R  Y  H  K  Z  U  J  D  J  B  V  R  B  E
Y  J  T  W  D  C  C  J  P  Y  W  A  G  Z  K
J  P  B  Z  Q  M  B  B  G  S  A  R  V  A  B
H  S  M  B  H  Q  B  B  P  I  W  A  E  M  I
J  M  G  I  L  O  J  X  P  K  W  D  H  Z  B
V  X  I  M  O  M  C  I  W  S  Y  M  H  Z  X
Y  Z  I  P  V  W  Z  D  T  Y  K  N  J  N  C
M  Q  K  N  Q  A  I  B  G  G  W  W  Y  Q  Y
Y  K  A  S  I  M  C  C  U  B  S  L  K  U  U
Z  H  N  N  Q  Q  I  I  O  J  D  M  H  B  C
B  S  J  Q  L  K  B  W  G  R  C  X  P  U  U
U  I  G  S  W  M  D  T  W  K  V  N  U  J  H
B  H  Q  J  C  C  X  B  G  X  W  A  C  M  C
A  L  O  S  J  M  D  W  K  J  A  X  W  W  H
L  S  J  Z  U  K  B  D  O  I  H  K  H  N  C
L  M  R  Y  C  C  L  X  T  X  I  L  K  M  D
D  J  T  N  J  A  J  X  P  X  W  R  Q  M  D
T  T  Z  T  U  A  C  X  F  J  F  T  O  I  H
C  Z  H  J  N  W  C  B  G  S  S  U  O  M  L
L  W  Y  Z  F  P  Y  B  P  I  W  W  P  I  I
J  M  O  S  H  V  H  T  W  R  W  R  Q  D  K
K  W  O  S  J  M  D  L  C  W  W  W  H  Z  Z
V  Q  M  Q  R  A  Y  B  P  X  K  V  X  J  Y
Y  R  O  Y  W  M  B  I  G  G  W  O  H  P  B
R  R  J  Y  W  M  B  X  H  T  B  R  V  K  B
C  T  T  Q  H  K  A  O  G  S  H  A  D  T  Y
H  S  R  Y  L  U  C  T  U  H  Z  U  H  Q  J
Z  Y  G  S  G  T  D  B  G  Q  V  N  W  M  P
B  W  A  H  N  L  U  H  N  G  W  O  H  P  B
```

In each of the columns, the most frequent characters, it will be observed, are as follows ($_c$ denoting cyphertext, $_e$ denoting plaintext):

```
Alphabet  1:   4 x J,  4 x L,  4 x Y,  3 x B
Alphabet  2:   4 x J,  4 x M,  4 x S,  3 x R,  3 x W
Alphabet  3:   4 x O,  3 x G,  3 x J,  3 x K,  3 x T,  3 x A
Alphabet  4:   8 x S,  4 x Y,  3 x J,  3 x N,  3 x Q,  3 x Z  ∴ S_c = E_p
Alphabet  5:   5 x H,  4 x U,  3 x J,  3 x L,  3 x Q,  3 x W  ∴ H_c = E_p
Alphabet  6:   9 x M,  3 x K,  3 x W,  3 x Z,  3 x A,  3 x C  ∴ M_c = E_p
Alphabet  7:   4 x C,  4 x C,  3 x B,  3 x D,  3 x I,  3 x Y,  3 x B
Alphabet  8:   5 x X,  4 x B,  4 x I,  4 x T,  4 x B,  3 x J  ∴ X_c = E_p
Alphabet  9:   8 x G,  6 x P,  3 x W  ∴ G_c = E_p
Alphabet 10:   6 X J,  4 x S,  4 x X,  3 x G,  3 x I,  3 x Y  ∴ J_c = E_p
Alphabet 11:  12 x W,  3 x A,  3 x B,  3 x F,  3 x V  ∴ W_c = E_p
Alphabet 12:   6 x R,  5 x N,  4 x A,  3 x W  ∴ R_c = E_p
Alphabet 13:   8 x H,  3 x O,  3 x V,  3 x W  ∴ H_c = E_p
Alphabet 14:   6 x M,  4 x I,  4 x Z,  3 x Q  ∴ M_c = E_p
Alphabet 15:   4 x B,  4 x H,  4 x Y,  3 x D,  3 x C
```

This, unfortunately, gives us no clear signs for E_p in alphabets 1, 2, 3, 7, and 15; but, as we have indicated, it provides hopeful indications in each of the others. The next step is, in the test section, to convert each character in these encyphering alphabets into plaintext.

Taking the first row, LXCFURYIBYBDUVE, as an example, U in Column 5 must be the product of plaintext encyphered with Alphabet 5. In Alphabet 5 cyphertext H_c represents E_p. This leads us to the assumption that U_c represents R_p. For, in polyalphabetic substitutions, the usual method adopted by the encypherer to provide and designate the various alphabets used is for him to write out a Vigenère square. In this, the top line is the letters of the alphabet in alphabetical sequence. This becomes the plaintext alphabet. Underneath it he writes out the same alphabet shifted one letter to the left, and so on, with each succeeding alphabet shifting one letter to the left. These are the encyphering alphabets, to each of which he gives an identifying letter, which he uses in the keyword. Thus, the usual Vigenère square is 26 x 26, with A at the top-left corner, the top row and the first column each extending from A to Z. But Detmers, the cyphertext indicates, was using the alphabet plus an additional four characters — A, B, C, and D. We assume, therefore, that his Vigenère square was 30 x 30. We also assume that, for ease of encypherment, he put the additional four characters in sequence at the end. Converting back into plaintext on this basis the characters encyphered with these ten alphabets, the sample section will read as follows:

Breaking Japanese Diplomatic Codes

Unfortunately, when we examine the plaintext above, it is evident that in Alphabet 4 S_c cannot represent E_p, for that would sometimes produce, as plaintext, letters that do not exist (e.g. C in Column 4, Row 3; D in Column 2, Row 4; Column 3, Row 6; and, Column 4, Row 4). For the same reason in Alphabet 12, H_c cannot represent E_p (this would produce as plaintext B in Column 1, Row 6; C in Column 2, Row 6 and Column 3, Row 4; and, D in Column 4, rows 3 and 4). Our solutions for these two alphabets must therefore be struck out. The string ZENT?AL in Column 4, Row 8 suggests that in Alphabet 12, A_c represents Rp, which would produce ZENTRAL (i.e. that N_c, the runner-up in our frequency count represents E_p). We shall therefore assume this.

It now remains for us to identify the unsolved alphabets by filling in the missing letters in obvious words in the plaintext that has so far emerged. TE?EFON?SC? in Column 3, Row 8 is obviously TELEFONISCH. This indicates that in Alphabet 7, B_c represents plaintet L_p (i.e. Y_c represents E_p); in Alphabet 12, R_c represents I_p (i.e. N_c represents E_p — confirming our assumption in the previous paragraph); and, in Alphabet 15, B_c represents H_p (i.e Y_c represents E_p).

If in Alphabet 15, B_c represents H_p, then U_c represents A_p. In the light of these identifications the string DEMK?MM?????TE in Row 5, columns 1 and 2 becomes DEMKOMMA????NTEN. This, obviously, is DEM KOMMANDANTEN, which means that in Alphabet 1, U_c represents N_p (i.e. L_c represents E_p); in Alphabet 2, I_c represents D_p (i.e. J_c represents E_p); in Alphabet 3, G_c represents A_p (i.e. K_c represents E_p); and, in Alphabet 4, S_c represents N (i.e. J_c represents E_p).

In this manner, each of the 15 encyphering alphabets has now been identified as follows: 1 $L_c = E_p$, 2 $J_c = E_p$, 3 $K_c = E_p$, 4 $J_c = E_p$, 5 $H_c = E_p$, 6 $M_c = E_p$, 7 $Y_c = E_p$, 8 $X_c = E_p$, 9 $G_c = E_p$, 10 $J_c = E_p$, 11 $W_c = E_p$, 12 $N_c = E_p$, 13 $H_c = E_p$, 14 $M_c = E_p$, 15 $Y_c = E_p$. This enables the whole passage to be decrypted. It reads as follows:

> es war jetzt nur noch ewerk zwem klar. Der Versuch des Pumpenmeisters die Feuerlochleitung von dem Aggregat im Schraubenmotorenraum unter Druck zu nehmen misslang weil in der Beschadigten Feuerloschleitung der Druck sofort wegfiel.
>
> 1745. Eins wach Maschinist meldet mundlich dem Kommandanten auf der Brucke zu dieser zeit gingen die Motoren durch. Kmdt befiehlt zu versuchen wenigstens einen Motor wieder klar zu bekommen. Alle Versuche in den Maschinenraum ein zu dringen waren erfolglos. Eins wm ubermittelte befehl Kmdt telefonisch von Leck zentrale an L.T. im Masch leitstand L.J. meldete zuruck dasl befehl ...

When devising a cypher of this type the encypherer usually prefers to designate each of the alphabets on his Vigenère square by a distinguishing letter, rather than by a number, and to form the cycle from a codeword; this is easier to remember than a string of figures, both during the encypherment process and afterwards. A convenient choice is the letters at the margin of the square. In this case the encypherer used the right margin — the column of letters encyphering D_p — and chose the code word:

1	2	3	4	5	6	7	8	9	10	11	12	13	14	15
G	E	F	E	C	H	T	S	B	E	R	I	C	H	T

This means 'Action Report' and probably served also as the document's title.

Reference to the other 24 sections indicated that they were consecutive parts of the one document, the encyphering of each section beginning with the first letter of the keyword. The divisions appear to have been made at random; their purpose may have been to make decryption by the enemy a more tedious process.

This Action Report purports to be the deck and the engine room logs for the period from the sighting of *Sydney* (3.55 pm 19 November 1941) until the scuttling of the *Kormoran* some $8\frac{1}{2}$ hours later. It provided the most reliable account of how *Sydney* met her fate. The material passage reads as follows:

> <u>1715 hrs</u> — Cruiser cuts across starboard at range of 800 metres.
>
> <u>1725 hrs</u> — Further signal: 'Hoist your secret call'. Further delay can only make situation worse … Thereupon at 1730 hrs identity declared. Strike Dutch flag, German colours clearly shown. Time taken to reveal identity 6 seconds. Order to stand by with guns and torpedoes. Enemy falls slowly astern … Salvoes 3, 4, 5 up four points — about 4 seconds later hits on bridge and control tower… . AA [Anti-aircraft] machine-guns and starboard 37 mm guns effective on bridge, pom-poms and AA guns. Until 5th salvo no reply, then X Turret opens rapid and accurate fire. Hits on [sc. our] funnel and engines. Y Turret only fires two or three salvoes, all wide. A and B Turrets silent …

In short, before verifying the raider's identity, *Sydney* approached to within point blank range and was crippled by fire from *Kormoran*'s main and secondary armament before she could bring fire to bear.

Disbandment

After the Japanese surrender, the Section was disbanded and its members returned to civil life. Bond joined the teaching staff at Scotch College Melbourne where he later became Vice-Principal. Eastway joined the postwar cryptographic organisation. The other three resumed their studies. Barnes went to Cambridge and was elected to a Fellowship at Trinity in 1950. He became Professor of Mathematics and Deputy Vice-Chancellor at the University of Adelaide. McKay went to Cambridge and took a First in the Classical Tripos in 1950. He became Reader in Classics at The Australian National University. Smith went to the Sorbonne, where he took his doctorate. He became Professor of Modern Languages at the University of Tasmania.

Chapter 3. Japanese Diplomatic Cyphers: Cryptographic Survey Report Of Special Intelligence Section HQ Australian Military Forces Melbourne 1946[1]

Introduction

Part I: The Codes

1. NU (Date and Number Code)
2. TO (Address Codes)
3. LA Code (JAH)
4. X Code (JAI)
5. CA (Head of Mission) Code (JAJ)
6. YO Code (JAK)

Part II: The Transposition Cyphers

1. FUJI (TSU) Cypher (JAF)
2. GEAM Transposition System (JBB)
3. BA (TOKI) Cypher (JBA)

Part III: The Recyphering Tables

1. Cypher Book No. 1 (JBC)
2. NE (JAM)
3. SOSOS (JBN)
4. 10101 (JBD)
5. JAO
6. 50505 (JBE)

---

[1] National Archives of Australia, Series A6923/2, Item 1.

Part IV: Breaking the Recyphering Tables
1. Letter-Figure Substitution
2. Placing of Messages in Depth
3. Breaking of Additives
4. Indicator Systems

Part V: Miscellaneous Cyphers
1. HINOKI Machine Cypher (JAA)
2. SAKURA Emergency Cypher (JBL)
3. Unidentified Cyphers

Part VI: General Remarks
1. Code-Building
2. Cypher Systems
3. Errors in Encyphering
4. Distribution of Cyphers
5. Cooperation with Linguists

Part VII: Personnel 1942–45

Appendices[2]
A: Best Groups
B: Starts and Ends
C: R7F Low-Power Far Eastern Diplomatic Network
L: Code and Keys for GEAM (JBB)
Q: Unused Emergency Cyphers

---

[2] The following Appendices, though referred to in the text, are missing in the xerox copy of the Report that is deposited with the National Archives of Australia — D: Copy of NU (Date and Number Codes); E: Copy of TO (Address Codes); F: Copy of LA; G: Copy of X; H: Copy of CA; I: Copy of YO; J: Standard Japanese Diplomatic Vocabulary (1620 words); K: Copy of FUJI and Catalogue of Recovered Keys and Cages; L: Code and Keys for GEAM (JBB); M: Complete Information on BA: N: [Title Unknown]; O: [Title Unknown]; P: [Title Unknown]. Presumably these were stripped from the original document some time between its creation and its examination by the Department of Defence for access clearance in 1996. [All footnotes in this report were inserted by Sissons.]

Chapter 3. Japanese Diplomatic Cyphers

Abbreviations

Three-letter nomenclature for diplomatic cyphers

JAA	HINOKI Machine Cypher
JAF	FUJI (TSU) Transposition Cypher
JAH	LA Code
JAI	X Code
JAJ	CA Code
JAK	YO Code
JAM	NE Recyphering Table
JAO	GEAM Recyphering Table (Repeated Indicator)
JBA	BA Foreign Office Transposition Cypher (TOKI)
JBB	GEAM Transposition Cypher
JBC	Cypher Book No. 1 (Foreign Office)
JBD	10101 Interdepartmental Recyphering Table
JBE	50505 GEAM Recyphering Table
JBL	SAKURA Emergency Cypher
JBN	SOSOS Foreign Office Recyphering Table

Introduction

Work on Japanese diplomatic cyphers was first begun by the Section in December 1941 under the auspices of the Navy. During 1942, the staff consisted of only three cryptographers, but after the Section was taken over by the Army in November of that year, the technical staff was increased to deal with new cyphers. Professor A. D. Trendall of the University of Sydney was in charge of cryptography, assisted by Lieutenant R. S. Bond and Lieutenant E. S. Barnes. Mr. C. H. Archer of the British Consular Service supervised the language and translation section, and on his return to England in December 1944, Mr. R. L. Cowley was sent to replace him.

When the Section began work on Japanese diplomatic cyphers in February 1942, there were in force four codes, LA (also known as JAH), X (JAI), CA (JAJ) and YO (JAK), and two cyphers, HINOKI machine (JAA) and FUJI/TSU (JAF). All were used in conjunction with the Number (NU) and Address (TO) codes. The four codes, together with NU and TO, had already been broken and copies were supplied to this section. LA, X, NU and TO were virtually complete, but CA and YO required considerable expansion and correction.

During 1942, all four codes and virtually all traffic in the FUJI cypher were being read locally, and the breaking of the daily keys for FUJI was the principal task of the section at the time. Traffic in JAA (the highest grade of Japanese diplomatic cypher) was sent direct to London where a copy of the HINOKI machine was held.[3]

Between 1943 and 1945, the Japanese introduced eight new cyphers — two transposition systems and six recyphering tables. The Section was the first to break the new Greater East Asia Ministry transposition cypher (GEAM) introduced in July 1943. The breaking of the Foreign Office transposition cypher (BA) followed soon afterwards, and the Section concentrated on working out the available keys, while London turned to the machining of traffic in the recyphering tables. Once London was able to establish preliminary facts about the recyphering tables, the Section contributed code-equivalents and many pages of the pads, although relying upon recovery by hand without any mechanical aid.

Approximately 90 per cent of traffic received in these cyphers was read.

Intelligence Derived from the Messages

Messages sent in code rarely contained any important information, as the Japanese themselves realized that their codes had little security value.

Low-grade cyphers were chiefly confined to financial and staffing problems within the various embassies, visas, couriers, rations and similar routine matters.

Traffic in high-grade cyphers showed the reaction of the enemy to naval, military and political events abroad, and in addition provided a reliable general picture of the situation within Japan itself.

An idea of the importance of reading diplomatic cyphers may best be gained by mentioning a few examples of information received.

Of considerable local interest was a message despatched by the Japanese representative at Dili which revealed that the enemy was reading the Australian guerrilla code in Timor.

---

3   In the American literature on this subject, JAA is often referred to as the PURPLE cypher and the HINOKI machine as the PURPLE, the Type-97 Injiki, or the Type-B, Machine.

Chapter 3. Japanese Diplomatic Cyphers

The official Japanese attitude to the general war situation was regularly circulated by Tokyo, with particular reference to their reaction to 'Big Three' conferences or negotiations with the Soviet. The earthquake off Nagasaki and the American bombings of Japan were reported in full, including complete details of damage and casualties.

Posts abroad regularly sent through diplomatic channels reports from their spies and agents. Spy reports on the European and Russian front were frequently received from the Minister at Stockholm; Kabul was the nerve centre of a spy organization throughout India and the reading of their reports enabled us to supply the Indian authorities with information about the movements and activities of these agents. In 1942 one message from Kabul revealed that a Japanese agent was present at a British naval trial, and was supplying full details of carriers and battleships stationed at Bombay. Spy reports, dealing with the internal situation in China, came from an agent at Chungking and were transmitted to Japan from the embassy at Canton. One of these messages disclosed that the French Minister at Chungking was in the pay of the Japanese.

Information about Chandra Bose and his puppet government was obtained from messages sent from Rangoon and other places visited by the Indian National Government.

Posts in occupied Europe constantly sent detailed accounts of the effectiveness of Allied bombings on their respective cities, and long reports upon local politics.

Russo-Japanese relations were always delicate, and from a survey of reports submitted by Ambassador Sato recording his interviews with Molotov and Lozovsky, the gradual hardening of the Russian attitude became apparent.

For several months before the Russian entry into the Far Eastern War, reports were coming through from Japanese couriers via the Vladivostok consulate on the eastward movement of troops and material.

Much material recovered from Japanese diplomatic cyphers was of use to the Ministry for Economic Warfare in London. Reports from Far Eastern posts were mainly of an economic nature, generally trade reports and statements of shortages. Up to the end of 1942 shipping information was often sent in diplomatic cyphers but thereafter this practice was discontinued. However, we were able to follow the progress made by the Japanese in the building of wooden ships in French Indo-China and Siam to alleviate their shipping shortage. In addition air raid reports came frequently from Bangkok, Hanoi and Chiengmai [Chiang Mai]. London displayed a marked interest in the Japanese need for supplies and commodities, particularly Swedish ball bearings and Turkish chrome.

Breaking Japanese Diplomatic Codes

Part I: The Codes

1. NU (Date and Number Code)

2. TO (Address Codes)

3. LA Code (JAH)

4. X Code (JAI)

5. CA (Head of Mission) Code (JAJ)

6. YO Code (JAK)

1. NU (Date and Number Code)

This code was used in conjunction with most Japanese diplomatic codes and cyphers.

The date and serial number of each message were contained in a single five-letter group generally immediately preceding the cypher text. In this group the first three letters designated the serial number, the fourth letter the part number and number of parts, and the fifth the date and the period of day (i.e. morning or afternoon).

The complete alphabet was used in each part of this code (e.g. *ADYIP* indicated No. 304, Part 1 of a two-part message, sent on the morning of the 31st of the month).

Serial Number

There were two separate codes used, one for ordinary (place-to-place) messages and the other for circulars.

In the 'hundreds' place, each letter of the alphabet was assigned a number from 0 to 25 at random. The numbers assigned to the one letter for circular and ordinary messages added up to 25 — e.g. B (ordinary) = 0, B (circular) = 25. For numbers beyond 2,599, two thousand was subtracted before encoding — e.g. 2600 would be encoded as 600. There was little chance of confusion, as few series ever reached such high numbers, and in those which did, several months separated the identically encoded numbers.

For the 'tens' and 'units' places, the figures 0 to 9 were distributed over the alphabet at random, a few letters being left blank in each column. In no case was a letter left without a figure equivalent in the corresponding columns of both circular and ordinary numbers. This fact sometimes helped in establishing doubtful cases (e.g. If E occurred in the 'units' place, the number had to be a circular because E had no equivalent in the ordinary 'units' code).

In June 1943 the circular and ordinary codes were interchanged. Thus whereas ADY had signified Message 304, it now became Circular Message 304. There was no further change in the code at any stage.

Message Parts

The fourth letter of the date-and-number group designated the parts of messages. Each letter was given an equivalent ranging from 'single-part message' to 'part six of a six-part message'. There were six optional letters for 'single-part message', and one for each part of two-, three-, four-, five- and six-part messages. When a message exceeded six parts, all its parts were externally encoded as single-part messages and numbered internally (i.e. within the cypher text). This practice often proved of real assistance in the breaking of recyphering tables and in the finding of initial 'fits' in BA. Occasionally the several parts of a multi-part message were designated in LA code before the cypher text.

Date

The final figure only of the date (except in the case of 31st) was encoded. Each of the figures 0 to 9, and 31 was allocated two letters at random, one for morning and one for afternoon. The remaining four letters were reserved for special cases (e.g. 'date in text'). Thus B in the final place of the date-and-number group could designate the morning of either 10th, 20th or 30th of the month, the precise date normally being clear from the date of transmission. In the case of delayed messages confusion could arise, but generally traffic records decided any uncertainty.

Reference Code

When a message referred to a previous message an additional five-letter group was inserted between the date-and-number group and the beginning of the cypher text. In this code the first letter indicated the source of the message referred to (e.g. 'my circular', 'your telegram (+2000)'), the second, third and fourth letters provided the number of that message and the fifth letter the part or paragraph thereof. The whole alphabet was employed for each of the five codes involved, alternatives being freely used. The fifth letter of the group was almost always one of the five choices for 'dummy' (used when the whole message was referred to and not merely a section of it).

Foreign Ministry Revised System

On February 15th 1945 the Japanese Ministry of Foreign Affairs made a change in the date-and-number system, although the Greater East Asia Ministry retained the old system. In the revised system the same code was retained for the numbering and reference sections, but an improved date code was brought into force. The original five- letter groups were each expanded to two groups by doubling each letter, and for the date a bigram was substituted, there being a separate bigram for each day of the year. Thus Circular Message 48, Part 2 of 3, on 28th March in the old system would be BZUXT, but now became BBZZU UXXRH. This new system may have been introduced to diminish the chance of error arising from corruption.

The new date code consisted of bigrams formed at random from consonants. No provision was made to differentiate between morning and afternoon. Sufficient traffic was normally available to establish the code on sequence of messages, but it was possible to check most bigrams by means of the JBC indicator system which employs the date of origin. Occasionally the old date code was used, reduplicated, in place of the bigram code. The new date code was established, virtually complete for dates from 15th February 1945 to early September 1945 when cypher traffic ceased.

For copies of the date-and-number code together with the reference code see Appendix D [Missing].

2. TO (Address Codes)

Both the Greater East Asia Ministry and the Foreign Ministry used the same system of addressing messages but each had its own code. These codes were originally supplied to the Section by London and were complete only in as far as the posts with the greatest volume of traffic were concerned. Efforts were directed towards filling in the missing sections by inference from the texts of messages and from number series, but neither code was recovered in its entirety.

Address codes consisted of bigrams and trigrams, the bigrams being instructions for the distribution of the message (e.g. 'This message is addressed to ...', 'Please forward to ...'); and the trigrams, place-names. To complete a five-letter group at the end of a series of addresses the fillers SIMO were used. Where re-addressing involved numbering a message in a different series, the original number and address always came last, i.e. immediately before the cypher text. Thus in the Greater East Asia Ministry address code, a message from Shanghai Embassy to Tokyo, which Tokyo is forwarding to Hanoi and Saigon as a circular, would leave Tokyo with the following address code groups:- QQFZQ FVBMO (my message to Hanoi, Saigon) (date and number group) NNCZS (message from Shanghai to me (date and number group). When a message addressed primarily to one post was repeated merely for information to a number of other posts, the primary addressee was normally indicated at the front, and the remainder at the end of the message.

Copies of the address codes will be found in Appendix E [Missing].

3. LA Code (JAH)

This is a simple code consisting of bigrams and tetragrams, indicated by the letters LA at the beginning of the text. Bigrams are of the form, consonant-vowel or vowel-consonant; and tetragrams are special combinations of two bigrams, the first bigram being, SI, TU, VE, WO or XY. All the letters of the alphabet are used except Q; and Y is regarded as both a vowel and a consonant.

The bigrams are patterned according to the order of the *kana* vowels, i.e. A, I, U, E, O and the tetragrams are arranged in blocks of related words.

LA code has little security value and is used extensively for communications the contents of which the Japanese merely wish to keep from post office officials. However, cypher clerks on rare occasions did make the mistake of sending confidential matter in LA code but, on the whole, LA messages contained little of interest and value.

A copy of LA code may be found in Appendix F [Missing].

4. X Code (JAI)

This is an unrestricted alphabetic code of bigrams and tetragrams, indicated by one of the five bigrams IP PA AP AN IK at the commencement of the text. The code book is not patterned and is thus of higher grade than LA. X was not nearly as extensively used as LA — most messages in X coming from Kabul — but its subject matter was usually more interesting.

A copy of X code is attached as Appendix G [Missing].

5. CA (Head of Mission) Code (JAJ)

CA is an unrestricted bigram code held only by the Head of the Mission and is indicated by CA at the head of the text. Its security value is the same as that of X.

The code was usually sent unencyphered, but was occasionally used in conjunction with any one of the current cypher systems.

As only the Head of the Mission was able to decode these messages, the subject matter of CA messages was usually confined to staff problems.

Encyphered CA messages usually contained general statements on policies which Tokyo did not wish to disclose to embassy staffs.

A copy of CA code may be found in Appendix H [Missing].

6. YO Code (JAK)

YO is an unrestricted bigram code indicated by YO at the head of the text.

This code was rarely used, but occasionally appeared encyphered in the same manner as CA. Owing to the small amount of traffic, this code was only partially recovered and is attached as Appendix I [Missing].

Part II: The Transposition Cyphers

1. FUJI (TSU) Cypher (JAF)

2. GEAM Transposition System (JBB)

3. BA (TOKI) Cypher (JBA)

1. FUJI (TSU) Cypher (JAF)

This transposition cypher was current between June 20th 1941 and June 30th 1943, and was the main cypher used by the Japanese for diplomatic communications over this period. The cypher system had already been broken in 1941, and a few basic code groups recovered. Such information as was known was supplied to the Section.

The indicator of FUJI is a five-letter group immediately preceding the cypher text, the first three letters being invariably consonant-vowel-consonant. The initial consonant classifies the message as (a) European, (b) Far Eastern, (c) American, or (d) a Tokyo circular, while the remaining four letters progress in a fixed self-checking cycle. The cypher was designed to be used for a period of one year, all four regions having a separate key for each day, thus giving a total of 1464 keys. At the conclusion of the cypher text a checked five-figure group gives the number of cypher groups (e.g. 13777).

The code is composed of unrestricted bigrams and tetragrams, the total vocabulary of 1576 groups comprising 676 bigrams and 900 tetragrams. This vocabulary is slightly smaller than the standard Japanese diplomatic vocabulary of 1620 words (v. Appendix J [Missing]). Bigrams are used for *kana*, numerals, punctuation and short commonly used words; tetragrams for paragraphs, place-names, weights and measures, and longer words and phrases. Those bigrams which form the beginnings and ends of tetragrams (e.g. AL, BJ, YM, ZB) are used for dates and spellers.

An encoded message is written into a single transposition form which varies in width from 19 to 25 according to a key supplied by the indicator. The form contains random blanks which are inserted according to the date and which normally change on the 1st, 11th and 21st of each month. The maximum number of blanks is 53, and they are arranged in sets so that no blank is ever isolated. The blanking pattern does not extend below the 12th row of the form.

The Breaking of FUJI Keys

Progress on FUJI was at first slow and difficult. The recoveries supplied to the Section were few and unreliable, and the only keys broken in this country prior to February 1942 had been obtained from short messages the contents of which were known or presumed (e.g. messages reporting the departure of such ships as the *Queen Elizabeth* or *Queen Mary* from Sydney Harbour).[4] As FUJI (apart from the HINOKI machine) was the only diplomatic cypher in use at the time, the first task of the Section was to discover a general method for reading all traffic within a few hours of receipt.

The first attack was made on the following lines: An arbitrary width of key was chosen and the cypher text was written out in strips. Efforts were then made to find two strips which when correctly placed side by side produced good basic groups (v. Appendix A). Messages under seventy cypher groups were not worked upon if it could be avoided, because as we had only an elementary knowledge of the code, everything depended upon finding a good 'fit' in the section of the message clear of the blanks. This method of attack was very cumbersome and seldom profitable as the arbitrary width was almost always incorrect, and after a week this method was abandoned.

In March 1942 a member of the British Foreign Office from Singapore who possessed an excellent knowledge of Japanese joined the Section.[5] On the basis of his knowledge of the language a new and more direct attack was made upon the cypher.[6]

---

4   FUJI came into operation on 20 June 1941. The *Queen Mary*'s departures from Sydney after that date during 1941 were 13 June, 29 June, 21 August, 3 September, 15 October, 1 November; the *Queen Elizabeths*'s arrivals were 13 June, 15 October, 15 December.
5   A. R. V. Cooper of the British Government Code and Cypher School.
6   Bond insists that it was Trendall, not Cooper, who devised 'zoning':
    I cannot really accept this paragraph which suggests that it was Cooper who introduced 'zoning'. It was Trendall, and the latent mathematician in him. I was there, and as a minion I did the hackwork. Does this statement mean that the author of the Report was not personally involved in 1942. But the details of zoning on this page are 'spot-on', 100% correct.
    (R. S. Bond to D. C. S. Sissons, 15 November 1998)

As the common *kana* symbols *wa, wo, no, ni, shi,* and *to* were bound to occur frequently in any message of reasonable length, a search was made for these groups by 'zoning' out the letters of the cypher text which formed these code groups. Owing to a weakness in code construction the common group *wa* had only one equivalent, AG. Consequently AG usually proved a profitable investment for the zoning treatment.

A given letter, say A, was 'zoned' by writing all the 'A's of a message along a line of graph paper and writing, above and below each A the 15 letters which respectively preceded and succeeded it. Although 'zoning' might appear cumbersome the writing out rarely exceeded ten minutes and invariably produced results.

After, say, 'A's and 'G's had been zoned in the above manner they were placed together in turn until a 'fit' was found. To be classified as a 'fit', a column had to contain a high percentage of good groups. Value of groups was the most important factor in determining a fit, but experience alone decided its validity; even though a column might be found containing *shi, wa, no,* and *to*, if it also contained several rare or unknown groups like AZ or LY there was little chance of its being correct. In addition a correct fit had to be mathematically possible (e.g. letter 178 could not fit with letter 180, however good the resulting groups might be!).

When a fit was found that seemed reliable, the numbers of the letters were studied in an endeavour to establish the width of the key. For example, if a line ending at letter 24 fitted with a line ending at 72, and the message contained 530 letters, the average length of a column was 24 and the key was probably 22 wide. Owing to the bigram and tetragram basis of the code an odd key (i.e. 23 wide) would give a column in which code groups would be formed only on alternate rows. An even key (i.e. 20 wide) would form code groups on every row. At first even keys proved more difficult than odd keys, as columns had to be found separately and then fitted together according to sense; but with odd keys each alternate row had a split group which was of great assistance in fitting on a third line to the original two. For instance if a split group H . Z occurred in a message from South America there was a high chance of this being EHZB, the tetragram for Chile.

If the blanking system for the period was already known, a set of four or five lines was usually sufficient to determine the width of the key and the position of the set in the cage. When this had been done, a very useful device, known as the principle of isolated columns, was used. An isolated line was a section of the cypher text whose beginning and end were determined but which had not yet been fitted. The lengths of all isolated lines were checked off against the calculated lengths of all the lines in the setting. If a certain length occurred only once, the corresponding isolated line could be immediately written into the form, irrespective of whether it had been fitted to other lines or not. Such isolated lines were extremely useful as 'bridges' in expanding the original fitted lines.

If the cage was not known, all the lines of the message had to be fitted together, the end-point of the message determined by sense, and the number of blanks in each line calculated. The cage was then broken purely on the sense of the message and was, of course, greatly assisted by stereotyped beginnings (v. Appendix B).

Using the method outlined above, by May 1942 we were able to read virtually all FUJI traffic; and all bigrams, except those of very rare occurrence, and most tetragrams had been recovered.

The technique and speed of breaking keys gradually improved to such an extent that 'zoning' could almost be eliminated and the following simpler method was usually adopted: Messages were typed out, numbered, and an 'apartage' marked (i.e. letters were marked which were at a distance of two or four apart, as these distances were easily noted and accounted for both even and odd key-lengths) — e.g. ... XZLAN AFKTA ... which would be checked with PAQLD GYYOG, giving (since AG = *wa*) two *wa*s. Groups like *wa*, *wo*, *no*, *shi*, *ni* etc were so common in the body of a message that there was a high possibility that they would occur over one another in the same column. If a search for a *wa* over *wa* proved unsuccessful, a *wa* over *no*, or *ni* or *shi* was almost certain to be found. By this method fits came quickly and easily, and from May 1942 onwards it was only in rare instances that the 'hammer' method of zoning had to be adopted to discover an initial fit.

Change 1

On July 1st 1942 the first of three changes in the encyphering of FUJI messages was introduced. In normal times a completely new cypher would probably have been introduced but distribution during wartime to overseas posts prevented the Japanese from changing their cyphers after the usual period. The first change was as follows: The top line of the original cage was removed and the key 'telescoped' (i.e. arranged in the order first, last, second, second-last etc). The instructions for this change were circulated in a SUPER FUJI message (see below) which could not be read, but as soon as a key was broken after July 1st the system was quite apparent.

Change 2

From October 1st 1942 messages to and from Europe and South America were encyphered by moving the fifth row of the cage to the top. Far Eastern posts continued to use the system introduced on July 1st 1942. Kabul now used European cages with Far Eastern keys.

Change 3

The third variation in FUJI cypher was introduced on February 1st 1943, when all posts with the exception of the Far East used cages formed by moving the original blanks ten columns to the left. In addition a new key was used, derived from the original key in the following manner: Step 1: To each key number the preceding was added, retaining only the units digit in the sum. Step 2: These digits were then numbered in ascending order from the left to provide the new key.

E.g. Original Key:

| 11 | 1 | 3 | 8 | 13 | 16 | 5 | 6 | 10 | 19 | 18 | 15 | 12 | 4 | 2 | 17 | 9 | 7 | 14 |

Step 1: Rewrite, retaining only last digits.

| 1 | 1 | 3 | 8 | 3 | 6 | 5 | 6 | 0 | 9 | 8 | 5 | 2 | 4 | 2 | 7 | 9 | 7 | 4 |

Step 2: Repeat this sequence but now put the final digit (4) first.

| 4 | 1 | 1 | 3 | 8 | 3 | 6 | 5 | 6 | 0 | 9 | 8 | 5 | 2 | 4 | 2 | 7 | 9 | 7 |

Step 3: Add above two rows in columns without carry

| 5 | 2 | 4 | 1 | 1 | 9 | 1 | 1 | 6 | 9 | 7 | 3 | 7 | 6 | 6 | 9 | 6 | 6 | 1 |

Step 4: The new key is obtained by entering down the numbers 1 to 19 in the order determined by first using all 0s, then all 1s, and so on up to all 9s.

0s																			
1s			1	2		3	4												5
2s		6																	
3s									7										
4s			8																
5s	9																		
6s							10				11	12		13	14				
7s									15		16								
8s																			
9s					17			18					19						

New Key

| 9 | 6 | 8 | 1 | 2 | 17 | 3 | 4 | 10 | 18 | 15 | 7 | 16 | 11 | 12 | 19 | 13 | 14 | 5 |

Although a new key could be derived from the old, no method was found for deriving the original key from the new.

The Ministry at Kabul used the new key method and the new cage while continuing to use Far Eastern and not European keys.

Instructions for the third variation of FUJI encyphering were circulated by Tokyo in a SUPER FUJI message which was afterwards put through the HINOKI machine.

FUJI cypher was discontinued on June 30th 1943. A catalogue of recovered keys and cages together with a copy of the code may be found in Appendix K [Missing].

SUPER-FUJI System

This is a special variation of FUJI with an extremely high security value, and is reserved by the Japanese for communications of a 'most secret' nature. The system was supplied to the Section by London who had read the instructions.

For this special cypher the normal FUJI indicator is repeated at the conclusion of the cypher text. The variation is as follows: Until February 1st 1943, the key in force at the time was reversed in pairs. The first 13 numbers of the new key were taken and the letters A through M were arranged in the order of these figures. Underneath were written letters N through Z in normal order. These thirteen pairs of letters were then used to provide a reciprocal substitution which was applied to the message.

E.g. Using the above mentioned key as original key:

| 11 | 1 | 3 | 8 | 13 | 16 | 5 | 6 | 10 | 19 | 18 | 15 | 12 | 4 | 2 | 17 | 9 | 7 | 14 |

Reverse the order in pairs

| 1 | 11 | 8 | 3 | 16 | 13 | 6 | 5 | 19 | 10 | 15 | 18 | 4 | 12 | 17 | 2 | 7 | 9 | 14 |

Keep only first 13

| 1 | 11 | 8 | 3 | 16 | 13 | 6 | 5 | 19 | 10 | 15 | 18 | 4 |

Insert A through M according to the order of these numbers

| A | H | F | B | K | I | E | D | M | G | J | L | C |

Write N through Z under these

| N | O | P | Q | R | S | T | U | V | W | X | Y | Z |

Thus AG in the original code is substituted as NW.

This system is virtually unbreakable, as each message has the equivalent of a new code. Efforts were made by London, Washington and Melbourne to break one SUPER-FUJI message which was known to contain cypher instructions; but without success.

On February 1st 1943 the system changed, but the instructions were circulated in JAA which London read.

This new system is one of double transposition without substitution. In encyphering, the first transposition form is identical with the current form for ordinary FUJI. The second form uses the original cage with the top line removed and a special key derived as follows: If the width of the original key is n, the first n actual digits of the key are written down in order. Underneath these are written the last n digits of the key read backwards. These two rows are then added and arranged in order as described above for FUJI Change 3.

E.g. Using the same original key:

| 11 | 1 | 3 | 8 | 13 | 16 | 5 | 6 | 10 | 19 | 18 | 15 | 12 | 4 | 2 | 17 | 9 | 7 | 14 |

First 19 digits

| 1 | 1 | 1 | 3 | 8 | 1 | 3 | 1 | 6 | 5 | 6 | 1 | 0 | 1 | 9 | 1 | 8 | 1 | 5 |

Last 19 digits

| 4 | 1 | 7 | 9 | 7 | 1 | 2 | 4 | 2 | 1 | 5 | 1 | 8 | 1 | 9 | 1 | 0 | 1 | 6 |

Add without carry

| 5 | 2 | 8 | 2 | 5 | 2 | 5 | 5 | 8 | 6 | 1 | 2 | 8 | 2 | 8 | 2 | 8 | 2 | 1 |

Use order of numerals to write new key

1s									1									2
2s		3		4		5					6		7		8		9	
3s																		
4s																		
5s	10				11		12	13										
6s										14								
7s																		
8s			15					16				17		18		19		

New Key

10	3	15	4	11	5	12	13	16	14	1	6	17	7	18	8	19	9	2

Messages in the SUPER-FUJI system were not numerous, perhaps owing to the cumbersome method of encyphering. From the material these messages contained there is every reason to believe that the Japanese believed implicitly that the system was unbreakable. However, they compromised the system by sending both SUPER-FUJI and ordinary FUJI messages in the same key, which meant that a direct attack on a SUPER-FUJI message was rarely necessary; for once the original key had been determined, the SUPER-FUJI could then be decyphered immediately.

2. GEAM Transposition System (JBB)

GEAM was introduced on 21st July 1943. It is a transposition cypher with a bigram and tetragram code, the bigrams being consonant-vowel or vowel-consonant and the tetragrams made up of double consonant and a bigram. All letters of the alphabet are used and Y is regarded as both consonant and vowel. The code is patterned after the manner of LA.

The transposition system has appeared in three forms:

(a) Originally messages were transposed in blocks of ten by ten without blanks. There were 26 indicators, each providing a column and a row order, the row order containing only nine figures, as the bottom row of the cage was composed of dummies, namely the first letter of the indicator repeated ten times. The 26 keys were designated by the letters A through Z and each key was indicated by its letter and the following letter of the alphabet in the form ABABA. The indicator was located at the head of the cypher text.

(b) Shortly afterwards a new system appeared which was used conjointly with (a), but which eventually displaced it. The code remained the same, but the size of the transposition block was altered to 13 by 10, the dummies now being omitted, and a figure check added at the end of the text as in FUJI. Thirteen indicators were used each providing a column order and row order, and were built up on the pattern AZAZA, BYBYB etc, the keys being lettered from A through N excluding M.

(c) A further change was introduced on October 1st 1944. The size of the block was altered to 13 by 13, nine blanks being inserted in the cells with coordinates (1,1) through (9,9). The columnar keys of system (b) were reversed and used as both column and row orders. Any two keys could be used in conjunction. For example, the indicator ABABA gave B as the column order, A as the row order.

The Breaking of GEAM

As this cypher was introduced in a simple form, the breaking of the original system and the two subsequent improvements was not a difficult task. The actual steps of the analysis were as follows:

(a) A frequency count of a few messages showed that consonants and vowels were used in almost equal numbers. As we already had an example of a vowel-consonant, consonant-vowel code (LA), the theory was straightway suggested that GEAM was such a code transposed. The regular occurrence of the dummy letter at intervals of ten gave the probable length of the lines as ten. Moreover, as the dummies appeared at shorter intervals at the end of a message (when the final transposition form was incomplete) and these final dummies always began after a multiple of 100 letters, it was obvious that the size of the block was ten by ten. When a few messages were tested on these theories, fits of the required type were quickly found, while the only discrepancies were groups of the form BB, HH etc. Experience of the Japanese method of code construction showed that these were parts of tetragrams, and the five separate fits for all messages were soon established.

It merely remained to put these groups together on repeats. This part of the job did actually present a few stumbling blocks, as the presence of a row-order was not at first suspected and we were unfortunate enough to have constructed all the repeats backwards. The code-breakers were therefore somewhat baffled when these texts were presented to them — although it was later found that the main difficulty was the fact that the early messages were encoded from an English text.

The first guide to the real solution was given by the incomplete blocks in which an incomplete line of five letters appeared at the end of the line instead of at the beginning. Thus we saw that we had our keys backwards; this was remedied and then long repeats were found going from one line to another, the second line not necessarily being the next in order. From then on the breaking of the code and row order was a relatively simple matter and the complete code and cypher system were known within a fortnight.

(b) On the appearance of the second type of GEAM, the first messages were immediately examined for fits of the required type, but without success. Next day, when two messages in the same key had been received, these were written over one another producing repeats of letters at distances of 13. Moreover these repeats were the letters A D F I S S T U U V V V Y Z; our knowledge of the code immediately showed that these could be anagrammed into the traditional telegram reference: SSZA TI VU VVDY UF (*kiden 12 ni kanshi*). When the letters were lined up correctly in this order it was seen that two adjacent lines contained both code groups and split groups, and therefore the cage had an odd width and a row order. All 13 keys were then broken as soon as traffic in the keys was received.

(c) The third variation of GEAM was broken by London shortly after its inception. A few keys were broken by the Section and by London, whereupon it was seen that the new keys were the reverse of the previous set.

GEAM was the main cypher of the Greater East Asia Ministry, its other two cyphers JAO and JBE being rarely and spasmodically used. Although GEAM was by no means a high-grade cypher, the Japanese appeared to have no fear in transmitting secret data encyphered by this system. When the Embassy at Bangkok was bombed out the cypher clerk was able to continue sending messages, relying upon his memory for code and keys. This the Japanese regarded as an excellent recommendation for their cypher.

The code and keys of GEAM cypher will be found in Appendix L [Missing].

3. BA (TOKI) Cypher (JBA)

This transposition cypher was introduced on August 20th 1943, and was the first of the new Foreign Office cyphers to be broken.

The code is unrestricted bigrams and trigrams, transposed in blocks 25 by 10. The keys for the blocks are given by a five-letter indicator located at the end of the text. The first letter of the indicator is one of the consonants B, C, D, F, G, the second a vowel (including Y), the third one of the consonants N through Z, and the last two progress in sets of five according to a fixed cycle. Each of the 1,500 indicators is assigned a key number, this key being used for the first transposition block. For the second and third blocks the two following keys are used (e.g. if the indicator BANAY is 127, the first three blocks would have keys 127, 128, 129). Any further blocks repeat the same keys in order.

First System

Ten nulls are inserted in each setting in Column 1 Row 1 through Column 10 Row 10 (according to the key), the nulls spelling out the originator's name, rank and post in English.

Blanks are inserted according to the date, the same blanking system being used for dates whose difference is a multiple of six. Such blanks are always in vertical blocks of five cells, and extend either from Rows 1 through 5 or from Rows 6 through 10. The number of blanks in each block range from 5 to 45, and varied for each block.

Incomplete blocks of more than five rows receive special treatment in that the first five rows and the remaining rows are taken off separately.

Second System

On December 20th 1943 a new system was introduced as follows: Nulls were abolished and fifty blanks were inserted in each block, their location depending upon the key; beginning from Cell 1,1 five blanks were inserted vertically, from Cell 2,2 five blanks horizontally to the right etc, as far as Cell 10,10. Incomplete blocks were now treated in the normal fashion.

Breaking of First System

First a frequency count was made which showed that the code was probably unrestricted as in FUJI. Tentative attempts were made at finding repetitive fits on the same style as FUJI, but no conclusive results were obtained. One message was received which from its count suggested that it was highly numerical, but although certain progress was made on it, the message was unfortunately too corrupt to be of any real use.

Some messages in the same key were written over one another giving repeats at intervals of eleven letters, whereupon it was found that these repeats were nulls. As in GEAM these nulls were regularly spaced except towards the end of messages, suggesting that the encyphering was done in blocks but here difficulties were encountered as the lengths of the separate sections could be 245, 235, 225, 215 or 205. The longer blocks tended to be those at the beginning, but apart from this no rule could be established. The unevenly spaced dummies were naturally examined, but the system by which they were distributed was not at all clear.

Within a fortnight of the introduction of BA, Minister Morishima at Lisbon compromised the system by sending identical messages in two different keys. London was fortunate in intercepting both of these messages and quickly pieced them together. As the message was less than one complete block, it first appeared that the two parts of the block had different keys but these two keys were obviously related and were seen to be identical when sets of blanks were introduced. An analysis of this message gave a few of the high frequency groups and one or two more keys were broken. Our technique was rapidly improving, although almost no code groups were known, when Tokyo sent out a six-part circular in both BA and GEAM. The GEAM cypher was already completely known by this time and all efforts were made to break the BA keys. This done, the equivalents of several hundred code groups were immediately recovered, the only small difficulty being the presence of trigrams, the form of which was not at all obvious. From now on the breaking of BA keys was merely a matter of technique and experience.

Although the complete system by which the blanks were inserted was not discovered for some weeks, it was roughly known that the blanks were fairly evenly divided between the top and bottom of the cage, the top blanks being in Columns 11, 12 etc and lower blanks in 20, 21 etc. So that if the length of a block were 235 letters, the blanks were either in Columns 11, 12 and 20 or in 11, 20 and 21.

The method of breaking the keys was simply to write out a block in its twenty-five columns, inserting the required number of blanks on the above tentative basis. Fits were not difficult to find as the position of every letter in its line was determined and the whole process was greatly facilitated by stereotyped starts (c.f. FUJI where the beginnings and ends of lines were initially indeterminate). However the presence of trigrams and dummies gave no regularity in the pairing and splitting of two letters as in FUJI.

Virtually all traffic in BA was read until the introduction of the second system.

Breaking of Second System

All attempts to break into the second system failed until in January 1944 we received two small messages in the same key. Both of these were found to possess all the requisite letters for a 'repeat request' (v. Appendix B), and were successfully pieced together although they were so small that the actual key and blanking system could not be completely determined. The result was sent to London who fortunately possessed messages with complete blocks in both the old system and the new. They were thus able to establish the blanking system and to show that the transposition keys had not changed.

New messages in known keys were now readable but the breaking of new keys presented grave difficulties. Doubts were expressed both here and in London whether the breaking of the new system would ever become a working and a profitable proposition in view of the complexity of the system and the necessity of breaking three keys in order completely to read one message. Moreover the main recyphering tables were now well in hand and occupying almost the complete staff of the Section so that for many weeks no work was done on BA.

However, the volume of BA traffic began to increase in April 1944 when it began to be used as an interdepartmental cypher in conjunction with 10101, and it was decided to make serious efforts to evolve a technique for breaking new keys. Progress was slow and very difficult in the early stages and only possible when there were several messages in the same key. Eventually an effective method of verticalising was found (v. Appendix M [Missing]) whereby we filled in the thirty blanks whose positions were known and distributed the remaining twenty horizontal blanks as evenly as possible. Fitting was of course difficult in view of the shallow depth of the blocks, the presence of unknown blanks, the lack of pattern in the pairing of the code groups and the uncertainty of the beginnings and ends of lines.

One of the main resources was as follows: Messages in the same key were written over one another and each was examined for a stereotyped beginning which would give possible beginnings for all the other messages. (e.g. JOR being *kiden* [meaning: 'your telegram'], letters corresponding to all the Js, Os and Rs in one message would be written down and all combinations of them examined. If for example one found the sets JSK, OBD, RKR, giving *kiden, Ōden* [meaning: 'my telegram'] and the first letters of '1', these lines would be written down and examined as potential fits).

Incomplete blocks were always virtually unworkable and even after a great deal of experience it proved almost impossible to break a key on one message alone. London was the first to discover the principle that the key of Block 2 of one indicator might be identical with the key of Block 1 of another indicator; it was then obvious that indicators could be linked together (See Appendix M [Missing]). This fact was most helpful in that additional depth was obtained when breaking keys. Furthermore if upon the breaking of Block 1 of an indicator it was found that the key was identical with Block 2 of another of which the key for Block 3 was already known, Block 2 of the new message could immediately be decyphered.

Employment of BA

BA was discontinued in April 1945, although the transposition system was used from then on to re-encypher JAA (HINOKI machine cypher) messages and for use in Super JBC described below.

BA was used only to a moderate extent and the material it contained was of varying interest ranging from general Tokyo circulars upon international happenings to dull routine matters about couriers. Most BA messages from Russia were on the subject of couriers, visas and rations. However Stockholm was in the habit of sending all his *chōhōsha* (spy reports) in BA and much information was obtained therefrom. Although the second system of BA cypher might well have proved unbreakable the Foreign Ministry did not regard it very highly and issued instructions that it was to be used only for routine matters; more confidential material was to be sent in the recyphering tables. This was satisfactory from our point of view as we encountered far more difficulty in breaking and reading the second BA system than we did in recovering recyphering tables.

Complete information on BA may be found in Appendix M [Missing].

Chapter 3. Japanese Diplomatic Cyphers

Part III: The Recyphering Tables

1. Cypher Book No. 1 (JBC)

2. NE (JAM)

3. SOSOS (JBN)

4. 10101 (JBD)

5. JAO

6. 50505 (JBE)

1. Cypher Book No. 1 (JBC)

This is a recyphering table using a four-figure code and sent in five-letter groups with the letter-figure substitution OLFSCGRNYK equivalent to 0 through 9. The code contains 1620 groups with the following restrictions: the first three figures of the groups are all even or all odd; there is no zero in the first, second or fourth places and no 9 in the second place (N.B. This applies only to the code as recovered: it has been shown that the true Japanese code is 1111 lower).

The additive pad contains 100 pages numbered 00 through 99, each page containing 100 five-figure groups arranged in ten rows and ten columns. The rows and columns of each page are separately coordinated.

A dummy indicator of the pattern, consonant consonant vowel consonant consonant, stands at the head of the text. There are two true indicators, one at the beginning and one at the end of the text. The indicators are decyphered as follows: To the first four figures of the actual cypher-text add the day of the month, repeated to form a four-figure group. Use the result to find a five-figure group in the pad, the first two figures being taken as the page, the third the row coordinate and the fourth the column coordinate (11111 must be added to this group in our figures). This five-figure group is now subtracted from the first indicator. Then the date tetragram with the addition of a zero is subtracted from the result. This final five-figure group denotes the starting point, the first two figures giving the page, the next two giving the coordinates, and the last giving the digit of the five-figure group at which encyphering begins (e.g. a message on the 12th, front indicator 68053 and first cypher group 99256; the control is 9925 + 1212 = 0137; page 01, coordinates 3.7 gives, say, the group 90981; this subtracted from 68053 gives 78172; subtracting 12120 from 78172 gives the starting-point 66052, i.e. page 66, coordinates 0.5 beginning at the second figure of the group).

75

The rear indicator, also denoting the starting point, is decyphered on the same system, save that the first four figures of the second text group are used as the control.

JBC was introduced on July 1st 1943. On February 1st 1944 the recyphering pad changed, but the second pad was quickly broken into and the first pages were recovered by this section in March. The complete pad was soon recovered, and all messages in this cypher have since been read on receipt.

Super JBC

This combination of BA and JBC was introduced on April 20th, 1945. Additives are obtained by transposing a page of the recyphering pad in a setting 25 by 25, using a BA key, and with 125 blanks inserted in 25 sets of 5 in accordance with the second system of BA blanks. Each page is used once only by each post and the pages are used in order. Separate BA keys and sections of the pad are allotted to posts abroad and to Tokyo. Full instructions were given in Tokyo Circular 383 of April 5th 1945, which was in BA put through a machine.

Only four messages in this system have been received to date, and consequently it is not yet known whether the BA keys progress similarly to the pages of the pad.

2. NE (JAM)

This recyphering table, introduced on July 1st 1943, has the same appearance as JBC, save that the indicators are systematic, are used in alphabetical order and are repeated at the end of the text.

A four-figure code is used, recyphered and sent in five-letter groups using the same letter-figure substitution as JBC, the middle letter of each group being a null. The code consists of 1,620 groups and has the following restrictions (N.B. These apply only to our recovered code; the actual Japanese figures are not known): The first three figures of a code group are all even or all odd. Even groups have no zero in the third place and no 2 in the fourth place; groups with a 2 in the third place begin only with 06, 20, 44, 46, 80 and 82; no groups begin with 08. Odd groups have corresponding restrictions: no 3 in the last place; groups with 1 in the third place are restricted to six pairs of starters which are not completely determined, although the pairs 17, 55, 57 and 93 are confirmed; no groups begin with 19. The main part of the code (elementary *kana*, numerals, punctuation and common words) is confined to the even groups, the odd groups corresponding roughly to the tetragrams of FUJI.

Two recyphering tables were employed, one for messages from Tokyo, one for messages to Tokyo. There is no figure indicator, the letter indicator giving the starting-point, though no relation exists between the order of the indicators and corresponding starting-points. Encyphering always begins at the beginning of a group.

In July and August 1943, NE was used extensively, particularly by Tokyo, but thereafter was almost entirely replaced by JBC, traffic in NE averaging only about one message per month. Consequently NE was left over in favour of the more commonly used cyphers until October 1944. When these had been exhausted, several pages of the NE pad together with code recoveries were soon forwarded to London. London in turn passed these findings to Washington only to learn that the Americans had already been working on NE for some months without informing the rest of the world. Their recoveries, when made available, proved to be based on a different code and were very unreliable, and therefore they were of little assistance to this section. London accepted our recoveries and basic code and resumed work on NE shortly afterwards. The combined efforts of London and Melbourne have only resulted in the breaking of certain sections of the two pads and the establishing of the commoner code-groups, as very little workable depth was available.

The Japanese regarded NE as their highest-grade recyphering table and, after the initial abuse of this confidential cypher by Tokyo, instructions were issued that its use was to be confined to highly secret reports.

3. SOSOS (JBN)

This recyphering table was introduced on October 1st 1944 for use between Moscow, Vladivostok, Petropavlovsk and Tokyo. Very little traffic in this cypher was received.

In appearance it is similar to JBC and is a four-figure code recyphered and sent in five-letter groups, with the group SOSOS at the head of the text. There is no dummy indicator, but two figure indicators appear at the beginning and end of the cypher-text.

The second and third digits of the code-groups are of the same parity, and the first two digits are restricted to the ranges 4 through 9 and 0 through 5 respectively. It is presumed that there is a one-figure restriction in the last place, reducing the book to the normal 1620 groups.

The pad is made up of five-figure groups and encyphering can commence only at the beginning of a group. No additives have been recovered owing to insufficient depth and work on the cypher was abandoned upon Russia's entry into the war against Japan.

4. 10101 (JBD)

This is the interdepartmental recyphering table, introduced on July 1st 1943. It is a four-figure code recyphered and sent in five-figure groups prefixed by the group 10101. The message-number and number of parts are sent in clear.

The code contains 1,620 groups with the following restrictions: the first digit is even, but not zero; the third digit is odd and the last figure not zero; no groups begin with 86, 87, 88 or 89 (N.B. This is the actual Japanese code).

The recyphering pad contains 100 pages numbered 00 through 99, each page containing 100 five-figure groups arranged and coordinated similarly to JBC. Encyphering always commences at the beginning of a five-figure group.

There are two figure indicators, one at the beginning and one at the end of the text, the front indicator denoting the starting point and the rear indicator the end-point. The control for the first indicator consists of the 4th through 7th figures of the cypher-text, the first two giving the page in the pad and the last two the coordinates of a group on this page. The group thus found is subtracted from the front indicator to give the starting-point as page, page, check, row coordinate, column coordinate. The control for the rear indicator is the 4th through 7th figures reading from the end of the text and it is decyphered similarly.

The basis of the cypher was discovered by Washington's machining, and this section began work on JBD in April 1944; in May we recovered and telegraphed to London the first consecutive stretch of additives together with basic code groups. London immediately joined forces with us and practically the entire pad and code book were broken.

A second pad was brought into force on October 21st 1944, but poor local interception delayed the recovery of the new pad until April 1945. With the discontinuation of BA (which was also used to a moderate extent as an interdepartmental cypher), JBD traffic increased enormously after April and the pad was almost entirely recovered by August in cooperation with London. The entire traffic in this cypher was read until the cessation of hostilities.

5. JAO

This is a recyphering table for use within the Greater East Asia Ministry, introduced on July 1st 1943. It has a four-figure code book, the text being sent in five-figure groups with the middle figure checking the first two. The indicator, which is repeated at the beginning, is a five-figure group, the first two figures being the originator's number and the last three the serial number in this cypher.

JAO has not been broken, but the following facts have been established:

(a) Encyphering is done in sets of 58 groups, so that the 59th group has the same recypherer as the first, and so on.

(b) The last code group of a message must be either 6300 (*tsuzuki*) or 0940 (*owari*). The actual number of the message is encyphered at the head of the text and is encoded in the following way: the number is divided into pairs from the beginning, each pair being made into a self-checking, four-figure group by the addition of its complement (e.g. 24 becomes 2486). If a single digit remains it is repeated to form a four-figure group (e.g. 247 becomes 2486 7777). The part of the message is treated in the same way.

(c) An unrecyphered message from Nanking has shown that the code is not built up on any apparent pattern.

London has informed us that their machining of this traffic has proved that it is not homogeneous. This cypher is not extensively used and the length of a message rarely exceeds 58 groups.

6. 50505 (JBE)

This is apparently a recyphering table, with the text sent in five-figure groups, the middle figure checking the first two figures of each group. The group 50505 stands at the head of the text, followed by two non-checking groups which are presumably indicators or encyphered message-numbers.

50505 has not been broken. A suggestion was made by Washington that it was encyphered in sets of 97 groups (this being the 'normal' length of a message) but no confirmation has been found. Machining by London and Washington has produced no results.

Part IV: Breaking the Recyphering Tables

1. Letter-Figure Substitution

2. Placing of Messages in Depth

3. Breaking of Additives

4. Indicator Systems

1. Letter-Figure Substitution

NE and JBC, which both used the substitution, were introduced on the same day and were examined in conjunction. The original machining done by London revealed that NE was a recyphering table, and it was observed that the letters of the substitution divided into two Classes, CFORY and GKLNS, such that the 1st, 2nd and 4th columns of the five-figure group depth were each made up mainly of letters of the same Class — e.g. a specimen depth would be:

CYKGN
ORRGL
FRGNY
FOYSO
GNOCG
FONLY

Columns 1 and 2 being Class I, and Column 4 Class II. The natural division of numbers into two Classes being evens and odds, it was deduced that the code consisted of five-figure groups in which the 1st, 2nd and 4th figures were either all even or all odd. Very soon after the introduction of NE, Tokyo sent out a three-part circular which proved conclusively that the middle figure of each group was a null: in one part of the message S was used practically throughout while in another part the middle place was filled with all the letters of the alphabet.

The actual recovery of the letter-figure substitution proved a tedious job. London decided to work on NE only (in view of the initially large volume of traffic), and it was several weeks before the problem was solved, whereas it was later seen that it could have been written down by inspection of a few JBC columns (in view of the 9 and 0 restrictions in the second digit).

The first method adopted was that of examining the frequencies of the basic differences with every possible system of substitution. As the only restriction known was that of the even and odd sets, the possibilities apparently ran into millions, but careful analysis showed that the relevant permutations of each set were only six in number. Assuming, for example, that CFORY represented 02468, then any cyclic permutation of this order gives the same frequency distribution of basic differences; furthermore, the common difference of the arithmetical progression CFORY can be altered to 4, 6 or 8 without altering the frequencies, so that CFORY, COYFR, CRFYO and CYROF are all equivalent. Thus the 120 possible permutations of CFORY are divided by 5 and then by 4, to give only 6 basic permutations.

This method would certainly have given the order of the two sets, but the depth available for differencing was unfortunately not great and was further reduced, as only columns whose first three digits were all of the same class could be examined. The six frequency sets proved to be distressingly similar, and no conclusion could be made with any confidence.

At this stage a further restriction in the code was discovered by London, who noticed that one of the five figures was always missing from the third column, while another figure was rather rare. In this way a relation was quickly established between the five letters of each set, as the missing figure (zero) and the rare figure (2) obviously bore a constant relation to one another. The orders OFCRY and LSGNK were proved correct, and further examination of the relation between the two sets in the third column of the depth indicated the complete order OLFSCGRNYK (The evidence for this was rather scanty, but was fortunately conclusive). As any cyclic permutation of this order could be used, the above order giving O as zero was decided upon, and was finally proved correct by the JBC indicator system.

2. Placing Of Messages In Depth

Although the general rule for setting messages in depth is to break the indicator system, or, if this is not possible, to run all messages through a machine, the structure of the various codes studied by this section made such arduous work unnecessary.

NE

Obviously, if a recyphering table is used to encypher groups whose first three figures are all of the same parity, then the 'pattern' of the even and odd figures of the table will be evident from an inspection of the encyphered messages (e.g. If a four-figure group of the table is E O E E, then any group encyphered with it must appear as E O E or O E O). The possible arrangements are only four in number, and so each group of a message was classified as 0, 1, 2, or 3 (0 when all three figures were of the same parity, 1 for the first two, 2 for the first and third, and 3 for the second and third digits). Thus a message was typified by a series of numbers, known as its 'pattern', or more correctly as the pattern of the section of the additive book from which it was encyphered. The problem of tying in messages was thus reduced to that of finding repeats in their patterns, which was easily done by logging sheets. An example of this patterning follows:

Additives:	3891	2675	3940	8827	6394	2831
Code:	3731	3578	8849	4408	3774	1775
Cypher Text:	6522	5143	1789	2225	9068	3506
Pattern:	2	1	1	0	3	1

which is the pattern both of the cypher text and of the additives.

It was established that the NE recyphering table consisted only of four-figure groups, encyphering always commencing at the beginning of a group, so that this method was sufficient to place all messages in depth.

JBC

The JBC recyphering table consists of five-figure groups with encyphering beginning at any figure of the pad, so that the above patterning system was not completely effective as it accounted only for messages whose starting points were a multiple of four figures apart. For JBC, therefore, a method of 'partial patterning' was evolved as follows: Numbering the figures of the additive page 000–499, a message is said to be on 'Cut' I, II, III or IV according as its starting point is 4m, 4m + 1, 4m + 2, or 4m + 3. Now if two messages on Cut I and Cut II respectively are examined, it is easily seen that the parity of the second and third figures of the groups of the Cut I message corresponds to that of the first two figures of groups of the Cut II message.[7] Accordingly, all messages were typified by the parity of the first two figures of the groups ('A' Pattern) and also by the parity of the second and third figures ('B' Pattern). The patterning was simply done by underlining pairs of figures which were both even or both odd and writing down the distances between them, e.g. 2294 8362 9004 3746 2215 0762 3485 0926 4408 'A' Pattern for this stretch would be (.) 3.1.4. ...

As Cut I was by far the most commonly used, the various Cuts of a page could quickly be established, and when the entire pad was known the NE patterning system was resumed (all four Cuts on any page having, of course, separate patterns).

7	Code Groups	3731	3578	8849	4408	3731	3578	8849	4408
	Additives	3814	5211	6963	4084	8145	2116	9634	0846
	∴ Cypher Text	6545	8789	4702	8482	1876	5684	7473	4244
		OE	OE	OE	EE	OE	OE	OE	EE

Chapter 3. Japanese Diplomatic Cyphers

10101

The initial machining of JBD by Washington revealed that, when messages were placed in depth, in every second column the figures in that column were of uniform parity.

E.g. 2<u>9</u>386   14<u>0</u>77   2<u>9</u>348   62<u>3</u>14
      4<u>8</u>728   06<u>9</u>53   8<u>5</u>754   50<u>4</u>36

This led to the assumption of a four-figure code book in which the first figures were of a uniform parity and the third figures were of a uniform parity. An elementary patterning system was devised: in alternate digits of the text the evens were marked and the distances between them noted down. This system was continued until it was discovered that the pattern of the odd digits of one message could be linked with that of the even digits of another thus showing that, of the first and third digits of a code group, one was even and one was odd and thus Cuts I and III and Cuts II and IV could be linked by patterns.

The obvious defect of the patterning system outlined above was that each message had to be patterned twice, once for its even digits and once for its odd digits. The following method was therefore devised: As the cypher-text was sent in five-figure groups, there were three relevant digits in the 1st, 3rd, 5th, etc text groups, and two in the 2nd, 4th, etc groups. The odd-numbered groups were classified as 0, 1, 2 or 3 in the same way as NE patterns. The even-numbered groups were classified as 4 or 5 according as the two relevant digits were of the same or opposite parity.

E.g.   1st   2nd   3rd   4th   5th   6th   7th
           20<u>9</u>46   34<u>8</u>57   00<u>4</u>28   39<u>1</u>56   35<u>3</u>38   29<u>0</u>44   28<u>9</u>27
Pattern   2   5   0   4   1   5   3

Thus messages on the same Cut or on Cuts differing by two had identical patterns, the actual cut being easily determined by the starting point.

The essential difference between JBC and 10101 was that, while all Cuts of the former could eventually be found from patterns alone, it was impossible to link Cuts I and III with Cuts II and IV of 10101. This difficulty was serious in the early stages, but when a good knowledge of the code had been acquired, it was not difficult to break a few groups of additives on two Cuts alone, pattern these additives and thus find the other two Cuts of the page.

SOSOS

The structure of the SOSOS code book presented by far the greatest problem in patterning. The text was divided into four-figure groups, and each of these was classified as O or E according to the parity of the second and third digits. These patterns were very difficult to distinguish, and of course it was impossible to relate any of the four Cuts. The total traffic received before the cypher was discontinued gave a maximum depth of only five, which was however sufficient to portray the restrictions on the first two figures of the code-groups.

A sample depth was:

0709	6914	9778	9278	6099
0851	4221	0512	8167	2120
2544	7315	5680	8293	4010
2679	5110	7466	8210	3766
4834	6916	7313	4233	1941

from which it may be seen that the first two figures of each group can always be limited to a 6-digit range, the actual ranges being as yet indeterminate.

The ranges were tentatively determined from an inspection of fillers (see Appendix B) as 4–9 for the first place and 0–5 for the second. This assumption was finally proved correct when London found a message on a Cut adjacent to that of a known depth.

The actual finding of such Cuts was an arduous process and was never completely developed, as the ranges were only established a week or so before Russia's entry into the war. The only method was that of writing down the possible additives for the first figure of each group of a depth and then searching among the remaining messages for one such that the second digit of its group could always be placed in the range 0–5 by at least one of these possibilities.

3. Breaking of Additives

Apart from the usual method of differencing columns, many other devices were used which depended on stereotyped starts and ends, fillers, the restrictions on the codes, and, of course, the actual sense of the Japanese.[8] There is no need to discuss these in great detail, as experience alone can allow one to 'spot' columns and 'prapse' effectively.[9] The information on starts and ends may be found in Appendix B; it is a simple matter to exploit the restrictions of each code: e.g. a column in 10101 —

---

8 Differencing columns: Where a large depth of messages has been established, two common words, e.g. *wa* and *no* (whose code values in 10101 are 8559 and 8416 respectively) will often occur in the same column. Where recyphered with the same additives their difference (0143), of course, remains constant. The cryptographer has beside him his list of frequently occurring differences and, in the same columns of cypher-text, subtracts groups from each other in search of these.

9 To 'prapse' — a verb coined by Professor Trendall from the adverb 'perhaps'.

Chapter 3. Japanese Diplomatic Cyphers

5675
7856
7499
3136
5811
5394
7311
5393
5255

has fairly certainly the additive 9 for the first figure, giving five 6s, three 8s and one 4; the additive for the second figure can only be a 3 to eliminate the combinations 86, 87, 88 and 89; two groups with a difference of 0001 and beginning with 60 are most likely to be 6096 (*wo*) and 6097 (stop), and a trial of the required additives 07 for the last two columns gives a result which is seen to be certainly correct: quote, *wa*, *so*, *ni*, *dai*, stop, unquote, *wo*, *ki*. The open and close quotes will require their complements; the stop will have a final verb or brackets before it, possibly a paragraph after it, and the '*so*' will probably either be in quotes or be followed by '*ren*' or '*gawa*' [meaning 'Soviets'], and so on. In this way the whole section may be extended without great difficulty, the restrictions showing quickly whether one's 'prapses' are possible or not.

4. Indicator Systems

These were not broken by this section, as the great labour involved requires either a machine or a very large staff.

Part V: Miscellaneous Cyphers

1. HINOKI Machine Cypher (JAA)
2. SAKURA Emergency Cypher (JBL)
3. Unidentified Cyphers

1. HINOKI Machine Cypher (JAA)

JAA is the highest-grade of Japanese diplomatic cypher. The indicator is a five-figure group at the head of the text and is made up of all the permutations of the groups 02468, 13579, 01234, 56789.

2. SAKURA Emergency Cypher (JBL)

This emergency cypher was introduced for use by posts which were forced to burn their cyphers, as the system can be easily memorised. It is a plain-language double-transposition without blanks, indicated by the group XXXXX at the head of the text, with a figure check at the end. The instructions were circulated in NE and JAA, both of which messages were read.

The key for the first transposition, in encyphering, is derived from the word *umiyukaba* by numbering the letters in alphabetical order from the left (Thus the key is 764985132).[10] The key for the second form is derived in the same manner from the word *umiyukaba* followed by the originator's name (e.g. *umiyukaba* Harada produces the key 13 11 9 15 14 10 1 6 2 8 3 12 4 7 5).

3. Unidentified Cyphers

Following is a list of unidentified Japanese diplomatic cyphers. With each the small amount of traffic intercepted did not justify any serious work being done on them.

Hanoi-Vichy Figure Traffic

This was sent in five-figure groups and was used only in the circuit Hanoi–Vichy–GEAM. Only five messages of this type were received.

9009

This cypher was mainly used between Canton and other China posts. It was indicated by the group 9009 at the beginning of the text and was sent in four-figure groups.

---

10   *Umiyukaba* is the first word of a passage from a famous patriotic poem of the Late Nara period (8th Century AD):

   We are the sons of the fathers who sang
   'At sea be my corpse water-soaked
   On land let it be with grass o'ergrown,
   Let me die by the side of my Sovereign!
   Never will I look back'.

When this was set to music by Nobutoki Kiyoshi in 1937, at a time of national fervour following the outbreak of war with China, it achieved wide popularity. The Japan Broadcasting Corporation used it as the background music for the declaration of war against the United States and, later, for bulletins announcing naval or military reverses.

Chapter 3. Japanese Diplomatic Cyphers

5005

This cypher was current in the GEAM area and was sent in four-figure groups. The indicator 5005 led to the suggestion that it might be a form of 50505 (JBE) in which the middle figure check was omitted.

Petropavlovsk Code

This was a simple code, which came into use simultaneously with SOSOS (JBN) and was used by the same posts. Only ten messages of this type were received.

Part VI: General Remarks

1. Code-Building
2. Cypher Systems
3. Errors in Encyphering
4. Distribution of Cyphers
5. Cooperation with Linguists

1. Code-Building

A great deal of evidence has been found that the Japanese regarded their cypher systems as completely unbreakable. However, it is not advisable when constructing codes to have patterns or restrictions; and alternatives for common groups are most necessary. Yet no alternative groups were ever found in the figure codes, while the letter codes had only two equivalents for a few common groups: the alternatives in FUJI were *wo, ni, no,* and *ga*; in BA *wa, wo, ni, no, ga,* and *mo*.

As the standard Japanese diplomatic vocabulary is 1,620 groups, their figure codes had to be tetragrams restricted in some manner. The obvious method is to choose 1,620 groups at random, but a patterned code not only reduces chances of corruption but also saves a great deal of time by allowing the decode to be set up on charts and facilitating memorisation of the code groups. A study of Part IV: Breaking the Recyphering Tables will show what invaluable assistance the patterned codes were to us.

2. Cypher Systems

The recyphering tables introduced in July 1943 were the first the Japanese had ever used for diplomatic communications. Hitherto transposition systems had been solely used, but curiously enough the Japanese regarded their recyphering tables as of such high grade that they were chary of using even the second system of BA for important messages, although this latter system proved to be the most difficult for us to read. Perhaps the swing from transposition to recyphering tables was most fortunate from our point of view, as it is impossible to say how complicated the transposition systems might have become.

3. Errors in Encyphering

[1 paragraph (approx. 7 lines) expunged][11]

(a) Both BA and GEAM were introduced in a reasonably simplified form, the complexity being afterwards increased by a series of changes in the cypher system while keeping the code consistent. [Concluding portion of the paragraph (approx 7 lines) expunged].

(b) [1 paragraph (approx 9 lines) expunged]

(c) [1 paragraph (approx 22 lines) expunged]

4. Distribution of Cyphers

A state of war invariably produces great difficulties in distribution, the usual result being that cyphers must be kept in force much longer than is safe. The Japanese, faced with this position, attempted to compromise by introducing changes in the existing cyphers (e.g. in FUJI — see Part II above). But however ingenious a new system may be, a knowledge of the previous system and code is usually sufficient to break it.

Another result of the war was that when the European countries were being overrun, the problem of cypher security became acute and the Japanese posts were forced to burn their cyphers and use emergency systems which could be memorized. The instructions for these systems had, of course, to be circulated in existing cyphers; they might have proved difficult to break, but it was fortunately not necessary to attack them directly.

5. Cooperation with Linguists

Although military and naval recyphering tables, with their great bulk of traffic, can be broken by purely cryptographical methods [1 paragraph (length unknown) expunged].

---

11 The expungements in this part were made by the NAA on 17 February 1998, pursuant to *Australian Archives Act* §33(1)(a) and (c) — 'information of a class concerning operational methods/techniques that remain current'.

PART VII: PERSONNEL 1942-45

Technical

Professor A. D. Trendall (University of Sydney) (January 1942 – June 1944)

NX139540 Lieutenant R. S. Bond (February 1942 –)

Dr Elizabeth Sheppard (September 1942 – March 1943)

N450470 Lieutenant E. S. Barnes (January 1943 –)

NX139427 Sergeant K. L. McKay (July 1944 –)

NX82807 Sergeant A. C. Eastway (February 1944 –)

VX94295 Corporal I. H. Smith (May 1944 –)

V143841 Sergeant P. Grange (Clerical Duties) (October 1943 –).

The following personnel were lent to Special Intelligence through the kind offices of Lieutenant-Colonel A. W. Sandford, Commanding Officer, Central Bureau, during heavy periods:

Sergeant A. W. F. Rogers, Sergeant H. W. MacKenzie (January 1945 –), Warrant Officer II P. Pledger (October 1944), Sergeant J. C. Davies (June 1942 – February 1943), Private K. McLeod (February – May 1944).

Language and Translation

Mr C. H. Archer (British Consular Service) (January 1942 – December 1944)

Mr H. A. Graves (British Consular Service) (February 1942 – September 1943)

Mr A. R. V. Cooper (British Government Codes & Cyphers School) (March – December 1942)

Mr J. O. Lloyd (British Consular Service) (December 1942 – March 1943)

Mr D. MacDermot (British Consular Service) (December 1942 – March 1943)

Mr H. R. Sawbridge (July 1943 – February 1944)

Mr R. L. Cowley (British Consular Service) (December 1944 –)

Mr E. T. Biggs (British Consular Service) (July 1944 –)

Miss Mavis Tilley (November 1942 –)

Mr L. R. Oates (February – November 1943)

Lieutenant C. A. James (British Army) (May 1944 –)

Lent by Central Bureau for short periods of heavy pressure — Warrant Officer II B. Pitman (British Army) (June 1945 –), VX128886 Private D. C. S. Sissons (April 1945 –).

Clerical and Typing

A staff of typists and women clerks was headed by Miss Reba Shearer (January 1942 –).

Clerical

Miss Mary MacRae Stewart (November 1942 – September 1943)
Mrs Marjorie Hattam (1943 –)
Mrs Catherine Gahan (September 1943 –)

Typing

Miss Pauline Dennis (1943 – June 1945)
Corporal Vailima Parbery (AWAS) (May 1944 –)
Corporal Thora Martin (AWA) (June 1945 –)

[Report of Special Intelligence Section ends.]

Sources

It was, I think, in 1978, that my colleagues at the Australian National University, Desmond Ball and David Horner, came upon evidence in recently declassified files that a diplomatic Special Intelligence Section headed by Professor A. D. Trendall had operated in Melbourne from about January 1942 until the war's end, its function being to intercept the encyphered signals traffic between the Japanese Ministry of Foreign Affairs and its embassies and consulates overseas and to decrypt so much as was possible. They suggested that I make an attempt to put together a history of that Special Intelligence Section.

At the time it proved impracticable. Persistent enquiries at the NAA elicited the suggestion that the records of the Section had either been destroyed in toto in the 1950s or were held by the Department of Defence which was unlikely to declassify them in the foreseeable future.

I attempted to prepare the ground by writing to former members of the Section for their recollections: Eric Barnes, Ronald Bond, Kenneth McKay and Ian Smith among the cryptanalysts, and Mary Stewart from the office staff. They were patient and indulgent and provided a treasure trove of background information.

Ronald Bond and Ian Smith remembered that before the Section was disbanded they spent much time compiling a detailed and comprehensive report on the

Section's activities. This prompted me in about 1986 to apply to the NAA for access to that document. This elicited a reply from the Defence Signals Directorate (DSD) that the Report had survived as had an Army Central Registry file, '37/401/425: Special Intelligence Section' (NAA Series A6923, Item 37/401/425) that, when declassified, might be of considerable help to the historian. These documents were eventually declassified in about 1997. At the same time, in 1986, DSD presented me with a Xerox copy of a file held by the US National Archives & Records Service containing translations of diplomatic intercepts cabled by Trendall's Melbourne Section to the US Navy's cryptographic department in Washington throughout 1942.

At the time of the 1997 declassifications, DSD also declassified what appeared to be two wartime office files of the Major I(x) in the Directorate of Military Intelligence who administered the Section (NAA Series A6923, Items: 'Diplomatic Message Traffic' and 'SI/2 Attachment') which cast some light on the Section's daily activities over certain periods.

It would appear, therefore, that the office records of the Section, which were complete and in good order at the time the Section was disbanded, have been destroyed in toto — including the leather-bound register, referred to by the office staff as The Koran, in which the particulars of every intercepted message was recorded!

Surely the time has come for Defence to declassify their files on the 'TRENCODE', used by Allied operatives working behind enemy lines, and its development. (Incidentally I remember that it was still in use in the British Commonwealth Occupation Force in 1947) There can no longer be 'security' objections. After all, it was never considered to be unbreakable — merely that it could resist decryption for a period of two or three days.

My impression is that the Section was essentially one of the overseas out-stations of the United Kingdom's cryptographic organisation, the Government Code and Cypher School (GC&CS). Following the recent declassification of GC&CS wartime files, their detailed listing by the Public Record Office indicates that GC&CS had a much less cavalier attitude to their records than our Defence Signals Directorate has demonstrated to its own. There should be a good deal of information about the operations of Trendall's Section in the GC&CS files available at the Public Record Office at Kew.

My editing of the Report is confined to:

(i) Re-arranging the sequence of some of the chapters;

(ii) The insertion of section headings;

(iii) In the interests of clarity identifying each of the codes by the title used by the Section at the time, e.g. GEAM, 10101, BA, JBC, Umiyukaba;

(iv) The addition to the list, Personnel 1942–1945, of a few names that the authors had apparently forgotten;

(v) The rewriting and expansion of a few sentences where Ian Smith agreed that, as written, the meaning was not sufficiently clear; and

(vi) My attempt to reconstruct, using American sources, Appendix L (which is one of the several Appendices missing in the file).

Appendix A: Best Groups

Following is a classification of the best groups in the Japanese diplomatic vocabulary (This list must be used with discretion, as certain 'position' groups such as *gokuhi*, jōhō etc which are often very good at the beginning of a message are on the other hand very rare in the body of a message).

Class I: *no, ni, wa, wo, shi, mo, to.*

Class II: *chi, dai, ga, i, ji, ka, kai, kan, ki, kō, ku, ri, sen, su, tai, tō, tsu.*

Class III: *bei, bu, bun, chō, chū, dō, doku, e, fu, gawa, gō, gun, hi, jō, ken, koku, kyō, mono, nari, naru, ru, ryō, sei, shin, shō, so, sō, suru, ta, taru, teki, tokoro, yō.*

Class IV: *ari, arita(shi), aru, bō, gen, go, jin, kaku, kin, koto, mi, migi, mu, ni oite, re, sho, shū, te, yori.*

To this must be added punctuation and low numerals, which are usually 'position' groups.

Appendix B: Starts and Ends

Starts

Following are the most common starts of Japanese diplomatic messages:

Ōden or *Kiden* [numerals] *ni kanshi. 1,*

Gokuhi or *(gai) kimitsu.*

Kanchōfugō.

For multi-part messages — [Numeral no numeral] or [numeral].

[Place) *hatsu* [place] *ate dempō dai* [numerals] *gō (ni kanshi).*

Date.

Paragraph.

Other traditional starts were sometimes used by certain posts. e.g. Stockholm sent many spy reports which almost invariably began with some variation of '*chōhōsha hōkoku* [date] *sa no tōri*'.

Tokyo circulars very often began with '*kokusai jōhō*'.

Ends

Apart from final verbs (of which '*nari*' was by far the most common), circulars could usually be relied upon to finish with a formula listing addresses, like one of the following:

[Place, place, etc] *ni tenden seri.*

[Place] *yori* [places] *ni tenden aritashi/o kō.*

Honden atesaki [places] *ni tenden seri.*

Honden zaiō kaku taishikan (*so wo nozoku*) *ni tenden seri.*

The number of parts of a multi-part message was also found at the end occasionally, also '*tsuzuki*'.

Fillers, if a whole four-figure group, were often stop, comma, or close brackets. The usual fillers, however, were of the type 0000, 0123, 1234, etc, (the sequence often carrying on from the last figure of the final code-group).

Very short messages were often requests for repetitions and, if so, could usually be written straight in on the following formula: *Kiden* [numerals] *kaiyaku funō ni tsuki chōsa no ue saiden aritashi/o kō.*

Appendix C: R7F Lower Power Far Eastern Diplomatic Network

Traffic on this low-power Far Eastern diplomatic network was first intercepted in Melbourne towards the end of August 1944. By far the greater part of GEAM and interdepartmental messages were sent through this channel and in the year preceding the cessation of hostilities only a very small portion of the total Far Eastern traffic passed over commercial links.

The transmission procedure was somewhat different from that used by commercial stations.

Breaking Japanese Diplomatic Codes

(1) Addresses were in code instead of in clear (v. Appendix E [Missing]).

(2) Signatures of originators were not sent.

(3) The text was not sent in normal fashion from left to right. Each page of the transmission form contained 50 groups in five columns, and the text was transmitted by reading down the columns, the end of each column being denoted by the *kana* break AL.

(4) In figure messages the following short figure substitution was used:

T	A	U	V	4	5	6	B	D	N
0	1	2	3	4	5	6	7	8	9

Appendix L: Code and Keys for GEAM (JBB)

[Ed. The original Appendix is missing in the xerox copy of the Report held by the National Archives of Australia (NAA). What follows I have reconstructed from information derived from the US Army Signal Security Agency's file, 'US/UK Technical Exchanges and Information on Solution of JBB' (US National Archives, Record Group 457, Box 1328, File 190/37/34/3 (19 pages).]

The following description is of GEAM in its final form, in use from October 1st 1944.

The Indicator and Keys

The indicator is the group of alternating letters (e.g. BKBKB) following the date and number group. These letters (A through N excluding M) indicate the horizontal row order and vertical column order respectively in the 13 x 13 transposition block, namely:

A	5	2	11	9	3	13	8	1	10	6	4	7	12
B	2	7	11	1	6	13	9	3	12	8	4	5	10
C	11	6	4	3	2	13	1	9	7	8	12	5	10
D	10	9	5	11	7	3	6	13	4	1	8	2	12
E	1	13	3	6	11	7	10	4	12	5	2	8	9
F	11	2	6	4	5	10	12	3	7	1	8	13	9
G	13	4	10	5	3	11	7	1	2	9	6	12	8
H	11	10	5	3	4	9	7	1	13	8	2	6	12
I	9	7	2	8	12	6	13	5	3	11	10	1	4
J	4	9	13	1	8	5	2	6	12	3	10	7	11
K	13	10	2	9	6	4	11	8	1	3	12	7	5
L	11	6	8	3	7	5	12	10	2	9	4	1	13
N	5	10	13	7	2	11	8	1	3	12	4	6	9

Chapter 3. Japanese Diplomatic Cyphers

These keys also determine the positions of the nine blanks, which are inserted in the cells with the coordinates (1,1) through (9,9). Thus, for example, the transposition block indicated by the indicator group ABABA would be as follows:

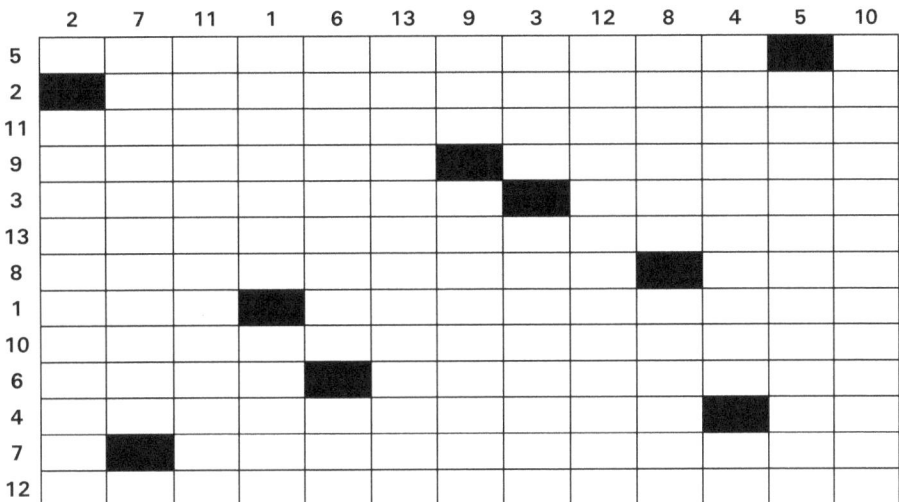

Encoding and Transposition by the Sender

In this example the originator sends the following message in GEAM using the indicator ABABA.

Janku yusō ni kanshi

Dai 20 ji

Kinmangen (*kane. yorozu. minamoto*) 78 ton

Fujōhatsu (*futsū no fu. senshū no shū. hatsushin no hatsu*) 33 ton

Dai 21 ji

Chinryūjun (*chinkōin no chin. ryūtai no tai. suna ...*

He encodes this into the appropriate digrams/tetragrams of the GEAM code and it reads:

```
           20                      40                      60
    JJXYERCURUDYVVDYUFAS    VUSAMIUFICAJELNICAGE    UKROKOMUUKJIGAJOFONU
           80                     100                     120
    UTEVOFUFHUYHIYNIHUIR    GOHUUKEDYFGOYFUKIYID    GOIYNUWEWEOFUFASVVTI
          140                     160
    MIUFIFYLTOERNIIFCYIB       GOIFUKYLWYGOWYUKDUGA ...
```

He divides this from the left into packets of 160 characters (i.e. 13 x 13 – 9) each of which he successively enters into the transposition block, row by row, from the left, in the numerical sequence indicated by the row key, as follows:

	2	7	11	1	6	13	9	3	12	8	4	5	10
5	U	K	J	I	G	A	J	O	F	O	N	■	U
2	■	V	V	D	Y	U	F	A	S	V	U	S	A
11	I	U	F	I	F	Y	L	T	O	E	R	N	I
9	I	Y	I	D	G	O	■	I	Y	N	U	W	E
3	M	I	U	F	I	C	A	■	J	E	L	N	I
13	L	W	Y	G	O	W	Y	U	K	D	U	G	A
8	U	K	E	D	Y	F	G	O	Y	■	F	U	K
1	J	J	X	■	Y	E	R	C	U	R	U	D	Y
10	W	E	O	F	U	F	A	S	V	V	T	I	M
6	U	T	E	V	■	O	F	U	F	H	U	Y	H
4	C	A	G	E	U	K	R	O	K	O	■	M	U
7	I	■	Y	N	I	H	U	I	R	G	O	H	U
12	I	F	C	Y	I	B	G	O	I	F	U	K	Y

Usually the final block of the message will contain less than the full 160 characters. In such cases he will reduce the number of rows accordingly, from the bottom. If the bottom remaining row is not full he will insert from the left edge the necessary number of blanks to fill it.

On completing the transposition he writes out for transmission the cypher text by reading off each block, column by column, from top to bottom, in the numerical sequence indicated by the column key. In the present example this would be:

IDIDF GDFVE NYUII MLUJW UCIIO ATIUO CSUOI ONURU etc.

Decryption

The recipient goes through the same procedures in reverse — he makes out the same transposition block as indicated by the indicator group, enters the cypher text column by column, reads off the encoded message row by row, and decodes it by reference to the GEAM decoding charts, which are here reproduced.

Chapter 3. Japanese Diplomatic Cyphers

Decoding Charts

Consonant-Vowel Digrams

	A	E	I	O	U	Y	
B	A	E	I	O	U	Ō	B
C	KA	KE	KI	KO	KU	KŌ	C
D	SA	SE	SHI	SO	SU	SŌ	D
F	TA	TE	CHI	TO	TSU	TŌ	F
G	NA	NE	NI	NO	NU	NŌ	G
H	HA	HE	HI	HO	FU	HŌ	H
J	MA	ME	MI	MO	MU	MŌ	J
K	RA	RE	RI	RO	RU	RŌ	K
L	GA	GE	GI	GO	GU	GŌ	L
M	ZA	ZE	JI	ZO	ZU	ZŌ	M
N	DA	DE	(	DO	)	DŌ	N
P	BA	BE	BI	BO	BU	BŌ	P
Q	PA	PE	PI	PO	PU	PŌ	Q
R	YA	YŪ	YI	YO	YU	YŌ	R
S	Ø	SATSU	KATSU	SHO	KETSU	SETSU	S
T	AI	ZAI	1	JU	KOKU	ZEI	T
V	100	ZATSU	GAI	JO	2	ZETSU	V
W	ATSU	3	NICHI	SUI	KONO	TAI	W
X	EI	SHA	GAKU	4	GETSU	TAKU	X
Y	KAI	GYO(BI)	KYO	SEI	SAI	←	Y
Z	KAKU	SHU	KEI	RYŌZI	SAKU	TATSU	Z
	A	E	I	O	U	Y	

Vowel-Consonant Digrams

	A	E	I	O	U	Y	
B	AN	EN	IN	ON	UN	KYŪ	B
C	KAN	KEN	KIN	KON	KUN	KYŌ	C
D	SAN	SEN	SHIN	SON	SUN	SHŪ	D
F	TAN	TEN	CHIN	TON	↕	SHŌ	F
G	NAN	NEN	NIN	↓		JŪ	G
H	HAN	HEN	HIN	HON	FUN	JŌ	H
J	MAN	MEN	MIN	MON	↕	CHŪ	J
K	RAN	REN	RIN	RON	⊙	CHŌ	K
L	GAN	GEN	GIN	GON	GUN	RYŪ	L
M	ZAN	ZEN	JIN	ZON	REP. VOWEL	RYŌ	M
N	DAN	DEN		DON		GYŌ	N
P	BAN	BEN	BIN	⊙	KYO	GYŪ	P
Q	PAN	PEN(?)	TAISHI	MYŌ	TOMO(?)	RYŪ	Q
R	DAI	5	N	TSŪ	SHINKU	KYOKUSHAKU(?)	R
S	CHO	KAI	MAI	REI	6	FUTU	S
T	SONO	CHO	AAI	REI	7	SHOKU(?)	T
V	TEI	SONO	8	HAI	NETSU	HEI	V
W	TEI	AAKU	MUGI	9	BEI	CHOKU(?)	W
X	TETSU	MURE	HARU	YAKU	NAO	RYAKU	X
Y	DOKU	RITSU	KATSU	SEIFU	HOKU	←	Y
Z	DOKU	RITSU	FUKU	YORI	MATSU	KYOKU	Z
	A	E	I	O	U	Y	

Auxiliary Chart for English Spelling

The use of this chart is indicated by the digrams OG or UJ ('Open Spell') and its discontinuance by the digram YY ('Close Spell')

Consonant-Vowel Digrams

	A	E	I	O	U	Y	
B	BE	BI	BO	BU	BY	BA	B
C	CE	CI	CO	CU	CY	CA	C
D	DE	DI	DO	DU	DY	DA	D
F	FE	FI	FO	FU	FY	FA	F
G	GE	GI	GO	GU	GY	GA	G
H	HE	HI	HO	HU	HY	HA	H
J	SPACE	☉	☉	'	☉	°A_P	J
K	B	C	D	E	F	▲	K
L	LE	LI	LO	LU	LY	LA	L
M	ME	MI	MO	MU	MY	MA	M
N	NE	NI	NO	NU	NY	NA	N
P	PE	PI	PO	PU	PY	PA	P
R	RE	RI	RO	RU	RY	RA	R
S	SE	SI	SO	SU	SY	SA	S
T	TE	TI	TO	TU	TY	TA	T
V	VE	VI	VO	VU	VY	VA	V
W	WE	WI	WO	WU	WY	WA	W
X	J	K	L	M	N	I	X
Y	T	U	V	W	X	←	Y
Z	CON	CH	GH	PH	SH	COM	Z
	A	E	I	O	U	Y	

Vowel-Consonant Digrams

	A	E	I	O	U	Y	
B	AB	EB	IB	OB	UB	YB	B
C	AC	EC	IC	OC	UC	1	C
D	AD	ED	ID	OD	UD	2	D
F	AF	EF	IF	OF	UF	3	F
G	AG	EG	IG	OG	UG	4	G
H	AH	EH	IH	OH	UH	5	H
J	‡	?	(	)	,	6	J
K	H	/	∴	∵	G	7	K
L	AL	EL	IL	OL	UL	8	L
M	AM	EM	IM	OM	UM		M
N	AN	EN	IN	ON	UN		N
P	AP	EP	IP	OP	UP	9	P
R	AR	ER	IR	OR	UR		R
S	AS	ES	IS	OS	US		S
T	AT	ET	IT	OT	UT		T
V	AV	EV	IV	OV	UV		V
W	AW	EW	IW	OW	UW		W
X	O	P	Q	R	S		X
Y	Y	Z	MENT	EX	SION		Y
Z	TH	WH	ST	PR	TION		Z
	A	E	I	O	U	Y	

SEQUENCES

A 5-2-11-9-3-13-8-1-10-6-4-7-12

B 2-7-11-1-6-13-9-3-12-8-4-5-10

C 11-6-4-3-2-13-1-9-7-8-12-5-10

D 10-9-5-11-7-3-6-13-4-1-8-2-12

E 1-13-3-6-11-7-10-4-12-5-2-8-9

F 11-2-6-4-5-10-12-3-7-1-8-13-9

G 13-4-10-5-3-11-7-1-2-9-6-12-8

H 11-10-5-3-4-9-7-1-13-8-2-6-12

I 9-7-2-8-12-6-13-5-3-11-10-1-4

J 4-9-13-1-8-5-2-6-12-3-10-7-11

K 13-10-2-9-6-4-11-8-1-3-12-7-5

L 11-6-8-3-7-5-12-10-2-9-4-1-13

N 5-10-13-7-2-11-8-1-3-12-4-6-9

Appendix Q: Unused Emergency Cyphers

Super – LA

Instructions for use of this refinement of JAH (LA code) were sent out in JAA in June 1942, but no traffic of this type was ever intercepted.

Method of encyphering

The message is first encoded in JAH. A figure bigram is substituted for each letter of the coded text according to a substitution table formed in the following manner: All the letters of the alphabet excluding Q are written in order into a square 5 by 5 beginning at the top left-hand corner. The columns are numbered from 0 to 4 beginning at the left and the rows from 0 to 4 downwards. The figure bigram to be substituted for a given letter is formed by combining the row co-ordinate with the column co-ordinate of the letter. Thus, if A is in the top left-hand corner of the square A = 00, and X = 42.

The figure text is then written out in blocks of 40 figures consisting of two rows of twenty. A block of less than forty figures is likewise divided into two.

Starting from the left of the block each upper figure is combined with the figure beneath to form a figure bigram which is converted to a letter according to the substitution table. This is the final cypher text.

The substitution square is altered for each message and is indicated as follows. The co-ordinates of A are encyphered according to the number code appendix to JAH (v. Appendix F). The resulting bigram is written before and after the letter Q. Thus if A = 00, then the substitution square indicator is BAQBA.

A five-figure group giving the data and serial number of the message is placed at the head of the text. 01001 would signify message No. 1 on the 1st of the month.

In March and April, 1944, when Rumania and Bulgaria were threatened by the Russian advance and the legations in these countries were forced with the necessity of burning their cyphers, each minister formulated an extremely primitive and cumbrous emergency cypher. Neither cypher was ever employed and in May 1944 instructions for the use of SAKURA (JBL), a much simpler and securer emergency system, were circulated from Tokyo.

Bucharest 'Consonant-Vowel' Substitution

Details of this system were sent to Tokyo in March 1944. It is based on the *kana* syllabary, the redundant '*wi*' and '*ye*' being omitted. Each syllable is written in reverse order against the remaining 45 syllables to form a substitution table. Thus '–N' is substituted for 'I' and 'SU' for 'RO'.

Each syllable, however, is always to be represented by a bigram of the form 'consonant-vowel'. If single vowels have to be substituted, they are preceded by one of the fillers V, X, or Z. Instead of '–N' 'Q: plus any vowel' is employed.

The consonants B, C, D, F, G, J, L, P, are used with any vowel to indicate the following:

B = preceding syllable is nigoried.
C = preceding syllable is half-nigoried.
D = long vowel
F = several syllables follow in quotes
G = stop
L = comma
P = close brackets

The text was to be sent in five-figure groups. The specimen text sent by the minister at Bucharest himself best illustrates the weaknesses of the system.

'*DAI NIPPON BANZAI*' was encyphered as follows:

Cypher text:	HU	BE	QU	MO	YA	HI	CE	XI	SE	BO	ZI	RU	BA	QE
Clear:	TA	nig	I	NI	TU	HO	semi-nig	N	HA	nig	N	SA	nig	I

In April 1944 Tokyo replied, adding a further process to the original system. The bigrams obtained by the first substitution are further substituted according to the following substitution table.

The letters from A to M are written above the letters from N to Z so that A is above N and M above Z. Substitution is effected in the following manner:

(a) Where both letters of the bigram are in the same row, the corresponding letters of the other row are substituted. Thus AB becomes NO; UV becomes HI.

(b) When the letters of the bigram come one in each row, the corresponding letter of the opposite row are taken in each case, but the order is reversed.

(c) Where the letters of the bigram are in the same vertical line, the letters immediately to the right of each are substituted. Thus AN becomes BO; MZ becomes NA.

(d) Double letters are treated as in (a) above. Thus LL becomes YY; XX becomes KK.

All tetegrams used in this method were to bear the prefix "BASBA".

Sofia Emergency System

Details of this emergency cypher were intercepted in a message from Sofia to Tokyo in April 1944, but were somewhat obscure due to the actual phrasing of the message and signal corruption.

The basis of the system is as follows: The message is first encoded in JAH and the coded text is written out in two rows. The first group of the first half of the final cypher text is formed by taking the first letter of the upper row, the first of the lower row, the second of the upper row, the second of the lower row, and the third of the upper row. The first group of the second half of the final cypher text consists of the third letter of the lower row, and the fourth and fifth letters of the upper and lower rows taken in order. Succeeding groups are taken off on the some alternating principle.

In the case of fillers the method employed is unknown and the specimen text given at the end of the instructions was so corrupt that no inferences could be drawn from it.

Annexes: Interviews, Correspondence and Notes

Annex 1. David Sissons to Alan Stripp, 9 November 1988............... 105

Annex 2. Notes from an Interview with with Professor Arthur
Dale Trendall by Desmond Ball on 10 May 1990.................... 115

Annex 3. David Sissons to Ian Smith, 3 August 1990.................. 119

Annex 4. Ian Smith to David Sissons, 8 August 1990................. 125

Annex 5. Interview of Dr A. P. Treweek by David Sissons,
11 October 1990...................................... 131

Annex 6. Ronald Bond, Notes on Sissons (3 August 1990),
Smith (8 August 1990) and Treweek (11 October 1990),
undated but probably late 1990.................................. 135

Annex 7. David Sissons to Desmond Ball, 11 October 1993............. 143

Annex 8. Steve Mason to David Sissons, 26 June 1994 145

Annex 9. Steve Mason to Desmond Ball, 7 July 1995 149

Annex 10. Ronald Bond to Desmond Ball, 29 September 1994........... 153

Annex 11. David Sissons to Desmond Ball, 22 May 1996 157

Annex 12. David Sissons to Desmond Ball, 9 September 1996.......... 163

Annex 13. David Sissons to Desmond Ball, 16 October 1996........... 165

Annex 14. David Sissons to Desmond Ball, 23 March 1998............. 167

Annex 15. David Sissons to Kenneth McKay, 9 November 2004.......... 169

Annex 16. Notes on the Breaking of GEAM Using the
'Winds – Set-Up' Message.. 175

Annex 17. David Sissons to Kenneth McKay, 28 November 2004......... 185

Annex 18. David Sissons to Kenneth McKay, 19 December 2004......... 189

Annex 1. David Sissons to Alan Stripp, 9 November 1988

The Australian National University

GPO Box 4, Canberra ACT 2601
Telegrams & cables NATUNIV Canberra
Telex AA62694 SOPAC FAX No. (062) 571893
Telephone 062 495111

Department of International Relations
reference

9 November 1988

Mr Alan Stripp

Dear Alan,

Many thanks for your letter (October 13th).

Congratulations on your success with the publisher. I very much enjoyed your *Intelligence and National Security* article and greatly look forward to your book.

Let me deal, in sequence, with the two points that you raise in your letter.

Mornington's Traffic Record, March 1943

I, too, assumed that the Jap OUT figure equalled the sum of the other countries' IN figures; but lacking your thoroughness I neglected to put it to the test. Your interpretation, that we were also eavesdropping on neutrals and our allies, is exciting and, if established, would confirm the existence of activities that the British Government has endeavoured, so far with considerable success, to keep under cover.

Apart from the Denniston memorandum, the best evidence I have seen that Britain read her Allies' traffic is Churchill's letter to Roosevelt of 25 February 1942 unearthed by Christopher Thorne in the Roosevelt Papers (*Enclosure A*). Similarly, an academic colleague recently volunteered to me information that indicates very clearly that GC&CS or one of its out-stations was reading Nationalist Chinese traffic in 1940 (*Enclosure B*).

The first instance judgment in the *Spycatcher* case in the N.S.W. Supreme Court cites the following as indicating that Britain was still intercepting Soviet diplomatic traffic in the later stages of World War II - *A Matter of Trust*, p.28, *Their Trade is Treachery*, p.47, *Too Secret Too Long*, p.39, and *The Spy Who Never Was*, pp.22-3. If my recollection is correct, one or more of these authors (and perhaps Wright himself) states that Australian interception stations were on occasion assisting in the latter activity. I think the place mentioned was Darwin. I see no problem in Darwin, Mornington (i.e. 52 Section) or any of the RAAF 'Wireless Units' on request watching particular Soviet stations for limited periods. Similarly, it would not surprise me if this was treated as a matter of the utmost secrecy and if strict instructions were given that it must not be referred to in the Traffic Record and War Diary. (I have heard that in early 1941 the interception of Japanese diplomatic traffic was approved by the Minister for the Army (Spender) in the Menzies Administration with some reluctance and only after he had consulted the Attorney-General about its legality. I wonder whether in 1944 the D.M.I. (or the C.G.S.) were prepared to risk referring to Ministers in the Labor Administration its extension to Soviet traffic).

Despite the above, Mornington's War Diary confirms my impression that their function was to intercept *Japanese* diplomatic traffic. With a War Establishment of 2 officers and 89 other ranks (of whom only 53 were wireless operators) they lacked the resources in personnel to do much more.

How, then, can we explain the figures in the March 1943 Traffic Record? In the table that follows I have done a few calculations for every tenth day:

1	2	3	4	5	6	7	8	9
Date	Total Messages	Sum of OUTs	Japan OUTs	Sum of Other INs	(5)-(4)	Japan INs	Sum of Other OUTs	(8)-(7)
1/3/43	58	58	14	21	7	37	44	7
10/3/43	62	62	31	31	0	31	31	0
20/3/43	90	90	44	46	2	44	46	2
30/3/43	74	74	33	35	2	39	41	2

Columns 6 and 9 tally in every case. Would it not be a sufficient explanation if the figures in these two columns represent messages sent from one overseas Japanese post *direct to another*?

If it is important for you to know whether or not all these overseas stations were Japanese, then the May 1944 figures may be of more use to you; for accompanying the Traffic Record table is a break-down according to the call-sign of the sending station of the 3348 messages intercepted during that month (*Enclosure C*). Some of these call-signs, no doubt, date from the pre-war period. If so, their owners may perhaps be identifiable in the lists of call-signs published by the international body that allocated frequencies.

One of the inadequacies of my explanation is that it doesn't tell us how messages with multiple addressees were dealt with in the Traffic Record. I should imagine that Tokyo was sending quite a number of these. Perhaps

Mornington entered them only under the name of the first of the addressees listed in the message.

Your enquiry has confirmed me in my feeling that I and the general reader need to know much more about the basic techniques of interception (as well, of course, as of decryption). How did Tokyo go about transmitting an enciphered diplomatic message to, say, Kabul (or for that matter how did Cable and Wireless Ltd go about transmitting an enciphered diplomatic message from London to Canberra)? Surely Kabul was not on listening watch for 24 hours each day just on the off-chance that Tokyo might have an occasional message for it. Was there a prearranged time each day? Did the sender 'Offer' the message and then transmit it only when the addressee replied 'Send your message'? Did the recipient 'Acknowledge' when he had received it? How did Mornington and the like find and identify senders and addressees? Did they just have to go to a book-store and buy an annual wireless directory which would list JUQ5 as one of the call-signs of the Japanese Post-Office and YAK as the address group of the Japanese Embassy, Kabul and would also list their authorised frequencies? I imagine that this type of know-how is merely esoteric and not highly secret. Such, however, is the aura of secrecy that necessarily surrounded 'Special Wireless', that I doubt whether there is a relevant pamphlet in that estimable series, *Signals Training (All Arms)*. Were you kept at arms length from the Signals people or did they tell you about this sort of thing as background to your training? Could any Boy Scout with a short-wave set pick up the call-sign and the addressee, or were these sent at machine speed? Maybe it's just that I'm not well-read in the public literature of cryptography. Does Kahn or one of the other standard authors devote a couple of pages to such 'basics'?

Citation of Traffic Records

The Traffic Records along with the rest of the War Diaries are available to the public at the Australian War Memorial where they have, after individual examination, been declassified and given 'OPEN ACCESS' status. The xerox copies were furnished to me by the War Memorial quite officially in the exercise of their statutory duties. They may be freely cited, quoting the AWM Series and Item numbers; but in the case of reproduction or extensive quotation the normal formalities for Crown copyright material apply.

Colossus Machine

Neither my colleague, Prof Desmond Ball, nor I can remember Christopher Andrew telling us that this machine eventually came to rest in Australia. This is news to us - although we have no reason to doubt it.

Yours sincerely,

D.C.S. Sissons

Encl: 3

Appendix 26

5E SECTION TRAFFIC RECORD FOR MARCH 1943
AUSTRALIAN SPECIAL WIRELESS GROUP
NUMBER OF MESSAGES RECEIVED

DATE	Number Productive Stations	JAP In	JAP Out	S.AMER In	S.AMER Out	FR.IN CH. In	FR.IN CH. Out	AFGH In	AFGH Out	SWITZ In	SWITZ Out	RUSSIA In	RUSSIA Out	ITALY In	ITALY Out	SWEDEN In	SWEDEN Out	CHINA In	CHINA Out	THAI In	THAI Out	FRANCE In	FRANCE Out	GERM In	GERM Out	PORTUGAL In	PORTUGAL Out	Total Messages	Total Groups	Average Groups	Forwarded Number	Forwarded L	Forwarded O	Forwarded T	Groups
1		17	37	14	1	5	10		6	2	6	1	8	7	5									5	4			58	3811	65	5	53	319	3493	
2		17	32	18	1		18			4		5		6	6		1								4				51	4837	94	13	38	107	3820	
3		22	30	57	3		8	9	2	1	6	3		3											3				90	5624	62	24	66	1509	3815	
4		19	53	33	2		9	27			4		4	4											6				86	7938	92	36	50	2948	4990	
5		32	32	20		14	10	4		6	3		7		1				2	6				6	7				59	6005	102	16	43	1294	4721	
6		20	56	36	3		24		4	1		5	3	5			1			5	15				6	14			92	7310	79	23	69	1401	5909	
7		15	29	34	4		10	7	1		2	3		8	6	8										12			63	4527	72	9	54	730	3997	
8		11	8	17				7		2		3		2	2		5			3	2					5			30	2047	68		30	—	2047	
9		20	27	32	7		3	8	1	2		9	5		3	4		3		3	2				4				62	5336	86	16	46	1275	4092	
10		14	31	31	1		6	7	1		2	5	5	2	1	11			10	9	4		1						62	4469	67	11	51	985	3484	
11		17	32	18	1		4	7	1		4	1	3		4	8	10	2	3	3	6				6				53	4119	78	12	41	850	3269	
12		17	35	55			7	9		4	3	1		14	12										23				90	5324	59	16	74	1219	4105	
13		21	51	23	1		6	16		4		2	2	15		5	1		6	11									75	5157	69	20	55	1598	3559	
14		14	34	34	2		3	10	1		1		3	6	17	2			8	12									78	5212	67	19	59	1645	3567	
15		12	42	11				7			2		2	3	31	1			1										54	5240	102	14	40	1125	4089	
16		24	58	76	8		7	24	3	2	6	11		14	9		5		7	5	3	6	3		1				136	8567	63	14	122	809	7758	
17		15	41	42	1		3	15			8	4	4	17	4				3	5						2			89	6354	71	35	54	3291	3063	
18		14	31	31	3			10			3	3		4	5				4	6					1				52	3913	75	12	40	1242	2671	
19		15	22	19			9			1	3		2	4					4	6									42	4446	106	16	26	1509	2937	
20		19	44	44	6		3	20	1		8	2		13	5		7	2	3	14	4	4			13				90	9475	105	26	64	2173	7302	
21		20	41	71	6		11	11	2		2			7	12	2			9	16		5		1	17				123	9364	76	21	102	1605	7759	
22		13	12	14	1		3				3	1		4	5		3		3	4					7				28	2905	75	4	24	429	2466	
23		13	24	15	1		5	12	1		2	2		4	6				3	4					4				45	3276	73	11	34	842	2434	
24		21	27	38	5		2	9			7		2	8	8		3		4	8					15				76	5469	72	12	64	733	4696	
25		10	13	13			2	12		1	2			13	6		3		2	4					12		6		92	8032	82	16	82	1368	6664	
26		17	14	45	1		1	10		6	2		1	24	5		1		4	2		2			4		1		68	8026	74	8	60	795	4231	
27		21	55	38						2	1			15	2		3		9	13		1	1	3	21				86	5527	61	19	67	1470	3817	
28		17	21	58							4	3		8	16		7		5	6					10				94	7156	76	26	62	1279	4977	
29		18	29	18	6		5	18	3		4	2		9	8		6		3	3					4				48	3358	70	11	37	752	2663	
30		18	34	33			4	18			4	3		4	2		4		3	6					13				74	5342	72	22	52	1806	3536	
31		23	31	42	3		6	16	3	3	3	4	2	14	7		6	2	4	3		2	1	2	7		8		77	5000	71	21	56	1878	3131	
Total			1085	1074	76	1	136	357	15	41	52	96	163	114	185	222	28	47	137	228	20	35	6	1	316			8		168830		229	1731	4089	127761

Annex 1

WAR DIARY of INTELLIGENCE SUMMARY.

Army Form C. 2118. (adapted.)
(Erase heading not required.)

Unit: 52 Aust Wireless Section, AUST SPECIAL WIRELESS GROUP

Date and Time.—From 1-5-44 To 31-5-44

Place.	Date.	Hour.	Summary of Events and Information.	Remarks and references to Appendices, Diaries, &c.
Mornington			**SUMMARY**	
			(a) Traffic totals - Countries. Traffic was received from the following stations for the month :-	
			JAPAN - ROA2 ROA4 JAI JAJ JAM JAR RNE JNF JNL JNO JNP JNJ JNS2 JNS4 JUI JUM JUN JUQ5 JUS2 JNU JYZ JFS3 JYD JNR JNA JIG4 JEK.	1108 messages "Feb Y
			CHINA (occupied) - XMA INA YON IOS XIG3	29 " Feb Y
			FRENCH INDO-CHINA - FZS FZQ5 FZS3	175 " Feb Y
			RUSSIA - RTZ	623 " Feb Y
			AFGHANISTAN - YAK	53 " Feb Y
			PHILLIPINES - XOa5 Xoa1	9 " Feb Y
			SWEDEN - SDM6 SDM4 SDM5	27 " Feb Y
			GERMANY - DFC DFN DFP DFT DGH DGO DGR DGM2 DOH DGD DEJ	817 " Feb Y
			NETHERLAND EAST INDIES -, PLK1 PLK2 PMA PMD PLV	484 " Feb Y
			THAILAND - HSP6 HSE3	84 " Feb Y
			SPAIN - EAI	1 " Feb Y

By Authority: L. F. Johnston, Commonwealth Government Printer, Canberra.

WAR DIARY of INTELLIGENCE SUMMARY.

(Erase heading not required.)

Unit 52 Aust Wireless Section, AUST SPECIAL WIRELESS GROUP   Date and Time.—From 1-5-44   To 31-5-44

Army Form (adapted)

Place.	Date.	Hour.	Summary of Events and Information.	Remarks and references to Appendices, Diaries, &c.
Mornington			**SUMMARY** (contd)	

Comparison of traffic to and from all countries for April and May.

COUNTRY	APRIL in	APRIL out	MAY in	MAY out
JAPAN	1901	1128	1621	1108
FRENCH INDO-CHINA	311	211	288	173
AFGHANISTAN	27	29	25	53
SWITZERLAND	62	nil	45	nil
RUSSIA	197	508	266	625
ITALY	nil	7	3	nil
SWEDEN	43	7	49	27
CHINA	15	1	10	29
THAILAND	63	136	50	84
FRANCE	30	nil	26	nil
GERMANY	280	1010	515	817
PORTUGAL	6	2	9	nil
NETHERLAND EAST INDIES	744	658	608	434
PHILLIPINES	10	8	2	9
VATICAN CITY	nil	nil	9	nil
SPAIN	8	nil	9	1
BURMA	1	nil	16	nil
HUNGARY	nil	nil	3	nil
	3698	3698	3348	3348

Comparison with previous month:—
Totals for the months of April and May compare as follows:—
April 3698 messages, 319541 groups. MAY 3348 messages, 268819 groups.

By Authority: L. F. JOHNSTON, Commonwealth Government Printer, Canberra.

Annex 1

WAR DIARY or INTELLIGENCE SUMMARY

Army Form C. 2118. (adapted.)

(Erase heading not required)

Unit: 52 Aust Wireless Section, AUST SPECIAL WIRELESS GROUP

Date and Time.—From 1-5-44 To 31-5-44

Place.	Date.	Hour.	Summary of Events and Information.	Remarks and references to Appendices, Diaries, &c.
Mornington			**SUMMARY** (contd)	
			Increases were recorded in traffic from:-	
			Afghanistan Russia Sweded China Phillipines Spain.	
			Decreases were recorded in traffic from:-	
			Japan French Indo-China Thailand Germany Portugal Netherland East Indies.	
			(c) New stations found passing Diplomatic traffic during May:-	
			Japan ....JIG4 JNU	
			Spain ....EAX	
			Phillipines.XoeI	
			Germany...DEJ	
			China ....XMA XNA XON XIG3	
				Attached as appendix Traffic Summary.

By Authority: L. F. JOHNSTON, Commonwealth Government Printer, Canberra.

Page 1.

AUSTRALIAN SPECIAL WIRELESS GROUP
52 SECTION TRAFFIC RECORD FOR MAY 1944

NUMBER OF MESSAGES RECEIVED

DATE	JAP IN	JAP PRO FTNG	JAP UN	S. AMER IN	S. AMER OUT	FRENCH IN	FRENCH OUT	APCH IN	APCH OUT	SWISS IN	SWISS OUT	RUSSIA IN	RUSSIA OUT	ITALY IN	ITALY OUT	SWEDEN IN	SWEDEN OUT	CHINA IN	CHINA OUT	THAI IN	THAI OUT	FRANCE IN	FRANCE OUT	GERM IN	GERM OUT	PORTUGAL IN	PORTUGAL OUT	N.E.I. IN	N.E.I. OUT	TOTAL MSGS	Total groups	Averaged groups	FORWARDED MSGS L	FORWARDED MSGS G	FORWARDED GROUPS L
1	16	24	10		1	2		1	2			2	9								2			6	28			23	8						
2	18	35			5	13	1	2	5			4	7											24	8			5	11						
3	12	41	32		6	5	1	5	1	6		14	15	2							3			13	21			6	11						
4	19	37	36		4	6	2	6	2			15	21			1					3	1		9	32			37	5						
5	22	20	39		17			2		2		5	5			1	1			2	4	3	4	12	22			21	21						
6	23	60	44		11	10	3	3		2		7	28			2	2	2		2	3	3	2	17	45			34	4						
7	19	57	46		22	10	3			2		5	29			3	1	2		3		2		5	55			44	5						
8	25	41	55		7	2				4		18	14			1	1	3	3	4				13	31			25	17						
9	16	54	16		6	1	3	1		3		3	40			3				3	1	2	3	18	21			16	9						
10	18	52	35		10	16	4	1		4		3	18	1		2				1	1		1	5	11	3		9	13						
11	18	35	20		5	8		1		3		7	8								1	2		5	15			8	11						
12	23	41	44	25								4	9					6		3	10	1		5	32			13	9						
13	22	69	31		8	11	1	3		1		4	16			1		5	1	5	15	1		11	31			24	22						
14	30	67	32		7	3	2	1	2	2	1	4	16					4	1	6	8	2		6	37			31	23						
15	32	68	41		12	14	2		1	9		15	21			6				8	8	3	3	11	23			19	24						
16	23	95	37		17	9		3		5		5	61					4		5	2	2		10	15	2		5	4						
17	27	60	46		15	5	3	5	1	6		9	21			3		2		3	3	2		15	25	1		20	17						
18	21	26	50		4	5	1	4		4		12	5			1		3		2	2	1	1	4	12			10	9						
19	17	50	54		16	6	3	4	4	3		6	6			4				3	1			21	5			3	34						
20	26	108	11		5	6	1	6		2	1	10	47							1	2			2	66			55	39						
21	19	57	20		4	1						12	23			10			3	3				8	34			17	17						
22	21	50	62		5	1	1	1		2		21	30					1		3	2	2	4	15	21			15	4						
23	15	32	16		10	9	10	1				6	3			2			2	2	2	2	2	1	22			10	4						
24	20	77	34		12	6	1	1		4		8	18			1		2	4		2	2		10	46	1		15	13						
25	27	55	33		5		1			4		8	26			1								4	14	1		15	19						
26	27	37	24		13	8				2		6	18					1			1	1	7	7	22			15	13						
27	16	54	46		8	5	2					10	23					4		4		1		17	29			24	13						
28	17	80	50		8	3	1					15	47						4	4	3			18	27			28	19						
29	14	28	39									3	21			5					5	1		10	46			7	6						
30	11	10	35		4					3		23	6			4				1				4	19	1		47	16						
31	11	37	8		3	5							25											3	7			13	7						
TOTAL		1621	1108		288	173	25	53	13	45		266	623	3		49	27	10	24	50	84	26		315	817	9		624	434						

PAGE 7. AUSTRALIAN SPECIAL WIRELESS GROUP
SECTION TRAFFIC RECORD FOR MAY 1944

NUMBER OF MESSAGES RECEIVED

DAY	AMER. NAVAL IN/OUT	SPAIN/PORT/HUNGARY IN/OUT	SHIPS IN/OUT	RUSSIA IN/OUT	ITALY IN/OUT	SWEDEN IN/OUT	CHINA IN/OUT	THAI IN/OUT	FRANCE-GERM IN/OUT	PORTUGAL IN/OUT	TOTAL MSGS	AVERAGE GROUPS/DAY	FORWARDED MSGS L/C	FORWARDED GROUPS L/C
1	1										58 5007	86 6	52 567	44450
2											76 4892	60 11	65 1654	32236
3											89 7328	82 7	82 841	6487
4											103 7468	74 12	91 964	6704
5		1									91 8272	89 24	69 2768	5563
6	1										135 9638	71 21	114 24488	7140
7		2									146 10384	71 20	136 2362	8422
8		2									131 13002	100 14	107 2206	9816
9											85 6986	82 6	79 780	6206
10											100 7633	75 21	79 1808	5725
11		1									67 6602	98 13	54 478	5126
12											105 9088	87 17	88 1493	7595
13											124 9860	80 19	105 2322	7538
14	1										136 9601	76 19	107 1913	7688
15	1 1										134 11357	85 21	121 13050	9442
16	3 4										147 9627	68 21	121 3050	6572
17	3 1										128 9221	72 31	97 3465	5756
18											86 9643	105 16	70 1981	7062
19	5 4										106 8117	77 21	85 2119	5998
20											193 11806	61 13	180 1763	10043
21		4									103 10267	100 18	85 2354	7808
22		1									128 10382	81 21	107 1992	8390
23	2	1									58 4305	73 16	42 1477	2728
24	4	2									127 10625	80 16	111 1251	8874
25		1									102 6906	67 14	88 1596	9310
26											96 7696	77 13	77 1903	5113
27											139 12846	84 12	117 6313	9273
28											138 14450	83 21	117 2483	8767
29											130 8723	68 5	125 4621	8372
30			3								74 4177	88 7	72 9656	6635
31	2	6 9									47 3265	69 1	46 244	3194
TOTAL											3348			
											263319	78 AVERAGE	480 2868	53619 200400

Annex 2. Notes from an Interview with with Professor Arthur Dale Trendall by Desmond Ball on 10 May 1990

Interview with Professor Arthur Dale Trendall, in his suite at La Trobe University, Melbourne, on 10 May 1990. (Introductions made by Professor J. D. B. Miller and D. C. S. Sissons).

Trendall moved to Melbourne soon after Japan's entry into the war. He returned to Sydney University in the latter half of 1944.

In 1940–41, when he was Professor of Greek at Sydney University, he used to get together from time to time, mostly at weekends, with three other colleagues to test their teeth on various coding systems. They were mainly Japanese transposition and substitution codes. The other members of the group were Professor T. G. Room and Mr R. J. Lyons, mathematicians, and fellow classicist Dr A. P. Treweek. On one occasion, probably in January 1940, they worked out a simple Japanese code from scratch, even without knowing the language.

Trendall was introduced to the group by Professor Room. 'I was approached by Room'. Treweek was a Lecturer in Trendall's Department, and a Major in Sydney University Regiment.

Room, Lyons and Treweek had done some 'practice' on Japanese codes before Trendall joined them, 'but I was with them for about two years before Japan entered the war'. Trendall had only moved to Australia in August 1939.

The 'practice' consisted mainly of becoming acquainted with cryptographic theory and techniques, rather than working on actual Japanese traffic. In 1941, they were given some messages encoded with the LA system. They found these 'relatively easy to decrypt'. They realised the code involved repetitive patterns; the clue was the repetition at the end of each sentence. It used two-letter combinations (one vowel and one consonant). LA was a very simple, straightforward code.

Nobody was doing any translation at this stage. The messages were not current. They were being used by the Sydney University group only for experimentation. Translation was not necessary as the content was not important.

Trendall was asked to join the Army in late 1941, but he preferred to remain a civilian and to take secondment from Sydney University. The Army reached an agreement with the University that he would be paid the equivalent of his Professorial salary; he was nominally given Lieutenant Colonel rank. The Vice-Chancellor was told that he was to work 'in intelligence'.

Treweek was in the Army Reserve already, but Trendall, Room and Lyons all remained civilians throughout the war.

Trendall stayed as a civilian mainly to preserve the option of returning to Sydney University at a time of his choosing. However, it had the incidental benefit that as a Professor he had more access to senior Army authorities than he would have had as a Lieutenant Colonel.

Trendall moved to Melbourne at the very beginning of 1942. He worked initially with the Royal Australian Navy's cryptanalytical group under Eric Nave. They worked in what is now a block of flats near Albert Park in St Kilda. He worked there for several months. His commanding officer was Commander Long, the Director of Naval Intelligence. Trendall headed the group at Monterey which worked mainly on Japanese diplomatic traffic, while Nave was mainly responsible for Japanese Naval traffic.

In fact, Trendall worked on both Japanese diplomatic and Service traffic. It was 'mainly diplomatic', but all personnel worked on 'whatever came in'.

Trendall never dealt with Japanese machine cyphers at any time during the war. He had 'no contact with them whatsoever'.

Trendall moved to the Army, and to Victoria Barracks, in November 1942. His commanding officer was now Lieutenant Colonel A. W. Sandford, the CO of Central Bureau. He has 'no idea' why the diplomatic activity was transferred from the RAN to the Army.

Trendall had no knowledge of the interception stations. An Army Sergeant simply brought the messages in on signal pads. He had no recollection of the station at Park Orchards. He remembered Ferny Creek, 'but only that a station was there'. He also remembered Mornington, 'but the stations were of no significance to us'.

When Trendall was with the Navy group, the cooperation was just with Britain, not the United States. The exchanges principally involved 'current keys'. After the diplomatic section was hived off to the Army, it worked almost entirely with the British. Trendall had 'no knowledge of contacts with Washington'.

The numerical code 10101 was introduced in 1943. Messages encoded with this system began with '10101'. It involved a 'block' from which some squares had been blacked out. It usually involved two-letter groups, but sometimes three-letter and sometimes four-letter groups. Trendall 'worked it out from the key'. 'We could be lucky and break one in no time at all — a matter of half an hour'. 'Sometimes we got a beautiful fit. Otherwise, we had to slog it out'.

10101 traffic came in the greatest quantities. It provided enormous amounts of material for 'depth'. It involved 'prepared groups of 5 random numerals', which were added without carrying. Patterns would emerge with sufficient 'depth' of messages. A 'considerable bulk of messages' was required. It was introduced in mid-1943, and 'it took considerable time before sufficient material built up'. We 'prayed for check and repeat' messages.

On Arthur Cooper: 'There was a somebody'. He was a really good linguist (Chinese). When he first appeared in Melbourne—having come by submarine from the Philippines—he had a gibbon called Tertius with him. (He gave Trendall a book, with an inscription dated 15 July 1942). His 'special knowledge' was Icelandic, but he was also especially good at classical Chinese. Tertius was later presented to the Melbourne Zoo. Cooper worked at Victoria Barracks for as long as Trendall was there; he was still there after Trendall returned to Sydney. Trendall tried to persuade him to take up a Chair at Sydney University. (In 1973, Penguin Books published Cooper's annotated and translated collection of poems by Li Po and Tu Fu). Cooper had 'a very fine brain'. 'For intelligence purposes, Arthur Cooper was very much at the top of the tree'.

On decryption: The patterns kept repeating, given the relatively small code books used. Cooper prepared a chart of the Japanese words likely to be commonly used. Often, the senders had to spell out a word, and that was very helpful. This was particularly the case with place names. 'Really, when you get into the hang of it, with practice, it becomes fairly easy. It was not as difficult as it appears to be'. 'So often it was a matter of luck'.

Trendall had an inexplicable ability to see the patterns in the encoded text underneath the jumbled bigrams and random additives. 'You get a feeling for it. Your eye lights up on something, and … bang'.

Trendall only ever worked on Japanese codes. He has 'no knowledge of any others, including Russian' codes.

He recalled that Miss Shearer and Miss Robertson 'worked with us at Vic Barracks'. He also recalled that Tony Eastway and Alan Rogers had joined Australia's post-War cryptographic organisation.

The TRENCODE: It was designed to fulfil the need for a safe means of communication that would be unlikely to be broken for at least some hours or even days. It was sufficiently simple to use in the field but difficult to break quickly. He developed it in Melbourne in 1943 (?). It is 'correct that Treweek got it out'. However, he 'cheated a bit', and it took him a long time.

Annex 3. David Sissons to Ian Smith, 3 August 1990

3 August 1990

Prof I.H.Smith

Dear Ian,

Please excuse me for troubling you in your well earned retirement.

Two of my colleagues in this Research School, Prof Desmond Ball and Dr David Horner, have for some time been toying with the idea of producing a book of collected articles on the history of signals intelligence in Australia. They wish to include an article on Australian interception and decryption of Japanese diplomatic traffic during World War II. They had hoped that Professor Trendall might have felt able either to write this or to tape his recollections. But unfortunately, when approached, Trendall felt that he had more urgent, academic tasks to complete. He was, however, prepared to be interviewed and speak freely, although he feared that his recollection of those years was not good -- particularly as he had deliberately in the immediate postwar period tried to purge his memory of such matters.

The interview took place in Melbourne a few weeks ago. Ball tells me that Trendall was in excellent form and gave him a full three hours. As a result Ball is convinced that the book should contain an article on the Diplomatic Section and has asked me to try and put one together! I have said that I shall see what I can do -- on the basis of the very fragmentary archival material that has survived, supplemented by the recollections of some of the people involved. I wonder, therefore, if I could trespass on your forbearance, and plumb your memory a little.

As you are probably aware, this subject has, since the Pearl Harbor Hearings in 1946 and, more particularly, since the fairly liberal declassification of official archives in the late 1970s, become considerably less sensitive than you and I were trained to believe it would always remain. I was quite surprised when Ball in 1978 drew my attention to the enclosed papers in Department of Defence file A816 43/302/18 which he had read at the Australian Archives (Enclosure A). I was even more surprised at the publication of

1

the Denniston memorandum (Enclosure B). Christopher Andrew came upon this in the Archives Centre at Churchill College and, after referring it to the 'D' Notice Committee (which made no objection), published it in the opening number of Intelligence and National Security in 1986.

Archival material regarding the Section is very meagre indeed. The present Head of our Defence Signals Directorate tells me that, after extensive searches, all that his staff have been able to find is a file of the translations of intercepted Japanese diplomatic telegrams that we sent to Washington during the year 1942 and a copy of our Special Intelligence Precis for the week ending 21 December 1942. The first is in the U.S. National Archives and was declassified in 1985; the second is in the MacArthur Memorial and was declassified in 1982. He was good enough to provide me with a copy of each; but I'm afraid that they are not wildly exciting. A bit more interesting has been the war diary of our friends at Mornington, 52 Aust Special Wireless Section, held at the War Memorial. Enclosure C contains examples of the kind of information that from time to time turns up there. Among the records of the Department of External Affairs, I have come upon the files of Hubert Graves's little Political Warfare outfit in M Block. From these it would appear that Graves joined the cryptograhic Section in about February 1942 and by the end of the year had been joined there by Archer. In March 1943 External Affairs requested that he be released for Political Warfare work. Army agreed that this could be done when Graves's successor, Sawbridge, reached Australia. Sawbridge arrived at the end of July; but Graves was unable to leave his cryptographic work until September 'because the enemy has recently made changes in his procedure'. In March 1944 External Affairs asked if Sawbridge, too, could be transferred to Political Warfare work; but before this could be effected he was admitted to an Army Convalescent Home with some psychiatric complaint.

Ball has given me the notes of his interview with Trendall. Essentially the story that emerges from these is as follows: Early in 1940 Trendall, at Prof Room's request, joined Room, Lyons and Treweek who, under the auspices of Military Intelligence (Eastern Command), were in their spare time (mainly at week-ends) practising cryptographic theory and techniques. During 1941 they were given some old LA traffic to try their teeth on. This they cracked without much difficulty -- without any knowledge of the Japanese language. It came in repeating patterns. The clue was the repetitive end to the sentences: YEIZ YEIZ. Trendall was taken on strength at the very beginning of 1942 when he joined Cdr Nave's outfit in a block of flats near Albert Park. There they worked on both diplomatic and Service traffic; but most of it was diplomatic. After a few months (before, he thinks, any Americans joined them) he and the diplomatic side were transferred from Nave's organisation to Victoria Barracks where they came under Army (ADMI) control. There he remained until the latter half of 1944, when he returned to Sydney University. During the whole of his time at Victoria Barracks he has no recollection of any exchange of information with Washington: it was all with the British. It was while they were at Victoria Barracks, early in 1942, that they were joined by Arthur Cooper, who, together with his gibbon, Tertius, arrived by submarine from the Phillipines.

Annex 3

Cooper was still with them at Victoria Barracks when Trendall left in 1944. In the middle of 1943 the Japanese introduced 10101. This was a numerical code and used a grid in which particular squares were blacked out. The code consisted mainly of two-letter groups with some three and four letter groups. It was reciphered with random additives. Patterns would emerge only with sufficient depth of messages. For this, an enormous amount of traffic was needed. One prayed for 'repeats': a repeat often revealed the message. Sometimes one got a beautiful fit and could break a message in half-an-hour: sometimes one just had to slog it out. It was in Melbourne -- probably in 1943 -- that he devised the TRENCODE. The specifications were that it should be simple enough for use in the field but proof against being read by the enemy within a few hours or days. Before its adoption it was given to Treweek to test. Treweek managed to break it; but it took him a long time and he had to cheat a bit.

So much for the material that I have to go on -- supplemented by my own worm's-eye observation of the period April-September 1945. I'm afraid that I can't remember much beyond tons of very dull economic and shipping information in the telegrams that I translated (These were almost entirely GEAMs). In terms of the history of signals intelligence more interesting, perhaps, are my recollections of who were on the door-step when, as one of our lowly doormen, I answered the bell: Lt Col Sinkov (CB), Lt Col Sandford (CB), and Lt Col Treweek (FRUMEL).

I'd be much assisted by anything that you can remember about the Section and its activities. To start you off, I wonder if you could help me on the following points.

Am I right in thinking that you joined the Section before Trendall's departure? In my time, I had the impression that Cowley rather than Bond was in charge but that the day-to-day communications with Mornington, London (and Washington?) seemed to be in Bond's hands. It was Bond that did most of the chivvying when Mornington missed particular stations; and only in the last resort would Cowley be brought into it and send them an acid signal over his own signature. It was Cowley, I think, and not Bond, that wrote the monthly Precis. What was the situation in Trendall"s day? Which part of our suite of rooms did Trendall occupy (Enclosure D is my attempt to represent the seating plan in my day)? Did Trendall or Archer write the Precis? When Trendall left, which survivor (Archer, Bond, Barnes, McKay, yourself) assumed which of his functiions?

A good deal has been written recently about how in Britain GC&CS (now GCHQ) recruited its future cryptographers from Oxbridge dons and the bright students that the latter recommended. You, Barnes, Bond and McKay are of that category. I presume that Treweek recruited Barnes, and that Trendall recruited Bond and McKay. But you, I think, are a Melbourne graduate; who was the talent scout in your case? What was Tony Eastway's function in the team?. Did he have a similar background? I seem to remember a 'corps troops' (MG bn?) colour-patch on his hat.

I was surprised that Trendall had no recollection of close liaison and exchange of information with Washington. My impression was that, of the outwards and inwards signals that passed Bond's desk, Washington would account for as many as London. Am I mistaken in this? Did we work with the British on one code and with the Americans on another? Was there any code for which we were, so to speak, the major player; or did we just play the minor role of covering those stations that for atmospheric or other technical reasons were more audible in Australia than elsewhere.

This brings me to a related point. I seem to remember Mornington regularly sending us machine-cipher traffic that we could not read. Why I remember this is that, during the few days between the bombing of Hiroshima and the Surrender, we, like the rest of the community, were very excited and eager to know what was happening. I can remember Bond pointing to a heap of traffic in his 'in' tray (messages to and from Sweden in machine-cipher, I think) and saying: 'The answer is in there'. Was one of our roles intercepting material for which we were not given the codes and bundling this off to those who could read them?

As I mentioned earlier, I was translating principally GEAMs. What were the other codes that the Section was working on? As well as 10101 that Trendall mentioned, I seem to remember the names, 'Bar', JBD, umiyukaba, 'Head of Mission Cipher' (in Japanese 'kanchō fugō'), and SOSOS (one of the ciphers that we could not yet read?). Could you describe any of these for me? Incidentally, I presume that, to avoid confusion, the Americans, the British and ourselves adopted a uniform nomenclature. The reason why I raise this is that, of the above names, only JBD bears any similarity to the system of nomenclature in use by the Americans at the time of Pearl Harbor. For example, the code in which the Foreign Ministry on 2 December instructed overseas missions to destroy their code-books was called by the Americans J19-K9 (J apparently stands for Japan, 19 identifies the code-book, and K9 identifies the transposition system) and by Nave and the British TU (its Japanese title).

I can remember very few messages that contained information that was either patently important, or dramatic. Only one of the telegrams that I translated fell into the former category. This was a report from a spy passing on that at the Yalta Conference Stalin had agreed to enter the war against Japan within three months of the defeat of Germany. This does not sound like a GEAM -- perhaps while Jac James was convalescing from his concussion I was translating some of the more high-grade material. I remember Jac's glorious translation of the Minister at Kabul's account of when the Afghans made him pull up the floor-boards revealing the small arsenal that he was amassing up (Which code would that have been?). I can remember one GEAM that contained information about the movement of POW to Japan by sea that would have interested our Chiefs-of-Staff. I remember one telegram that gave the name and address of a Japanese spy in India (Which code would that have been?) and Miss Shearer's telling me that there had been a similar telegram some months earlier about a spy named 'Bengal Tiger'. Eric Barnes told me of the sinking of a German submarine en route to Japan because the Japanese codes were being read; but I received the impression that it was not our Section that had decrypted the signal in question. Ken McKay told me that we had picked up information about the movements of the German submarine U-862 and its depredations in Bass Strait in December 1944 (Which code would that have been?). Are there any particularly significant or dramatic telegrams that you can remember?

Were there any particular triumphs in the field of cryptography that the Section had to its credit? Eric Barnes told me of some long battle that Trendall and Archer (or was it Graves) had with a system of bigrams, at the end of which one announced victory to the other in a letter commencing: 'Myves Gradear', or words to that effect. This sounds a little like a GEAM.

Lastly, could you please have mercy on me and explain to this mere translator the implications of what, I understand, is one of the most basic of the axioms underlying the craft -- that one can begin to read a message sent in a reciphered code (for which one has neither the reciphering tables nor the key to the 'indicator' that tells the recipient which page of the additives to use) only when one has access to another message in which the same stretch of reciphering tables is used and several of <u>the same code-groups appear over the same additives in both messages</u>. For example, taking a four-figure code , one needs something like the following:

Message 1	Code-groups	4416	2089	1526	9734	....	5771
	+Additives	9046	7127	8168	3072	....	8643
	=Signal	3452	9106	9684	2706	....	3314
Message 2	Code-groups	7298	1492	1526	9090	....	5771
	+Additives	9046	7127	8168	3072	....	8643
	=Signal	6234	8519	9684	2062	....	3314

In other words, it is by observing the same figures 9684 and 3314 separated by the same distance that the ball is set rolling. This seems logical enough. What I want to know is how on earth you managed to do this time and time again in practice. So far as I can remember, you had no punch-cards, computers, or adding-machines to assist you. Surely you didn't just go through hundreds of past signals at random until such a similarity appeared. What was your system of filing past messages? Perhaps a ritual that we indulged in from time to time is part of the explanation. All hands were called to the pumps and, like some card game, Bond dealt each of us a hand. He then started to read aloud a series of numbers which we each tried to follow in the document before us. Frequently this would get out of hand -- one would find oneself lost and shout out 'I'm off the rails`. Whereupon , Bond and Barnes would become furious. What was this all about?

How did the Japanese construct the 'indicators' and how did anyone ever manage to break them?

It seems to me completely inappropriate that I, the most junior and a very transitory member of the Section,should be asked to undertake this article. If anyone else with the time and the inclination wishes to do it, I'd be only too happy to make way. About three years ago the present Head of the Defence Signals Directorate approached me and put out feelers as to whether I should be interested in writing an in-house history of the Directorate since 1939. Someone in khaki produced such a volume about ten years ago; but apparently they are not satisfied with it. I didn't rise to the bait --for a number of reasons. First, I had more urgent things to do. Secondly, the archival back-up that they offered appeared very amateur and haphazard. Although they were well acquainted with F.H.Hinsley's volumes on signals intelligence in the European theatre (<u>British Intelligence in the Second World War: Its Influence on Strategy and Operations</u>, London, HMSO, 4 vols, 1979-88), they seemed unable to appreciate the extent of his reliance on extensive, well organised records and well trained registry staff. In Australia the care of our signals intelligence records appeas to have been entrusted either to sleuths or quartermaster-sergeants who made great bonfires of intercepts, registers and all in the late 1940s. Hinsley is of the opinion that most of the material that we sent to London by bag or signal would have survived. But our DSD didn't seem to be thinking in terms of sending the historian on visits to London and Washington. But a more important factor was that, as one who had, during the passage of the Australian Archives Bill, said a good deal in professional journals and in testimony before Parliamentary committees about 'open access', I didn't feel that I could participate in the writing of a secret in-house history. They eventually signed a contract with Peter Hastings (who served in Central Bureau during the War) to do the job for $100,000; but he threw in the towel after a few months. He found that my fears about lack of expert archival back-up were all too well founded.

I do apologise for burdening you with a letter of such length. Any help that you may be able to give me will, I assure you, be very greatly appreciated.

With very best wishes,

Yours sincerely,

D.C.S.Sissons

Encl: 4

Annex 4. Ian Smith to David Sissons, 8 August 1990

Excuse handwriting, I cannot type, & no longer have access to typists.

8 August 1990

Dear David,

Your letter of 3/8 came to hand to-day. Please do not apologise for intruding on my retirement, on the contrary I have spent a pleasant few hours trying to remember one of the happy periods of my life.

I fear you will have a difficult task, if the records of that diplomatic section have been destroyed. I have a clear memory of participating in the composition of an archive sometime in the spring or early summer of 1945. Eric Barnes was in charge of this operation, I think, and it was well done. Description of the codes and the work done, &, I think, the files containing each weekly report put together by the head translator. Alas! it is no good weeping over burnt paper.

If you do take on this task, I should think that Ron Bond and Eric Barnes would be good sources, in some ways better than Trendall, since they were there till September 1945 (Ron Bond is retired from Scotch College some 3-4 years now, and lives at 30 Hortense Street, Burwood, Victoria, -- we have remained in touch over the years, tho' we do not often speak of the Vic Barracks room & its work -- conditioned by the tabus of 1945?). Eric Barnes finished his career at the University of Adelaide, but I have not seen him for about 10 years (he was at a conference in Hobart) -- he was then fascinated by his war work & used to give talks on cryptography, -- he was also familiar with modern cryptography (it sounded diabolically sophisticated -- I gather it is in great demand for computer security).

Tony Eastway retired from CSR early (in his early fifties), -- he spent a few years in the peacetime successor of the section, but his wife grew fed up with Melbourne & he went to CSR in Sydney. His address is 15 Ruby Street, Mosman, NSW -- he keeps in contact with my mother & we write at Xmas, but I have not seen him since the early 70's.

Ken Mackay must have retired from ANU, but I have lost touch.

Jac James (now, alas, Cyril James, as he was baptised) is retired in UK, at a fiendishly long address, Rosebery House, Elenby Road, Ashton-under-Hill, Evesham, Worcs, WR11 6SW. He sends a news circular at Xmas, mainly about his four children, who seem to be all "trendoid" -- not seen since 1972, when we passed thru' London and played "battleships" again in memory of old times. He may have memories of the actual material that was handled.

I arrived in the unit in May 1944 (via Central Bureau, where I spent a miserable month after basic infantry training). Trendall presided when I arrived, sitting in the corner where RB sat later. His absences became more & more frequent and he returned to Sydney some time in the spring of 1944, perhaps as late as November. I have memories of him taking us each Thursday to the Society Restaurant for lunch for quite some time after my arrival. I stayed on until November 1946, I think, intending at one stage to seek a position in the postwar section, which began crystallizing with people who had been in Central Bureau and who must have begun arriving by October or November 1945. I have memories of playing endless games of bridge & chess during this interim period. When I got a p/g CRTS scholarship, I abandoned any idea of staying on & have no regrets, the more so as it quickly ceased to be a game for amateurs.

Tho' I worked on an equal footing with Eric Barnes (of course I had nothing like his creative talents), I did not really see what happened in the actual administering of the department. We were under Col.Little (ADMI) in my time and RB used to take his orders (I have a feeling Trendall kept a paternal eye on what went on -- I can remember him telling me I was to be promoted corporal, which would have been on a fleeting visit to Melbourne after his departure). I have a feeling that nothing very dramatic or crucial came out in the decoded material during my time, but I was so fascinated by the game of cryptography that I really took no interest in the end result, -- it could have been a treatise on Zen philosophy for all I cared. As long as the messages used new sections of the cipher book, I was happy. The ciphers that we worked out were transmitted to UK & much more rarely we received material, often of poor quality, from them (UK) -- I cannot remember clearly whether our material was transmitted to Washington but I think so. The weekly reports went to Blamey, and (once again, I think, but am not sure) also to McArthur. I have vague memories of spies being identified in Kabul & New Delhi.

A postscript on the personnel: Arthur Cooper (a character -- Trendall's memory deceives him on the dates of Cooper's presence -- I never knew him) had left before I arrived (he returned to work in the postwar section in the 50's but I never met him). There was also John Davies, who left for Central Bureau before my arrival, -- he became Prof of French at New England & then Adelaide, now retired, living somewhere in Adelaide, -- he would have memories of 1943 & early 1944.

Recruitment, -- the connection was Sydney University, but also Sydney high schools. Like Tony Eastway, I was put in contact with Trendall by a brilliant Classics master at North Sydney Boys' High School (my family moved to Melb, so I studied at Melb), -- Tony & I were exact contemporaries, Ken Mackay a year ahead. Ron Bond would have known Trendall as an u/g at Sydney, but would have put him in touch with Eric Barnes & John Davies (they were all at Canterbury High together & Treweek, I think, had

Annex 4

taught Classics there before the war & before getting a post at Sydney University

Trendall's recollections of the cipher 10101 are blurred. When I came in May 1944 I was assigned to this cipher working under Eric Barnes. The code-book consisted of 4-figure groups, representing kana syllables, but also common words or phrases, also things like 6378...8014 which enclosed kana transcriptions of English phrases (eagerly welcomed; for one could guess the transcribed phrase -- I remember "heiseibingudebaisu" -- face-saving device). "No" was 8416, "wa" 8559, "to" 2758", -- if only I could remember the details of my present life as vividly! The message was encoded, then enciphered using the cipher-book, with the second 5-figure group (the first was 10101) indicating the beginning in the cipher-book. Your assumptions given on p.5 about the decipherment method are correct for normal ciphers of this kind, -- a large number of messages are usually needed to build up the "depth", but we were helped by the old-fashioned spirit of the Foreign Office in Japan. The full 10000 4-figure groups were not used in the code-book, the first figure being restricted to 2,4,6,8, the second to 1,2,3,4,5, the third figure to 1,3,5,7,9, the fourth alone being unrestricted, except that 0 was not used. The basic pattern in the code even-anything-odd-anything meant that whenever the same cipher numbers were used, the number groups of messages would have a common pattern and it was very easy to line up messages using the same passage, once you had catalogued the even-odd patterns of the messages.

When I arrived the code-book was fairly well-known & the main task was deciphering the messages, when they had built up to a certain "depth". In some cases with the help of Jac James, one could work on a "depth" of two, particularly when the code-groups overlapped by two, or when the subject-matter was routine.

By early 1945, or perhaps before, Eric Barnes had discovered the secret of the indicator. This was the second 5-figure group. The third group (first of the actual message) was subtracted from this & the result was the cipher-book reference in clear, page reference, column, line. I cannot remember how he hit on this, but he had brilliant intuitions. From then on the messages were read using the same method as the Japanese cipher clerks (JBD, by the way, was the reference for 10101).

There had been another 4-figure code, NE, I think, was the name, in use until just before I came; but it fell into disuse and the other main code in my time (apart from GEAM, which was easily read & and left to Paul Grange & McKenzie to decipher mechanically) was called BA (from the two initial letters of its indicator; JBC was its reference). Ron B & Tony Eastway used to work on BA, and when 10101 was easily read, Eric used to turn his mind to BA, -- I, too, but with very middling success.

BA was a transposition cipher, with a grid, I think, 20 across (but maybe 25), and about 10 or 15 deep. The code consisted of bigrams, with a smaller number of trigrams. The message was encoded, then written across the grid, then read by columns in a random order indicated by the group BA... at the beginning. Further there were groups of blanks in fives, horizontal alternating vertical, their position being determined by the first ten columns. I think it wnet something like this:

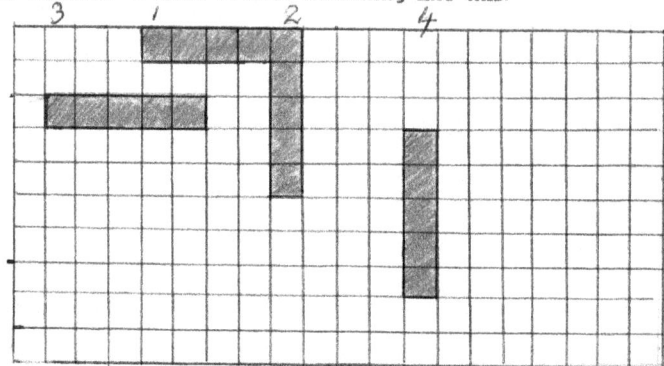

This cipher was broken before I arrived, I think, because a message had been badly enciphered, was repeated using the same indicator & so the same grid with the same blanks. This gave a break into the nature of the grid.

Your SOSOS was in fact 50505, -- it was thought to be a one-time pad cipher (i.e. the pages of figures were used only once), as it was never broken -- the traffic in it was very small. I remember learning after the war, probably late in 1945 that it was in fact a one-time pad cipher. No doubt they were terrified of using up their pads, hence the small traffic & the general use of the vulnerable 10101 & BA in 1944 & 1945.

Until this point I have been following my own thought train. I turn now to your letter & its questions (if I have not already answered them above).

The relationship between Cowley (of whom I have no memory) or his predecessor, Archer (whom I remember vividly because he had piles and was always scratching his arse), and RB I cannot know for sure. I suspect that technically RB was in charge under Little, but that Cowley was deferred to, Archer likewise. Biggs I remember with distaste, my first experience of an arrogant Pom (he married Kiwi Boot-Polish, a Miss Ramsey, and was prominent in Japan-Aust cultural relations at one stage). The Nips had interned him & mistreated him despite his diplomatic status, -- I cannot find it in my heart to blame them.

In my time Archer wrote the précis, but Trendall was consulted. Cowley would have taken over. The military bods simply decrypted or translated (Jac James, Pitman, yourself).

I have a feeling Trendall is wrong in saying no information went to Washington, -- on the other hand, having slept on this sentence (it is now 9/8) perhaps he was right. Certainly all our solutions went to UK, -- little came in return, either because they despised colonials or , more likely, they weren't very bright. Jap.

Annex 4

diplomatic ciphers would have been low down the pecking order in Bletchley.

I believe we simply worked on all traffic that was available to us, mainly thru' Mornington, but also in either late 1944 or early 1945, on traffic from an Indian station (quite a lot of 10101 stuff missed by Mornington).

To what extent our section was responsible for actual breakthroughs I am not sure. At some stage (before Smith) someone must have noticed the even-odd pattern in 10101 messages using the same passage of the cipher-book (the occurrence of the same code-group with the same cipher-group would have given sufficient "depth" of messages to see this), but who was it -- London, Washington, Eric Barnes? -- I do not know. Did Melbourne break BA thru' the unwise repeat? I think so but cannot swear it. Eric Barnes certainly solved the 10101 indicator problem. I have a memory that Trendall made a crucial contribution to the solutiion of a transposition code called "Fuji" which they used round the time of Pearl Harbour, but the details have gone.

The Jac James Kabul message would have been in BA, from memory the favoured code of the Kabul man. All non-GEAM messages would have been either 10101 or BA in your time.

I have no vivid memories of the decoded material.

In my day the number ciphers were indexed by the pattern of 1st & 3rd figures in the group (for 10101; NE had another pattern, alas! forgotten) The indexes were made out by hand & the method was considerably simplified by Eric Barnes (no time for details). The original discovery of similar groups would have been done by hand-made indexes (oh dear departed days!) It was believed UK had punch-cards & vast technological resources badly used!

I have no memory of the Bond number ritual & and your inadequate attempts to obey the master.

I suspect that you are fitter than anyone to undertake a history of what went on in the Jap. Dip. ciphers section. I fear, however, you are gravely handicapped by the disappearance of the archive, which would have given you a basic canvas on which to embroider. Lacking that, you are really obliged to rely on your own memories (remarkable, in my view, -- I am particularly impressed by the accurate reconstruction of the physical premises & the positions of the dramatis personae) and those of the other participants. All this will be pretty messy stuff. I cannot help feeling that Trendall -- top of your p.3 -- has mixed up 101001 and BA (the latter, often, by the way, needed only one message to be solved, -- the letters of common bigrams were matched & with luck the columns of the original grid were put together like a jigsaw puzzle -- one needed to know the trick with the horizontal & vertical blanks to do this successfully) and that some of the 3-hour interview will need cross-checking. Likewise with my outpouring. I would like to think that you will take on the task, but it would certainly need a visit to UK where some material from Melbourne may survive.

Your remarks about the destruction of our intelligence archives perhaps explains something that puzzled me 3-4 years ago. A volume appeared on the sinking of HMAS Sydney, written, I think, by the son of an officer who went down with her. He postulated the presence of a Jap sub to explain Sydney's failure to cope with the German raider. I found this odd, because at some time in 1945, probably before VE-Day, Eric B & I were asked to decipher a coded narrative written by the captain of the "Kormoran"(?) in a small notebook, confiscated from him in Tatura (I can see it now, -- the brand was VANA, common at the time, for notebooks and exercise books). It was a simple Vigenere substitution & gave an account in German of the battle, which I translated, --"Sydney" was deceived & came too close, -- the first shells mortally crippled her, -- it was very clear proof in my view that "Kormoran" alone was responsible. This material must have disappeared, too.

I must stop. I have written in haste, but with some consideration. We leave for 3 weeks on Magnetic Island this coming Sunday & I was anxious to let you have something before we left. We shall be back 5 September. I shall be curious to know if you go ahead with the project, but would not be surprised if you didn't. Sad that the record of all that labour is lost.

I pray that you have had a happy career and are far removed from the follies of Dawkins & his cowboys. They drove me out a year early. One day there will be a massacre of economics graduates, -- get out of Canberra before that happens.

With all best wishes,

                                                    Yours

                                                    Ian Smith

Sorry for the scrawl, --but it is better than silence.

Annex 5. Interview of Dr A. P. Treweek by David Sissons, 11 October 1990

INTERVIEW WITH DR.A.P.TREWEEK 11/10/90

Prewar

When compulsory training was abandoned in 1929 I decided to continue in the Militia. I was commissioned in the Field Artillery in 1932 and remained on the Active List throughout.

I considered it likely that Australia would be involved in hostilities with Japan and therefore taught myself some Japanese during the 1930s. I did not enrol in Prof Sadler's classes; but I received some help from one member of his staff, Miss Lake.

When war broke out with Germany I tried to join the A.I.F; but as a university lecturer I was 'reserved occupation' and the University would not release me. As time went on the University did release people. They let a fellow gunner officer join the 8th Division (He survived imprisonment); I was next in the queue.

The Cryptography Group at Sydney University

The group (Room, Lyons and Trendall) was already in operation when I joined them, at Trendall's request.

Sessions at the Barracks were less frequent in my time than, I understand, they were previously; but when we did meet there, the officer from M.I. who paricipated with us was a Maj Wilkins. I knew Mander (the Ia); but he was in a completely different part of M.I. -- a rather childish, 'dirty tricks' crowd who tried their hands at entering premises and pinching things. We had occasion to vet some of the ciphers that Mander and his team used; they were terribly unsophisticated.

Among the things we were given to practise on were consular telegrams in LA (provided to us through the good offices of A.W.A.). These were often news reports. LA is a simple substitution cipher. I solved it fairly readily -- largely by observing common patterns in different messages. Take for example the following:

Cipher	U F B I U K G E O V G E O T U K I K U K G E O V G E O T
Plain	i O gatu nichi O wo O gatu nichi month day month day
Trans	(i) O month day O (i) O month day

I could not have done this if I did not know Japanese. Cryptanalysis is impossible without some knowledge of the language. Trendall is a gifted linguist. He absorbed the language naturally.

In the Australian Archives file those LA messages with the similarity in opening groups that you have just shown me read as follows:

Message 1	M X P D G	L A I B K	I I J I G	I F F U T
Message 2	M X D D K	L A I B K	I I J I G	I F C U T
Message 3	M K I D C	L A I B K	I I J I G	I F F U T
Message 4	A S D D S	L A I B K	I I J I G	I F F U T
Plain	*group*	*Address*	*Discrum inent*	o ri mo no
Transl				textiles

For practice they sometimes sent us letters that Postal Censorship suspected contained coded messages. I remember one that superimposed a dot code between the lines of ordinary handwriting, transforming it into a torrid and most explicit love letter. We toyed with the idea of adding in the same code: 'Careful! --The Censor'

It was as one of these practice exercises that I solved the TRENCODE.

I've no recollection of our using any cryptography text-books (either commercially published or in-house).

At the Navy Office

I was the first of the Sydney University group to assume full-time duties.

When I arrived, Eric Nave, Jim Jamieson, Ian Longfield Lloyd (from Fiji) and Keith Miller (R.A.N. Emergency Reserve) were already there. Room, Lyons and Trendfall came later.

Nave's best years as a cryptanalyst were already behind him. He was in his forties (which is a bit old for such work), and Japanese codes had become much more sophisticated than in the days of his great successes. He had also become rather secretive, and this held up our work. One would wait for his rest-day, open the safe, and find much that speeded us on our way. We had another R.N. linguist with us, Alan Merry, who also was obsessed with security. On one occasion he destroyed the ciphertext, the plaintext and the translation!

Room and Lyons were not a great deal of use. A purely mathematical mind can be rather restricting in cryptographic work. Room could spend days devising some theoretical solution to a problem that a linguist would solve intuitively in a few minutes. A garbled text will bring the mathematicians to a standstill; and most texts are garbled. Room was a remote person rather out of touch in coping with the world. He had little conversation -- Jamieson found him pretty heavy going at Singapore. At the University, Room was known for his tantrums and childish bickering (e.g. with the Professor of Applied Maths over precedence).

It was while we were at the Navy Office some time before Japan entered the war (perhaps in about October 1941) that Customs brought us a reciphering table they had found on a Japanese merchantman. Naturally, the Japanese

Annex 5

ceased using it immediately afterwards. Nevertheless, it was of help to us in showing us how the system worked.

Arthur Cooper arrived in about December 1941 by steamer from Singapore along with a number of R.N. wives, who were taken on to our payroll. I don't think Cooper was ever at the Navy Office. He went off with Trendall and his show before the rest of us moved to Monterey. He remained with Trendall's show throughout.

I well remember the excitement as everyone waited for the 'Winds'-execute message. Jamieson and others were given receivers to take home so that they could extend the watch. I'm not sure that Nave was reading diplomatic traffic at that time. He may have received the 'Winds'-setup message in translation from Singapore.

As regards naval traffic, I should be very surprised if we received anything that in any way suggested an attack on Pearl Harbor.

We exchanged information directly with the Dutch, the New Zealanders, the Canadians and with Kilindini (Mombasa). Initially the New Zealand outfit had its own cryptographer, King. He joined us in Melbourne after we had moved to Albert Park Barracks. Kilindini's cable address was AMBITION. There was a famous occasion when Trendall replied as follows to one of their signals: 'Ambition should be made of sterner stuff. Your solution shows marked absence of serendipity.'

I think it was at Melbourne that we were given your Maj Mason. He was a 'red-tape-worm'. He expended great effort in trying to organise useless information. Trendall got rid of him.

It may have been before we moved to Monterey that Trendall left us. I think he was in a different building from us before he settled in 'A' Block.

After the Americans Joined Us

The Americans worked on JN-25 themselves, leaving the other codes, like JN-40, to the Australians.

Intercepted Navy messages gave us foreknowledge of the Japanese landings at Buna and at Milne Bay. Unfortunately MacArthur didn't believe the first; but timely action was taken regarding the second.

The following are a few codes that I remember us breaking.

There was a weather code. It used a 50 x 50 block. We had a message of 20 or 30 groups -- just enough to solve it. Here again the restricted vocabulary and the common pattern in different messages were a great help: 'Tenki jōhō. Unryō .... Shikai..... etc. ('Weather Report. Cloudy ..... Calm sea....'. etc).

There was a code in which diplomatic messages were sent from Dili over Navy circuits. We had about eight messages in this at Monterey in 1942/43. Here again it was the stereotyped pattern of the messages that helped: e.g. enumerations beginning (i), (ii), (iii).

There was a Navy machine cipher (JADE, I think). We solved it without coincidences. IBM books were a help. Eventually Keith Miller (who was very good on transposition ciphers) made a mock-up of a JADE machine. Unfortunately the Japanese quickly abandoned this particular cipher.

3

There was a transposition device consisting of a large peg-board and sticks recovered from a Japanese submarine off the Phillipines. It never came into use.

You mentioned the enciphered account of the Kormoran-H.M.A.S.Sydney engagement in Detmers' diary. It was Keith Miller who solved this. He did it over a weekend when I was on leave. The key-word was GEFECHSBERICHT ('battle-report').

You mentioned the story told to you by Eric Barnes in 1945(The Japanese included in a message the itinerary of a German U-boat bound for the Far East. The Allies read the message and, after duly despatching the mandatory reconnaissance aircraft to the appropriate spot, sank the U-boat. The Allies also read the ensuing exchange of messages in which the Germans queried the Japanese about their signals security and the Japanese assured them that it was impregnable!) This story rings a bell; but I've no recollection of FRUMEL being involved.

My visits to other establishments were not encouraged by the U.S Navy. To see Sandford and Central Bureau at Brisbane I went on leave. Similarly, my calls at 'A' Block were under the lap. In this way I was sometimes able to pass on useful bits of information to Trendall. The Foreign Ministry emergency cipher UMIYUKABA is a case in point. Among the material that Washington sent us at FRUMEL was the message from Tokyo to overseas posts explaining the UMIYUKABA cipher and giving a worked example: NICHI DOKU I HISSHŌ ('Japan, Germany and Italy will win the war'). I passed this on to Trendall thus enabling him to turn the tables on London -- informing them rather than being informed by them

Although you are right in remembering that Kingston at the CSIR was a friend of mine, I don't think that it was he who overheard the loose talk that breached our security. I think it was John Merewether at APM (who was a clubman) rather than Kingston (who was not). I remember a much worse example. I was travelling down St Kilda Rd in the tram. As we passed Monterey the conductress pointed to it and said 'That's where they break Japanese codes!'.

Room and Lyons left us long before Nave. I think Nave was still at Monterey for part of 1943. The Admiralty were trying hard to get him back; but he was resisting this. I think he went straight from Monterey to Central Bureau.

D.C.S.S.

Annex 6. Ronald Bond, Notes on Sissons (3 August 1990), Smith (8 August 1990) and Treweek (11 October 1990), undated but probably late 1990

(i) Notes on [letter from] Sissons to Smith on 3 August 1990

Page 2: When Trendall and I left the Navy block at Vic Barracks early in March 1942 to go to Monterey, Graves *and* Archer were in the next room to us at Monterey, together with a few female clerical staff. So it is not correct to say that Archer joined Graves at the end of 1942. (Archer incidentally was much more senior than Graves in rank and influence). When Trendall and I moved to 'A' block in Vic Barracks in early 1943, Archer, Graves and their staff came with us and worked in the adjoining room. They stayed there 1943, 1944 and, I think, were still there when I started to break loose about September 1945, though Graves might have disappeared just before then. (I cannot be sure about Graves, as I was by then tired, bored, and exploring possibilities for early discharge).

Trendall must have come to Melbourne in January 1942. He was certainly here in February 1942, because he met me at Spencer Street and took me to Nave's office at Vic Barracks. I wrote several times to Trendall from Georges' Heights, (NSW) begging him to extricate me from my pit of misery, and I am 90% certain that I wrote to him in Melbourne.

I think it was 28th February 1942 that I arrived on 'The Spirit' — much to everyone's surprise! — and Trendall took me firstly to Nave, then arranged for me to be a Corporal, so that I could afford to live with him in a boarding house in St. Kilda Rd, so that we could work for 30 hours each day! Working conditions in the Navy block were overcrowded. I think we were there for about a fortnight, if that, before moving to Monterey. I have sketched for David Jenkins our location in Monterey (which I believe is about to be demolished for a huge block); RAN people moved in simultaneously, and so did the United States Navy (USN). USN provided armed guards at all (or most) entrances. Commander Newman was the RAN chief. An American cypher section (machine sent messages) was on the second floor. This I know, for sure, having taken information to it.

We moved to 'A' Block at the beginning of 1943 and came under the aegis of Lt. Col. R.A. Little D.S.O. Mr. A.R.V. Cooper worked with us at Monterey. He arrived from *Singapore* (with two very beautiful young ladies!!) where he had been working. I vaguely recall that previously to that he had worked in Hong Kong. We had already moved to Monterey before Cooper arrived. [The fall of Singapore fits that time table.] Cooper was still at Monterey in December 1942 when I got a few days leave to go to Sydney for Christmas. Cooper was summoned to the UK (A.D.T. [Arthur Dale Trendall] jokingly says by his mother — 'Arthur, come home to be married!'), and *did not come with Trendall to 'A' Block at the start of 1943*. (He did return to Australia 1949 (?) and worked with J.I.B. [Joint Intelligence Bureau] at Albert Park)

Trendall went back to Sydney University on 13th March 1943 (the day my commission came through). He returned in July/August (?) 1943, when the great change arrived and we had come to a grinding halt. Trendall sent me home to Sydney for a short break. I was more than a little tired, as Eric Barnes (who had arrived in late February (?), early March) and I were the only people in the diplomatic cryto section during the period March/July '43.

Page 3: 'TRENCODE' was born at Monterey in *1942*. It had been ascertained that the Japanese were reading the traffic sent by our troops on Timor, and this wasn't very surprising considering the quality of our cyphers. Trendall, with a little help from Cooper, devised this simple cypher which, if not unbreakable, would have, even with heavy traffic, taken a long time to unravel. Treweek, who had alarmed Aust. Cypher Production, by breaking the codes/cyphers in use on Timor very quickly, claimed to have broken into TRENCODE. Whether he did or not, I don't know. Perhaps Sissons' observation is pertinent. Whether our (Aust.) cypher section put TRENCODE into operation, I know not. At the time I suspected some rivalry between Ath [Athanasius P. Treweek] and Dale: perhaps Ath was a trifle piqued that A.D.T., a civilian, and not he, had been asked to produce a product??

By the time D. C. S Sissons arrived in April 1945, we were all very tired, a trifle bored, and, as Sissons considered, quite ga. ga. — which we probably were! I sensed that we were not militarily-minded enough — we ignored rank, did not stand on ceremony and engaged in friendly abuse of one another's incompetence.

Who is this 'Cowley'? As the years went by (There was never in my time any question about who was the Army senior in our section) our section had imposed upon it 'odd-bods'. The Central Bureau occasionally used us as a holding station for people in trouble e.g. Sgt Hickling — he had wife problems — a big, strong, fellow of some charm. As an inexperienced youth of 21 it distressed me to see such a fine man in tears. I can remember he disappeared for weeks: I finally found him to tell him to come back (to keep my attendances correct!!)

When Trendall was present, he dealt with Archer and Little. When Trendall was not there, I regarded Lt. Col. Little as my chief (while according to Archer due deference), though I had little personal contact with R.A.L. [Robert Arthur Little] and generally dealt with his Adjutants(?), initially Capt. Scholes, then Major George Mullenger (now deceased — but who returned to Scotch to teach junior classes after the war) and Capt. Stuart (Stewart?)

It was Archer who wrote the [weekly] Précis [of the Section's decrypts].

D.C.S.S. [Sissons] is not correct in assuming that Treweek recruited Barnes. It was I who mentioned Barnes to Trendall: When I was on leave at Xmas in 1942, I approached Eric in a roundabout way. It is more than likely that Professor Room had mentioned Barnes to Trendall. Eric had been dux of Canterbury Boys' High in 1939 and had graduated in Dec. 1942 with firsts in French and Maths. In 1942 Ron Downer had been recruited by Treweek: Downer had a first in history (1941) but apparently Stephen Roberts did not know him!! ('Modern Times'?). Alas, Downer is out at Springvale, having died of meningitis in 1943 — my first military funeral!

Ken McKay was not unknown to Trendall. He was in his second year Arts in 1941. He came to us late — 1944, perhaps 1945 — he was a Sgt. in artillery — I think his father had died.

A. C. Eastway (Tony) was a contemporary of Ian Smith's at North Sydney Boys' High (both were fans of their Classics Master Mr Gibbs — whom I met in 1944, after he had been transferred to Canterbury Boys' High). How he came to us, or was acquired by Trendall, I know not. He had been with 2nd/3rd Machine Gun Bn at Merauke (Dutch New Guinea), arriving at the end of 1943, or early 1944, and left early in 1945 (?) for Central Bureau. After the war he rejoined J.I.B. and in 1947/8? — could have been 49/50/51 — went to Cheltenham UK, returning to reside temporarily with A. R. V. Cooper in a remote (then) house on Oakleigh/Ferntree Gully Road. Later he rejoined CSR, and Ian Smith told me in 1990 he had departed, as a result of a heart attack while surfing/yachting. A competent athlete, Tony was not of the same intellectual capacity as Ian Smith or Ken McKay. His duties with us were 'general purpose': he lodged with Jackie (Cyril James) in Tivoli Rd South Yarra.

Ian Smith. I do not know if Gibbs had mentioned him to Trendall, but Ian was Prof. Chisholm's (Melbourne) bright boy and doubtless mention had been made.

While we were at Monterey, there was contact with the Americans, who resided a floor below. On several occasions we gave them info about ships leaving Saigon, Hanoi, info which the USN subs used to telling effect (I can verbally supply instances): and we gave them info about agents in Peru and Chile. Japanese 'machine encyphered' intercepts we could not handle and at Monterey we passed them on downstairs to the USN and to London: what happened to these when we moved to 'A' block in 1943 I'm not sure: I think Col. Little was given them. While we were in Monterey we received some (not much) help from Washington, but more from London and vice-versa. After January 1943, I think D.C.S.S. [Sissons] could be closer to the truth.

Page 4: When I arrived 'in medias res' LA was well known and generally disregarded, because being a straight code it had little matter of importance. 'FUJI' was the encyphered code to which I was introduced. Who had broken the encyphering system and the code, I do not know: possibly London or one of its subsidiaries/Singapore/Hong Kong.) One item of the encyphering system changed daily — and therefore this had to be cracked daily — the other item changed three times a month. Occasionally the 'CA' code, 'Kancho fugo', was used which was for the eyes of 'Head of Mission only', but the material in these messages did not appear to be of greater importance than the ordinary 'FUJI'. 'Hot' information was entrusted to FUJI double encyphering, indicated by a repetition of the encyphering keyword at the end of the message. This system was unbreakable at that time, if you did not know the encyphering system for that particular day. FUJI messages began with a priority word e.g. SIKYU ('requiring early attention'), followed by a five letter group giving the date of origin, and if this msg was part 1 of 3 etc. This second group code was well known by the time I had arrived in Feb. '42.

Trendall devised an ingenious system whereby the daily FUJI cypher could be broken — and then to be sent by our ULTRA system to London for their breakfast: it became a daily challenge and a matter of kudos! It was at Monterey that this system was evolved. I can supply details, but, as I told David Jenkins, I feel that it is Trendall's copyright, and I shall reveal it, only if he is disinclined to give details. 'FUJI' code, consisting of two letter and four letter groups was 50–66% known by February 1942, and in the next two years, Archer, Graves, London and Washington were able to fill in many of the remaining gaps. In my wakeful hours in senility I can still recall the AG = *wa* KY = *no* HL ... VB was '... ...' EHZB was Chile etc. etc. So much for the sins of youth!

Greater East Asia Ministry (GEAM) commenced their own cypher system after July 1943. It was much simpler than FUJI, but with certain similarities. London broke into this quite early and from then on we had little difficulty in breaking the daily cypher. The material was, as DCSS says, dull, mainly economic, boring. I seldom read any of the translations. Basically these GEAM messages would have delighted economists and statisticians.

(Page 4): I have no recollection of intercepts from the Japanese ambassador to Sweden. Our intercepts came from French Indochina, Tokyo, Afghanistan, Peru, Chile, some German occupied capitals e.g. it was from Budapest that the Japanese ambassador told his Foreign Affairs Office that the Germans had suggested that the Allies were reading his messages, but he assured Tokyo that this was unlikely, nay impossible, because Japanese was such a difficult language! Why I remember this piece of trivia, I do not know, but I do, quite well.

The military value of the contents of 'FUJI' traffic declined after July 1943. Up till then we had been able to supply information to the USN (and RAN) About shipping movements out of Saigon etc. — it was rewarding to read the subsequent messages to the effect that Mr. ... would not be returning by (such and such date) as there had been 'an accident' — and we tracked down a few spies (agents) of the likes of 'Mr. Gonzales Smith'. Perhaps the Japs sensed that their diplomatic cyphers were not as secure as they had thought. Perhaps, it was just a routine change, which would have been normal every six months or so, but in 1942/3 was delayed by distance and opportunity.

(ii) Notes on [letter from] Smith to Sissons, 8 August 1990

Page 2: John Charles Davies who worked with us for only a brief time (3 to 4 months) had been in my class at Canterbury Boys' High School. Early in 1942 I had suggested to Trendall that he could be a helpful minion; he was bright and had a first in Latin and in French. He arrived at Monterey about May 1942, worked with Trendall, Cooper and me for a few weeks and then worked with Treweek downstairs in Monterey. For some reason he fell into Trendall's bad books and Trendall had him shipped out to the Central Bureau which had just moved up to Brisbane. As far as I know he spent the rest of the war with CB, and I did not see him, or hear of him, again until he passed through Melbourne about 1955/6 on his way back from Queens Belfast to New England at Armidale.

John Thomas Laird also arrived in Melbourne about June 1942. He was also a classmate at Canterbury, but I don't think Trendall was interested in him and he went to CB at Brisbane. John, after the war, lectured in English at Duntroon.

Page 3: Paul Grange came to us in 'A' Block when he had moved into our larger room. He seemed to me 'elderly': he was a Czech-Jew who had served in 1914–18 war with the Austro-Hungarian army. (I remember him telling us that when they captured some Roumanian officers they were all wearing corsets!) Quiet, docile, he did clerical duties honestly without fuss. I thought that he had been a Sandford cast-off and I was surprised to learn that he had been formerly a translator with 52 ASWG. Paul and his wife lived in East St. Kilda (or Balaclava?)

Page 4: Ian mentions 'Cowley' — who is this man? I have no recollection of Biggs. Perhaps they arrived after September/October 1945. I had been summoned to Sydney in Sept/October (I think the latter) to the University of Sydney where, under Trendall's eagle-eye, I was to write the war diary (history) of our section, presumably because I was the only one with continuous knowledge of its work from Feb '42 to Sept. '45. I clearly remember writing down every detail of our experiences, etc. etc. (dates, codes, cyphers, personnel) — not once, but twice, and in parts, thrice — until Trendall was satisfied. What happened to this document forged over for nearly a fortnight? Did Trendall keep it, pass it on to someone's obliviontray? It was sufficiently detailed to answer any question posed by D.C.S.S, David Jenkins etc. etc.

I have no knowledge of Pitman — arrived after I left?

(iii) Notes on [letter from] Smith [to Sissons 8 August 1990] on 52 ASWG

(a) I have no idea how, from where, intercepts reached Trendall during our short stay with Nave and Co at the Navy Office.

(b) When we were in Monterey, intercepts came from Park Orchards by dispatch motorcyclist. Sometimes they arrived late, which made Trendall a trifle testy. I cannot recall hearing anything of Ferny Creek. I had no contact with any ASWG personnel.

(c) 52 ASWG moved to Bonegilla. When, I'm not sure. Why, I know not. However, by the time we had settled into 'A' Block in early 1943 somebody, (Col. Little?) had arranged with the PMG [Postmaster General] to run a direct 'sound' line from Bonegilla to our office. Two ex-PMG telegraphists manned our end, Sgt. Harry (?) Watson, who lived at West Footscray, and Cpl. Brown(e), the latter being a (6th or) 7th Division man who had served in Crete, and perhaps Greece. (I don't know if he was there with Ryan and Ballard). This direct line meant that we had last night's intercepts pronto in the morning, with confirmation copies coming next day, or on the next but one, from Bonegilla! Presumably by 'safe hand' D/R [dispatch rider]. It also allowed us to request checks or replays of garbled texts. This direct line was retained when 52 ASWG moved to Mornington, a move occasioned I did hear because it was a better reception area. 52 ASWG was quartered at Mornington racecourse.

(d) I did not ever hear KALINGA mentioned.

(e) I had virtually no direct contact with 52 ASWG personnel. I *vaguely* remember Lt. Col. Ryan coming to see Trendall and Cooper at Monterey in 1942.

In the winter of 1944, (or was it 1943?) I went to Bonegilla for two nights to see the unit at work, and to deliver an explanatory pep talk to the AWAS who were becoming 'browned-off' by the meaningless maze they were required to intercept. Being inexperienced in public speaking, I made quite a mess of this public address, mainly because I was unsure (and not briefed) what I could, or could not, reveal. At some time (cannot remember) Archer went to Bonegilla for a 'pep' talk, and I'm sure this experienced gentleman was more effective.

(f) I paid a flying visit to Mornington — once only — with several more senior officers. The reason for the visit I either did not know or have forgotten. As a humble lieutenant amid senior officers, I remember I kept a discrete [sic] silence.

(g) From the little I saw, I think the AWAS did a good job, especially as they could never be told the final fruits of their labours.

(iv) Notes on Interview by D. C. S. Sissons with A. P. Treweek 11 October 1990

I was not conscious of Treweek (who had been my Classics master at school and lecturer at University) during the short time we were in the Navy Block in Feb/March '42, but I am surprised by his comment on p. 3 about Trendall being in a different block. Treweek was with Nave and Co. on the first or 'second' floor of Monterey, and Trendall, Cooper and I on the 'third' (or do you say 'second') for nearly a whole year. Ath and Hazel occasionally had both us and sometimes AW Sandford for dinner in their Jolimont flat!

A.P.T. is correct about Arthur Cooper coming by ship from Singapore, but astray on the length of Cooper's stay. Still in those days movement was very restricted: you moved and lived only with those with whom you worked directly, and were told 'only what you needed to know' for your work.

Annex 7. David Sissons to Desmond Ball, 11 October 1993

11 October 1993

Prof Desmond Ball
Strategic & Defence Studies Centre
Australian National University
G.P.O. Box 4
Canberra, A.C.T.,2601

Dear Des,

I'm afraid that my work on our wartime 'D' Special Intelligence Section has struck a serious snag -- unwillingness of members to talk because of their secrecy undertakings at the time.

Earlier in the year I wrote to Eric Barnes (later Professor of Pure Maths and Deputy Vice-Chancellor, University of Adelaide). I received an enthusiastic and most informative reply in which he was able to describe each of the codes the Section were reading from the time of his arrival in January 1943. In addition to the low grade ciphers LA and GEAM these were essentially: (i) the blanked columnar transposition, FUJI (the successor to TSU?), and its successor, BA; (ii) the numerical reciphered code, NE, and its successor, 10101. He also described the cryptological problems characteristic of each. He offered to answer any further questions that I wished to put to him.

In his letter, however, Barnes asked for my assurance that he was now free to discusss such matters under what he termed the 'Official Secrets Act' (Enclosure A). I had no alternative but to indicate in my reply that I could not give such an assurance (Enclosure B). I addressed some more questions to him but received no acknowledgment. This I can interpret only as meaning that he is not prepared to talk unless authorised.

Until I encountered this set-back, my intention was next to seek information from Ronald Bond, who joined the Section virtually at the same time as Trendall (January? 1942) and succeeded him as Head in 1944. Although Bond, obviously, could provide much more information than any other member, I had reasons for leaving him until last. In 1945 he was inclined to be tense, impatient and supercilious with his more junior subordinates. While I was fairly confident that Smith, McKay and Barnes would take my enquiries seriously and go to a good deal of trouble providing answers to them, I felt it quite possible that Bond would give Pte Sissons, the lowliest of the linguists, the brush-off. I thought that the best strategy was to leave him until I could demonstrate to him that I had, as a result of patient and systematic research, amassed and digested a good deal of information about the subject and that I had, so to speak, the blessing and cooperation of the rest of the Section.

My other reason for leaving Bond until last was that, of all of us (including those who remained with the organisation after the War), I felt that he, both by temperament and life-style, was the one most likely to refuse to talk on grounds of security.

Yet it seems that both Barnes and Bond have been prepared to talk to David Jenkins. According to Barnes's letter, he gave Jenkins several long briefings. And at p 38 col 1 of his S.M.H. article Jenkins quotes Bond. I understand that you know Jenkins and that he is a frequent visitor at the Centre. I wondered whether, the next

1

time you see him, you could mention my problem to him and seek his advice. Am I right in thinking that Bond is going to be, at best, cagey? The only information that he attributes to Bond is comments about the examination questions that Treweek set in high-school Greek! Was this all that Bond would discuss; or was he prepared to talk about other things 'off the record'? Or has Bond (like, I hope, some of the rest of us) mellowed and become a more relaxed and more helpful person over the half-century that has passed?

In short, I don't think I can write a useful and informative article without Bond's help as an informant. I don't want to foreclose this by writing to Bond out of the blue, if Jenkins's feels that he is likely to reply with a refusal to help. If that seems likely, I might, instead, get in touch with Trendall and see whether, when I return in March, he could, perhaps, bring the two of us together over a cup of coffee in his rooms at La Trobe. In Trendall's presence Bond might, I think, adjust to regarding me as an academic and not as the Section's thick-head and odd man out.

Now, at last, as a result of the patient briefings by McKay, Smith and particularly Barnes about what the Section was doing and how it did it, I feel that with a couple of hours with Bond and Trendall, the whole thing can be brought into shape.

I've had one other set-back. Through Drea (who has been most helpful) I've managed to make contact with the Head of the Historical Section at Fort Meade (H.F.Schorreck). Unfortunately, he confirms that the only file of Australian diplomatic decrypts that they have is the 1942 volume!

Some months ago I received a letter from Stripp. He asked me if I could suggest Australian reviewers for a volume of reminiscences of Bletchley Park old-boys that Hinsley and he are editing (ISBN 0-19-820327-6; due to be published last August). I suggested Treweek, Barnes, yourself and David Horner. Stripp tells me that, like his own book, it was submitted to GCHQ before publication. It will be interesting to see whether the censorship has in the interim become less (or more?) onerous.

With best wishes,

Yours sincerely,

David S

(D.C.S.Sissons)

Encl: 2

Annex 8. Steve Mason to David Sissons, 26 June 1994

June 26, 1994.

Dear David,

Thanks for your letter- I was pleased to hear that you were able to make some sense out of our findings. One of the great difficulties that we now face in ascertaining facts of 50 years ago is the understandable desire at that time to restrict information to people exposed to the work to only what was needed for the task that they had to perform. With Kana operators, it was always a risk that our intelligence successes could be extracted in the event of capture.

Further to your enquiry on call-signs, Bob Suttie has confirmed that call-signs were unenciphered and no Kana was used at the time of Ferny Creek (Bob did notlearn Kana until he got to Bonegilla). Operators were given call-signs and frequencies to monitor and those stations sent high grade, high speed messages for long periods. He had no knowledge of any low grade, hand sent messages, although later, Margaret Griffin mentions that hand sent messages were intercepted in Mornington. Thus, it would seem that consulates would use the main networks and stick to set frequencies. Bob cannot recall ever discovering a new diplomatic link on his dial searching operations, but he could have without knowing it.

It is thought that the intercepted traffic was forwarded to Victoria Barracks for analysis.

For what it is worth, a rough old poem written by Joe Walters, the cook/check at Ferny Creek mentions the following:
JUM, JUF, JNB, JNP, JUX, JAR, RGE, YAK, HSP, RIKUGUN and KUIBEY-CHEV. 52 boys called themselves "the Koshi boys". I guess the 'J' stations would be Japanese and the R's Russian.

As regards DF, their detachments were usually sited away from their section, and it was later that our unit became involved in this aspect. 52 Section never had a DF, but instructions could have been issued to any of our DF establishments to obtain a line on a station. We had a station operating at Bald Hills, outside Brisbane, at Wanegilla and Kerema near Port Moresby and later at Nadzab (with RAAF 1 WU) and Finschaffen. The latter two installations had Collins machines. I was personally involved at Nadzab, where it was difficult to get cross bearings, although we were able to give the Ack Ack and the Fighter planes up to an hour's warning of an impending raid.

I have been advised of a couple of corrections to information given in my last letter.

Press Section Page 2, about half way down: Translators were: Mickie POSANNA and Boris LAWRENCE (not Lawson).

That's all for the moment, but please let me know if I can help further, and if I come across more information I will advise you. I enclose copy of our latest Newsletter, which may be of interest.

With kindest regards,
Sincerely, (Steve Mason)

AUSTRALIAN SPECIAL WIRELESS GROUP, DIPLOMATIC AND PRESS SECTIONS.

Because of the nature of their work, sections dealing with diplomatic and press tended to be pretty much self contained and their personnel tended to be isolated from the much larger and probably more prestiguous areas of interception.
In addition, the translators were mostly of foreign origin and their off-duty interests rarely corresponded with Australian-bred operators. The gap of 50 years has not made the task any easier.
Accordingly, it is difficult to piece together an account of these operations, the more so because many of the key players were older and now are no longer with us.

However, with the willing cooperation of several of our Association members, in particular, Bob. Suttie, Beryl Leopold (nee Enright), Margaret Griffin (nee McBrien), Betty Davies (nee Hurtig), Nev. Wintin and Bob. Edwards, who have put their memories on 'search', it has been possible to build up the following account:

Frank O'Loughlin has on record that Press operated at Park Orchards from early 1942. It may be that some diplomatic traffic was also taken there, but Bob. Suttie feels that our first coverage of Diplo. traffic was performed when the detachment went to Ferny Creek in March 1942, where both Press and Diplo. were dealt with.

Bob. Suttie enlisted in January 1942, first reporting to Caulfield Race Course. Then followed his first real job in peeling spuds in Park Orchards whilst a member of LHQ Sigs. His Lance-Corporal there was Dave Drummond, later to be a Captain in ASWG.
In March 1942, Bob, in company with Bob. Parker and Harry Ginnivan, was posted to Ferny Creek, where a detachment from the Group, then known as 5 W/T Section set up business to take Diplo. and Press wireless messages.
The dates correspond with your references to Major Mason, but our members have no knowledge of the Major.
The camp was on One-Tree Hill, where several houses, including one owned by Senator Leckie (a relative of Bob. Menzies) were taken over. Amongst the operators were : Diplo.: Bill Redpath, Ross Kirby (now managing director of Village Drive-ins), Ivo Riley, Tom Collins, Frank Walsh, Bob. Suttie and i/c was Jack Paterson.
Press: Bill Ryan, Ray Dolling with Gerry Jennings i/c.
Joe 'Gunga Din' Walters was the cook.

In mid-June, some original members of 5 W/T and presumably the Press Section from Park Orchards joined the detachment, which functioned there until July/August 1942, when they moved directly to Bonegilla where the Group had already been formed (at end of May).

Diplo. traffic was high speed, so was recorded on Edison circular wax cylinders, to be played back later and taken down by the operators. Messages started with the call sign, followed by the preamble including an identification of source, e.g. JG for Japanese Government, then the text. Messages were sent, no acknowledgements from receiving stations were received, at least on the transmitting frequency, and messages were never interrupted with repeats, requests for signals strength etc. It is thought that our operators' receiving sets were AWA's.

In May 1942, Park Orchards contained many sig. units, including 5 W/T Section. I think that the Sig. Training Battalion was the largest of the units and they also moved to Bonegilla at about the same time that our section moved.

Diplo. work carried on in Bonegilla the same way as had prevailed at Ferny Creek until August 1942, when the first of the AWAS joined the unit. Corporals Barbara Thompson (nee Nichols) and Doss Black (nee Jury) were among the first to report in. Beryl Leopold recalls being met by the Administrative Staff consisting of Lieut. Peg. Sitlington (nee Harrison-Owen), Miss Pettigrew, Miss Flowden, Miss Stacey, Miss Marg. Seabrook and Miss Sharp, together with C.O. Lieut.-Col. Jack Ryan. The girls came from S.A., W.A., N.T.,Vic., N.S.W., Tas. and Qld. Uniforms, straw paliases and dixies were issued. They were billeted in huts and soon started morse training, route marches, rifle drill and lectures on hygiene and security.

During October 1942, AWAS recruits were divided between Diplo. and Press sections.
Lieut. Litchfield, Sgt. Bill Ryan, Sigs. Jack Timberlake and Ray Dolling served as editors, proof readers and supervisors of the Press Section. The translators were: Mickie ? (Dutch), Werner Miebach (German), Boris Lawson (Russian), Frank Scally (Spanish), Frank O'Loughlin and George Perry (French),and Bill Thompson (Japanese), together with Paul Grange who had 6 European languages. The operators were: Gwenda Furness, Barbara Christie, Win. Menzies, Joan Bungey, Elsa Glen, Mavis Ball, Lea Leggo, Nance Newland, Pat. Thompson, Joan Baxter and Beryl Enright.
Receiving sets were 101's and Kingsley Broad Bands. Reuters, Japanese Kana and Tokyo Rose were taken.
Operators were given set frequencies to monitor, but the dial was searched when there was no activity on set frequencies.
The information was edited and bulletins sent to Army, Navy and Air-Force H.Q.
In September 1943, sections were formed and sent to Perth, Mornington, Cairns and Kalinga. There were 25 AWAS personnel in Cairns.

Margaret Griffin was involved solely in Diplo. work. She trained in Bonegilla, moved to Kalinga then to Mornington. Press work was carried out as well at most locations, but Mornington's Section 52 was all Diplo.
Transmissions were both high speed, interceptors using Edison cylinders, and hand sent. Most operators took messages on typewriters and later had the use of special typewriters which were adapted to Kana.
Kana 5 letter code was mostly used.

Receiving sets were Halicrafters, AWA's and Philips.
Many of the messages were designated JG and many were signed off by Tojo.
Mostly operators were given frequencies to monitor, but dial searching was carried out in inactive moments.
Many messages originated in Truk and call signs remembered were: YAK (Afganistan), RTZ (Russia), D.. (Germany) and I.. (Italy).
No acknowledgements were received on transmitting frequencies and there were no repeats or requests for signal strengths.
Jap. operators were skilled and transmission was good, although replaying the Edison records sometimes gave problems.

Our operators had their first Kana lessons before they left the Middle East, under British instructors, starting about December 1941.

It is not known how the frequencies given to operators were obtained, but it was later that the unit became involved in DF operations. It would be usual procedure for any instructions issued to Section 52 to emanate from HQ. ASWG. It was very rare for a station to change frequencies.

In December 1945, the AWAS left Mornington to be discharged and male personnel from Kalinga replaced them.
I had the unenviable task of bringing a party of 30 returned men from Brisbane, through their home states of NSW and Vic. to Mornington, and with the war over and the men awaiting their discharge points to come up. Six men were with me when we reported into Royal Park, but we managed to squeeze 4 days' leave there, allowing a full complement to be present at the first parade at Mornington Race Course.
Understandingly, enthusiasm for the work was at a low ebb, but we took mostly Russian high speed traffic. On occasions, with the use of incentives, full logs were produced- I can remember one night's work which yielded more than 1000 messages.

A liasion officer, W.O. Harry Dempsey was appointed (he had previously been with our Middle East Section and Section 55 in New Guinea) and each Wednesday he took our work to Mic. Sandford at Victoria Barracks.
Kingsley Receiving sets were mostly used.

The people whose names you mention from the War Diary are mostly not now available:
Frank Walker, Gwenda Furness and Gerry Jennings are all deceased. Miss Jury became Mrs Black, but her address is unknown. Tom Wastell (spelling?) lives in Caringbah NSW. Jack Butler was not known to be involved in Ferny Creek or Bonegilla- he was in New Guinea at this time seeking possible locations for Section 55 when it arrived.
In any case Frank Walker was O/C of a reinforcement of Section 55, which later merged with Section 53 at Finschaffen from December 1943 to mid 1945. Please advise if we can assist further.
Steve Mason.

Annex 9. Steve Mason to Desmond Ball, 7 July 1995

July 7, 1995

Professor Desmond Ball,
Strategic and Defence Studies Centre,
The Research School of Pacific and Asian Studies,
The Australian National University,
Canberra   ACT   0200

Dear Professor Ball,

Thank you for your letter dated July 3, 1995 and enclosures relating to your most interesting work, "A true Spy Story".

I am afraid that I can't add a great deal to that which I have already given to David Sissons- I presume that you have a copy of this, but one is enclosed anyway.

I have four main problems with the diplomatic part of ASWG operations:
1. 50 years is a long time.
2. I personally was not involved in diplomatic work until December 1945 when I arrived in Mornington.
3. Security was such an important part of all of our operations that personnel were given only the information that was necessary for them to perform their job.
4. My duties and rank were not high enough to warrant possession of much more information than was available to signalmen.

By way of background, perhaps I could outline some of my own experiences showing how we functioned:
   As a Lance-Corporal and then a Corporal, I was in charge of one of four shifts, each having from 6 to 12 intercept operators. After returning from New Guinea, I acted as Orderly Sergeant for some months, so had little to do with the operating side. At Mornington, as a Sergeant, I acted mostly as a Company Sergeant Major, although whenever possible I got onto the sets, either solely or by plugging in on one of the operators.
   As a shift supervisor, you were occasionally given frequencies and less often callsigns to monitor, and then a set or sets were dedicated to that work. Generally, the supervisor spent a lot of time on the sets, assisting operators when reception was poor or in training operators. At the end of a shift the messages would be sorted, counted and passed on to their next point of treatment (being the 'I' Staff in the field or a Don-R at HQ to take to Central Bureau.). Occasionally an 'I' Staffer or an officer with knowledge of Japanese (Captain Bob. McNamara, mostly) would inspect the operators at work, and if anything looked interesting, he would direct that the operator continue to monitor that station. If it looked very interesting, Bob. would plug into the set and take the traffic in Japanese.

Operators and supervisors were rarely told of achievements resulting from their work, although you could have some thoughts when subsequent news of a bombing, a sea battle, an air raid or a point or town taken came to notice.
At one time in Dutch New Guinea, rumors were strong that we were all to receive some honor from the Dutch government. Really, just in the last few years have I learnt much more about what we did 50 years ago. We were never sure that much progress had been made in cracking the Jap. codes.

But all of that does not help you much, so let's turn to your questions:

1. The Move to Mornington:
   We were told that, with the war over, Kalinga was to close, the AWAS (and a few 'B' Class men),who had done the work at Mornington over the years, were due for discharge and it would be some time before our discharge points came up, thus my task of taking 30 men from Brisbane to Mornington arose. At no time were we briefed on the Russian task and we weren't given to understand that there was any particular importance in the work. Our operators unenthusiastically took over the work that the AWAS had been doing. Everything was low key, Japanese traffic was reduced and no emphasis was placed on chasing it or any other traffic.

2. The Mornington Activity:
   We operated 24 hours a day, on four shifts, with 5 or 6 operators on each shift.
   Names??? Problems here:
   Officers: Maj. Ralph Thompson, Lieut. Jim Murray (dec.), Lieut. Jerry Jennings (dec.), Capt. Tom. Eastick (dec.), Lieut. Reed, Capt. Pascal, Maj. Hastings (in succession).
   OR's: Bob. Edwards, Jack Daniel, Ray. Lees, Bill Carse, Ron. White, Allan Jarman (dec.), Pat. Spicer (dec.), Nick Bisas, Joe Pritchard, Jim. Mackey, 'Blue' Fairweather, Gordon Tye, Wal. George, Alan Hansford.
   Harry Dempsey died 5 or 6 years ago.
   We took over from the AWAS just before Christmas 1945 (about December 20).
   I can't recall whether traffic other than Russian was taken, RTZ is the only callsign I know, traffic was all morse, diplomatic and mostly high speed, taken on Edison wax cylinders and transcribed later. Location of the transmitters is not known, but the operators were first class, signals clear, and as no repetitions were apparently requested, it seems that the messages were broadcast to be picked up by stations as arranged.

3. Mornington:
   Situated in the Race-course, club buildings were used for the set-room, orderly room and messes, and a series of galvanised huts served as sleeping quarters.
   From memory, the aerials were rhombic, directional, 90 degree span and sited in the middle of the race-course.

Annex 9

I picture our old faithful Kingsleys as the sets used, but note that Margaret Griffin remembers Halicrafters, AWA's and Philips.
I have been unable to ascertain whether any other Russian intercept activity was undertaken during the war.

4. Mic. Sandford:
Our only news of Mic. came from Harry Dempsey. Before Dempsey arrived, we sent our messages to Victoria Barracks by Don-R, but it is not known to which block.
I can't recall any feedback concerning our intercept activity. The operators were certainly not in top gear but would have risen to the occasion had any need been made known to them.

5. Boris:
His surname should have been given as Lawrence and he was in the Press Section in Bonegilla. His movements after that are not known.

6. Closing Down Mornington:
I was under the impression that the section continued to operate until October 1946. (I was discharged on October 15). I also understood that 101 Wireless Section took over the job and they were based at Balcombe and then moved to Mornington Race-course, but I could be wrong there, and certainly would not know whether they took over the Russian intercept activity.
Any of our people who wished to continue in the Army and did not wish to join the Occupation Forces transferred to 101 Section.
I can recall taking a convoy of trucks up to Carlton to hand them in, just days before heading for Royal Park, Melbourne for discharge.
Most of my group left Mornington in the first half of October, as we had been 18 years of age on enlistment, had overseas service and were unmarried, making our discharge points pretty well the same.

It seems that I can't help you all that much, particularly concerning the Victoria Barracks arrangements. Ralph Thompson would have been my reference, but you have spoken to him.

Further removed, reading your account on Page 31 reminded me that in early 1945 (I think) I was one of three ASWG personnel who performed signals work for the Australian Security Service when they were investigating lights flashing off the Queensland coast at the Gold Coast, first noticed after some Lutherans who had been released from internment and then purchased and occupied a property overlooking the sea.

Annex 10. Ronald Bond to Desmond Ball, 29 September 1994

29th September '94

Dear Professor,

As you can well see from the two enclosed sketches, the Good Lord did not intend me to be an architect! Neither sketch is to scale.

I am not sure about the number of windows in Room C, but next time I pass Vic Barracks I shall look up and count them – if that info is vital.

When we first moved in we occupied Rooms A, B, and C. Room D was used by a Group – I know not who – and both Archer & Trendall considered it unwise to have uninitiated people so close. When we left Room A for Room D (a much larger area) I cannot recall precisely, but I do remember working on GEAM traffic in Room A. So it would suggest we went over to Room D towards the end of '43 or early '44. We were well entrenched there when Ian Smith arrived.

In rather sharp contrast to Monterey, security to the Barracks in general & to 'A' block in particular was somewhat perfunctory. We had passes, but the guard at the front entrance to 'A' block appeared to be a "commissionaire" (unarmed).

For the life of me I cannot recall how and where we got paid while I was at Monterey!!

May speedy success await your labours.

Yours sincerely,

R.S.Bond

Breaking Japanese Diplomatic Codes

MONTEREY

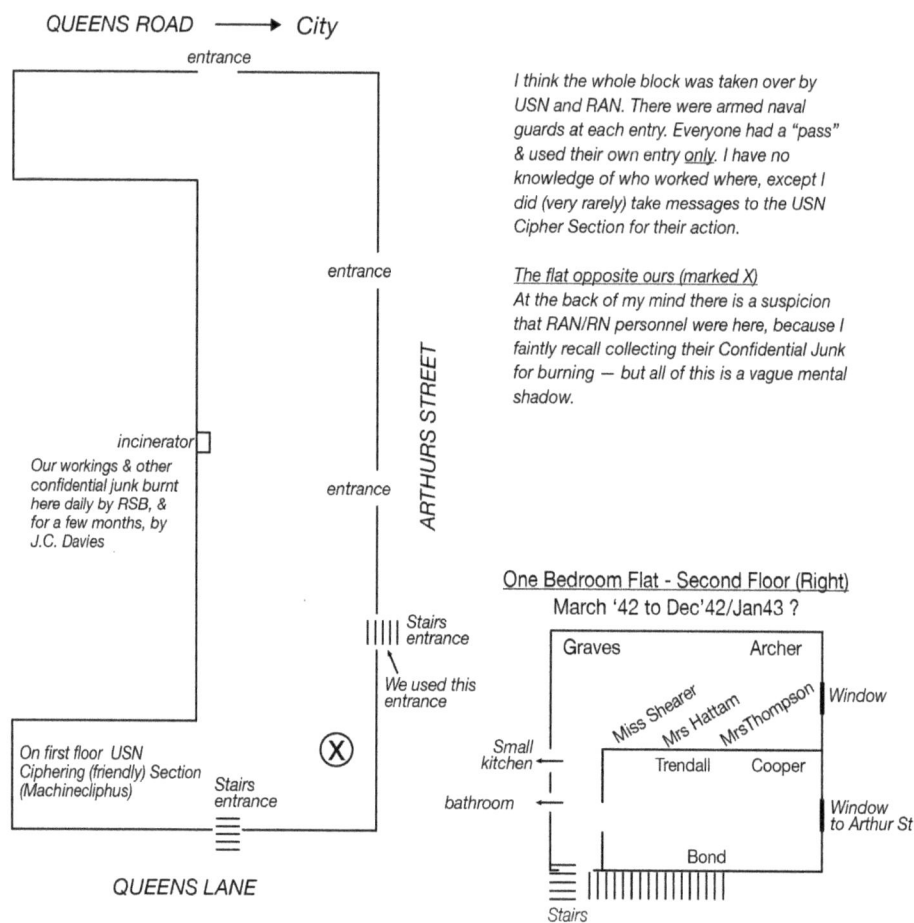

Monterey had not any earlier occupants. It was new, without any heating!

Annex 10

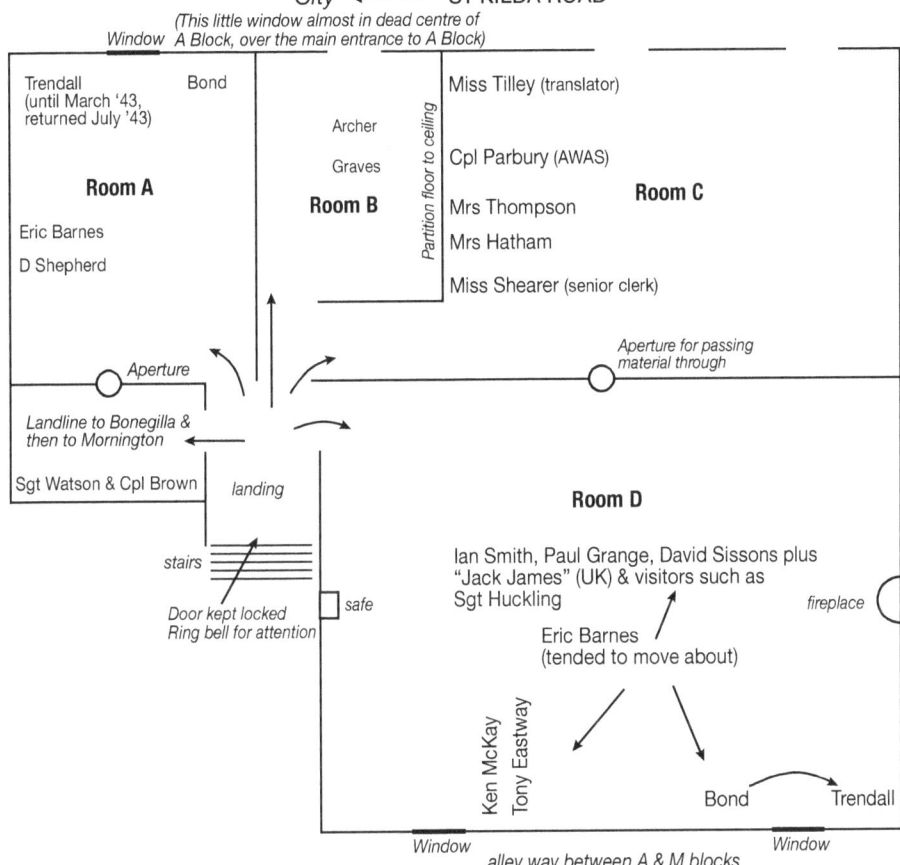

Moved in January 1943 — I left December 1945, but away quite a bit from July/August 1945.

(might have been late December 1942, but I don't think so)

Annex 11. David Sissons to Desmond Ball, 22 May 1996

22 Savige St
Campbell
A.C.T., 2612

<sissons@coffee.dialix.oz.au>

22 May 1996

Prof Desmond Ball
Strategic & Defence Studies
A. N. U.

I think that Emma Craswell's search of the SRDJ series for the three Harbin-Tokyo telegrams has now gone as far as it need. My report on it, The Search in the SRDJ Series for the Harbin-Tokyo Telegrams is enclosed (Enclosure 1). Also enclosed is my complete correspondence with her (Enclosure 2) in case any points should require elaboration.

My inference is that these three telegrams are among the 'Temp' numbers that she has listed as missing in Box 156, i.e. among those in the 'Temp' series witheld by NSA at the time of declassification.

It seems to me that, if you wished to continue the search, there are three lines of approach that could be followed: (i) search for the telegrams, as John Taylor suggests, among the mass of wartime material released by NSA last month; (ii) seek their production in the U.S.A. under their Freedom of Information legislation; (iii) seek the production of 'D' Special intelligence Section LHQ's register of intercepted Japanese diplomatic telegrams for the relevant period under Section 40 of the Australian Archives Act 1983. Let me outline these approaches one by one:

(i) The NSA Material Released on 4/4/96

The enclosed diskette (Enclosure 3) contains the National Archives press statement on this latest transfer (NSA.HTM) and the inventory of file titles of the 4923 items constituting it (NARAFIND.HTM). These I downloaded from the Internet. I suggest that you get your staff to copy the diskette and run you off a hard copy for your records.

This inventory runs to about 167 pages (A4) and a number of the items will interest you quite apart from the current search. Note well the three caveats in the press statement: (i) The transfer includes, in addition to new material, some copies of files already available (E.g. Item 3414, 20 Mar 1942, 'FRUMEL Outgoing/Incoming Messages', may be a file that you have already xeroxed); (ii) Related records are scattered throughout the collection; (iii) File titles often do not reflect the full content of the item. To this I would add a fourth caveat: the date attributed to the item (Column 4) is no indication to the date range of its contents. Take for example Item 2738: the item is dated 9 September 1940 but the file title is 'Chronology of Cooperation Between

SSA and GCCS [i.e. Bletchley] 1940-45'. Presumably the item date means the date of the earliest paper in the file.

Be this as it may, the transfer contains much that for me sounds exciting, e.g. cipher texts, work-sheets and solutions for the systems that were our stock-in-trade – FUJI (J-19), NE, JBC and JBD. So far as I'm aware, this is the first time that NSA has released cipher text and work-sheets since the Pearl Harbor Attack hearings. This will make it hard for our DSD to continue to rule that such material is still sensitive. Very exciting is Item 3428, 6 Apr 1943, 'Copies of Messages Supplied by Australia with Clarifying Notes'. This could be the long sought after succeeding volume to SRMN-006, 'R.A.N. Support to U.S.N. through A.C.N.B.: Summaries/Translations of Japanese Messages Feb-Dec 1942, which , you will remember, contained translations of some 200 diplomatic telegrams that Trendall, Bond & Co had solved.

I have been through the inventory twice. None of the titles appear to me to be likely to contain the specific Harbin telegrams for which you are searching. It would be looking for a needle in a bottomless pit rather than in a haystack. I do not recommend it.

In her Email to me of April 17th (of which David Horner has a copy) Emma Craswell passed on John Taylor's suggestion that, if this latest inventory contained no likely titles, she should contact Tom Johnson or David Hatch in the historical section at NSA to see if they can confirm whether or not this latest transfer contains any SRDJ translations hitherto witheld. This seems to me well worthwhile.

<u>(ii) An Approach to NSA under F.O.I</u>

If in her dealings with Johnson or Hatch she found them knowledgeable and on the ball, then she could take up with them the practicability of seeking the production of these particular telegrams (and their transmission details, ascertainable from SIS's logs — particularly call-sign, power of transmitter, frequency, and precise time of day) under F.O.I.

<u>D Sect LHQ's Register</u>

Since my return from Japan I have been in correspondence with some of the women in our D Section (they were girls when I last saw them). The cryptanalysts and I were in Room 86; the women were the other side of a communicating glass hatch, in 87; the British Consular officers were next to them in 87A. These ladies are proving very good value. Mavis Vernon, a fellow linguist, has confirmed, without any prompting from me, that it was Trendall and Graves that broke the GEAM cipher (with a bit of practical help from her) — before the British or the Americans. (Barnes told me this in 1945 but has no recollection of it to-day). But more relevant to our present inquiry are the recollections of Mary Stewart, a young Melbourne Arts graduate straight from the University who, when Bond & Co had solved the transpositions, used to apply the daily grids. She writes (28/9/95):

> Prof Trendall usually brought the work in himself for Reba [Shearer] to log and later a T(ranslation) number. The log, known as the <u>Koran</u>, was a large brown hard-backed book which was meticulously kept by Reba, or deputy, with all details of the traffic and translation titles, and a card index of the subject matter.

I am quoting from her letter exactly as she wrote it. Although the syntax

Annex 11

leaves something to be desired (She was dashing off a long letter to catch the mail) the meaning is quite clear. This log would answer conclusively the question whether or not the DMI got these Harbin intercepts from us.

I suggest that you make out an application on the prescribed form (Enclosure 4) for access to this log under Section 40 of the Act. You might also consider whether, for good measure, you should in the same application apply for access also to the history of the Section that Bond was required to submit before he was demobbed (Peter Hastings and I were shown this at DSD in 1987) and to the wartime history of Nave's organization submitted by Jamieson in similar circumstances (Australian Archives B5554). The cost of the ensuing proceedings in the Administrative Appeals Tribunal will be ths same irrespective of whether the application is for a single document or a number of different documents.

What will happen is that DSD, despite the statutory requirement to give an answer within 90 days, will drag their feet interminably for as long as Archives and you will let them. They will then refuse access. Archives will convey to you their refusal and at the same time inform you of your right to request within 30 days an internal reconsideration by Archives of the decision. In this internal reconsideration Archives will uphold DSD's decision and inform you of your right to take the matter to the Administrative Appeals Tribunal. When you exercise that right there will follow conferences between you and DSD who may, in the course of these, offer some concessions in the hope of avoiding appearing before the AAT. I understand that it is not until after these preliminary conferences that the applicant has to pay money into court.

Why I suggest that you, rather than I, make the application is that you and the Centre have a high reputation for conducting serious work on the subject. This will undoubtedly impress DSD and the AAT (who will also be mindful that the press and public opinion will take a similar view when the Canberra Times reports the proceedings). I, on the other hand, can be made to appear as some senile old Dig (rank, Private) who never got nearer to the front line than Melbourne, trying to write his 'war-ee' based on the activities of his superiors — despite his signing in 1945 the standard undertaking (preserved in his dossier at Central Army Records Office) not to divulge such matters on pain of prosecution under the relevant provisions of the Crimes Act.

ASWG's Occasional Interception of Soviet Diplomatic Traffic

We know from its War Diary that the Australian Special Wireless unit in the Middle East at times intercepted Soviet signals traffic for Bletchley. When I last saw you I undertook to commit to paper the basis of my belief that the Aust Special Wireless Group on at least one occasion between the return of our troops from the Middle East and April 1945 was required to intercept Soviet diplomatic traffic. My belief is based on the clear recollections of two different conversations.

The first converstion was with Bond in Room 86 and therefore at some time between April and September 1945 (and probably closer to September than to April). I asked him whether we ever intercepted the diplomatic traffic of countries other than Japan. He promptly replied 'No' and then, after a few seconds, qualified this as follows: 'Only once. One message. It was to be handled with the utmost of secrecy and went straight into that safe', or words to that effect. He did not say that it was Russian. I assumed so; but I suppose it could have been French. I didn't press him for further details; for I could see that he was speaking very reluctantly and probably regretted having spoken. I was rather puzzled; for his expression and gestures suggested that the document was still in the safe. Why go to all this trouble to intercept this message and treat the matter with such secrecy if it got no further than the safe — i.e. if you didn't send it on for solution/translation to whoever had requested the interception? But perhaps what he meant was 'I still have our copy of in in the safe'.

I don't see how it could have come into Bond's hands unless it had been intercepted by Mornington: ASWG dealt with DMI or with Bletchley direct and not through Bond. Unless reception conditions rendered it unsuitable, Mornington and not one of the other ASW Sections was the appropriate place for DMI to use for the interception of Russian diplomatic traffic.

The second conversation was with WO2 Allen Clifton who, as Ballard states in his book, at no time made any secret of his Communist sympathies. In conversation with me, he deplored the distrust and unfairness with which the Allies were treating the Soviet. For example, he said, ASWG were reading Soviet traffic. Unfortunately I cannot pinpoint the date at which this conversation took place. It was certainly not before October 1945, when I was sent to Labuan. I'd be very surprised if it was later than my arrival in Japan (February 1946). It was during that interval that I saw a lot of Allen. At Labuan in November and December we were in the same Mess and usually ate at the same table and went to the cinema together. We had adjoining bunks on the voyage from Labuan to Morotai just before Christmas. At Morotai we once again were members of the same Mess and then, as he states in his <u>Time of Fallen Blossoms</u>, we flew from Morotai to Japan together on the same D3 (a 3-day journey) in February (1946). I probably saw him a couple of times in Japan. (There we were in different units: he was Tom Millar's interpreter with one of the battalions in Kure and I was with the New Zealand field battery at Yamaguchi). The next time I saw him was for a couple of days at the General Details Depot at Royal Park in February 1947 when I was being demobbed. He had been taken on strength there pending his projected return to Japan while DMI conducted a security check on him. Apparently they reported adversely and he was discharged a few weeks later. I don't remember any prolonged conversations with him at Royal Park. After that I may have seen him or spoken to him on the phone a couple of times in Melbourne while I was an undergraduate. I distinctly remember in October 1950 telling another wartime associate that Allen had once told me that ASWG had been intercepting Soviet traffic.

I have given you this long rigmarole beacuse it is important for you to know within certain limits when this conversation with Allen could have taken place — whether he could have been referring to the interception of Soviet Traffic that, we now know (Steve Mason's note on <u>ASWG, Diplomatic and Press Sections</u> enclosed in Ballard to D.C.S.S 24/5/94), ASWG resumed some time between the War's end and the disbandment of 52 Section at Mornington (16/2/46). I reckon that it was at Labuan that this conversation took place and that it therefore refers to interception during the war.

Allen was with ASWG for a time. We know from Ballard, who was with 51 ASW Sect at Darwin from January to mid-December 1943, that Allen was there with them for some time, arriving later than he did. How long he was there, I don't know; but it was longer than the period required for eligibility for the Defence Medal, whose ribbon he wore. He must have left Darwin before 30/4/44; for DMI's War Diary shows him on the staff of the Army Japanese Language School in Melbourne on that date. He remained there until posted to Labuan after the War's end.

4

Annex 11

I don't think 51 Sect was intercepting Russian traffic while he was with them. If it was, I think he would have said so in as many words. There are, I think, two possibilities. The first is that he was moved from 51 SEct on security grounds and that this was because they were about to intercept Russian traffic there. He was nobody's fool and would have set about finding out why. The other possibility is that one of his mates in ASWG, whose Section was engaging in Russian interception, told him about it over a glass of beer when he looked Allen up during a visit to Melbourne.

Allen died on 12/6/95. There is an obituary in the Melbourne Herald Sun 5/7/95.

Emma Craswell

I think David Horner has already arranged payment for her services to date. If not, this should be done promptly. I think she has done a good job and has not wasted time spent on the job. She has done a lot in her 35 hours.

I think we should ask her to make the enquiries with Johnson or Hatch at NSA that John Taylor suggests. In her Email of April 17th she says she has some free time after the end of this month.

If you required further browsing to be done at College Park, I think you could probably get a less qualified person to do it for a good deal less than $Aust25 per hour. My daughter, Miranda, who found Emma for us, tells me that part-time work for students is at present very hard to come by. Miranda is now at Yale and, though quite as well qualified as Emma, has to take jobs at less than $US10 an hour. Although the employment situation at New Haven is worse than in Washington, she thinks there are probably students in the Washington area who would do it for between $US10 and $US15 per hour. Unfortunately Miranda would not be able to find one for us; for all her friends in Washington are friends of Emma's.

My apologies for writing at such length,

(D.C.S.Sissons)

Encl: 4. (Please copy any that you wish but return the originals to me for my records).

P.S. I once again have an Email address <sissons@coffee.dialix.oz.au>. I hope this will be more permanent and more satisfactory than the last.

Annex 12. David Sissons to Desmond Ball, 9 September 1996

22 Savige St
Campbell
A.C.T., 2612

9 September 1996

Prof Desmond Ball
Strategic & Defence Studies
A.N.U.

Dear Des,

THE HARBIN TELEGRAMS

Last week I forwarded to you by Email Emma Craswell's latest report (dated 27/8/96).

In this she passed on Hatch's observations that: (i) if the Americans had intercepted these Harbin telegrams, the translations would have been in the boxes that Emma has examined; (ii) because of reception conditions, the Americans were unable to intercept much traffic from Harbin. This is as close to an expert opinion as we are likely to get. It would therefore, I think, be futile to search further for them in the U.S. National Archives

Is it worthwhile pursuing the search elsewhere?

I still think it possible that it was Mornington, Bond & Co that intercepted at least some of them. On rereading Blamey's letter to the Acting Minister of 6/1/45 I see that he described the 24/11/45 message as a 'Special Spy Report' from Harbin. SRH-254: The Japanese Intelligence System, to which Hatch refers us, at page 24 (Aegean Park edition) describes 'Harbin Special Spy Reports' as a series of reports issued by the Army General Staff. If this be so, then Mornington would not have intercepted them; for we handled only diplomatic traffic. But in a later chapter on 'The Japanese Diplomatic Intelligence System' it refers at page 95 to intelligence reports from Harbin containing informtion provided by a contact within the local Russian consulate-general. There are references to these latter Harbin intelligence reports from time to time in the Magic Summary (e.g. No.788 of 22/5/44 p.11; No.1032 of 21/1/45 p.9; No.1180 of 18/6/45 p.1; No.1190 of 28/6/45) that state that these telegrams were sent by the Japanese Consul-General (Yamagiwa). If any of the telegrams to which Blamey refers were from Yamagiwa, then it is possible that Mornington intercepted them.

But if Bond and his colleagues had solved these particular messages, would one not expect them to be still rooted in their memory? I raised this point in a recent letter to Prof (then Cpl) Ian Smith:

> If they had passed through our hands, then these are telegrams that, one would have thought, everyone in the Section would remember (like the identification of 'Bengal Tiger', and other spies in India from time to time, which passed by word of mouth immediately through both rooms and caused great excitement). But no-one has any

recollection at all of these three Harbin telegrams. Des Ball visited Ron in Melbourne and Vai Parbery at Malua Bay and I wrote to Mavis Tilley, Mary Stewart and Midge Hattam; but, though each was frank and helpful, it rang no bells.

But perhaps I'm wrong in thinking that the significance of these telegrams would have been obvious to Jac or Mavis when they translated them, and to Archer when he analysed them. To any of us, the only useful deduction that would emerge from them might have been that some clerk in our Soviet ally's Harbin consulate was in the pay of the Japanese. And this was perhaps hardly exciting enough for one to want to share it with one's mates at the adjacent tables or with the ladies in the next room. Any of us would probably have assumed that the Soviet military attaché at Canberra was on the circulation list of the AMF Weekly Intelligence Summary. It was the boys in MI(b) that would have known that he was not, and would have been able to draw the deduction that there must be a Soviet mole at work in Canberra.

So my conclusion is that these telegrams probably passed through our hands but created no great stir amongst us.

One of my colleagues of those days, Mary Stewart, has reminded me that we logged in a register every intercepted message that Mornington sent us. She writes (28/9/95):

Prof Trendall usually brought the work in himself for Reba to log and later give a T (translation) number to. The log, known as the Koran, was a large brown hard-backed book which was meticulously kept by Reba (or her deputy), with all details of the traffic and translation titles, and a card-index of the subject matter.

Even if it is true that DSD have reduced their wartime records to 1 metre of shelf space (and I find this hard to believe), I can't believe that they destroyed our Koran. So I think that we should immediately apply for its production under Archives Act §40. With the Koran we should be able to tell in an instant whether it was we that intercepted the telegrams in question.

Shall I E-mail to Emma Craswell asking her to submit her final bill; or have you further tasks for her?

Yours sincerely,

David S.

(D.C.S.Sissons)

Annex 13. David Sissons to Desmond Ball, 16 October 1996

22 Savige St
Campbell
A.C.T., 2612

<sissons@coffee.dialix.oz.au>

16 October 1996

Prof Desmond Ball
Strategic & Defence Studies
A.N.U.

Dear Des,

I was recently in correspondence with my wartime colleague, Prof Ian Smith, about his solution of the Kormoran cryptogram. As he was the last of us to be demobbed (He remained with the Section until November 1946) I took this occasion to ask him whether they were working on Soviet traffic after my departure in September 1945.

I quote from my letter to him of August 29th:

"To my surprise, I've been told that in late December 1945 Mornington were working on Soviet traffic. Steve Mason, the Secretary of the ASWG Association, writes (26/6/94):

> In December 1945, the AWAS left Mornington to be discharged and male personnel from Kalinga replaced them. I had the unenviable task of bringing a party of 30 returned men from Brisbane, through their home states of NSW and Vic, to Mornington. . . . Understandably, enthusiasm for the work was at a low ebb, but we took mostly Russian high speed traffic. On occasions, with the use of incentives, full logs were produced – I can remember one night's work which yielded more than 1,000 messages. A liaison officer, WO Harry Dempsey, was appointed . . . and every Wednesday he took our work to Mic Sandford at Victoria Barracks.

Were you and Eric involved in this or was it kept secret from the Section?"

Ian's reply (September 29th) (on audio-tape as the fingers of his right hand were temporarily out of action with arthritis) reads as follows:

> I have a recollection of reading and translating Russian plain-language messages picked up by Mornington – after the arrival of the Central Bureau people from Brisbane – probably December 1945. They were, I think, Russian Post Office messages between individuals – or else office messages, mainly from economic units in the Far East referring decisions to Moscow for approval, or statistics – monumentally banal.
>
> I remember Bob Botterill among the arrivals from Brisbane. He was working on various codes including, I think, French codes. They had been stolen when sent to Djibouti on an English naval ship and had been photographed.

I thought this might interest you

Regards

David S.

Annex 14. David Sissons to Desmond Ball, 23 March 1998

22 Savige St
Campbell
A.C.T., 2612

23 March 1998

Prof Desmond Ball
Strategic & Defence Studies Centre
Australian National University

Dear Des,

You were interested in whether any Section of the Australian Special Wireless Group ever intercepted Soviet Traffic during the later years of World War II. I told you that something that Bond said to me in mid-1945 indicated that one such intercept passed through his hands at some time before I joined his Special Intelligence Section (April 1945).

Last week I came upon the enclosed document in the I(x) box-file of the Assistant Director of Military Intelligence (ADMI) at Victoria Barrracks Melbourne, declassifed by the DSD last December. I wonder whether this could refer to the intercept in question.

'Box-file' usually means a file in which an office keeps an additional copy of its outwards letters irrrespective of subject. The file in question, in fact, contains only outwards memos/signals. Its date range is October 1943 to October 1945.

The initials for the signature are those of the A.D.M.I. himself, Lt-Col R.A.Little, and together with the filing instructions, are in his own handwriting.

I wonder whether the subject heading 'Red Traffic' is Little's or Clark's. 'Red' could, of course, refer to something other than Soviet. The soldiery of several nations seem to have had a penchant for colours for code-words, e.g. REDLAND v. BLUELAND in war games, ORANGE I II III for the U.S. Navy's standing defensive plans for war against Japan, the RED Machine for the Japanese diplomatic cipher machine of the 1930s, etc. (It certainly does not refer to the latter; for according to Kahn the RED cipher machine was eventually withdrawn from service during 1941). If RED here does mean Soviet, then I'm a bit surprised that, with a matter of such 'delicacy', this was blazoned unnecessarily into a letter-heading. But Clark may have felt that he had to name the file in such a manner that it could be indexed and retrieved by subject. It was after all a TOP SECRET file, which he may have felt afforded it sufficient security. The classification 'Top Secret and Personal' is rather unusual — suggesting a higher degree of confidentiality than Top Secret alone. For example, no other paper in that file has that classification. It may have been the classification imposed by Clark; and it is customary for the recipient to use the same classification as the originator. In which case it is surprisng (and perhaps savours of a rebuke to Clark) that a memo addressed to Bond 'Personal' should be replied to by Bond's superior. Either way, it is bit odd for Little to be marking a memo as 'Personal' to Clark. This could be construed as deliberately to be witholding it from Clark's C.O., Sandford — which, I'm sure was not intended. I don't think Bond had authority to communicate with Central Bureau other than through Little or Little's Captain I(x). Hence there is nothing surprising in a memo to Bond being answered by Little (or by the I(x)).

In the symbol SRIC/P/393/44, the SRIC obviously stands for S.R.I.Clark; but the symbol seems too long for a mere typing code. The 44, no doubt stands for the year. It is probably the P/393 that is the suject category of the file; but the Index to Central Bureau's registration subjects has doubtless been destroyed.

In military communications it is sometimes difficult to distinguish between the simple future tense (e.g. 'It will rain to-morrow') and the imperative (e.g. 'This correspondence will cease forthwith'). In this memo the 'will not' could be either. If the former, Clark had asked Bond not to send him such traffic in future and Little's reply amounts to WILCO. If the latter, Clark had been sending Bond such traffic and Little is instructing him to desist. I think the former is the more likely. If it were the latter, I think the instruction would have come from Sandford after discussion between Little and Sandford.

On the related question, whether any ASW Section other than our dedicated 52 Section was ever put on watch over diplomatic circuits, the answer is affirmative. In the same file, a memo from A.D.M.I. to C.O., A.S.W.Group dated 2/3/45 thanks them for successfully covering Japanese diplomatic traffic on the Far Eastern (R75) low-power network during the preceding month when 52 Section because of atmospheric and local conditions was unable to do so. The memo continues that 'a similar arrangement regarding station RTZ [i.e. Kuibyshev] was employed early last year with considerable success'. (Interception of Japanese diplomatic traffic on the Kuibyshev-Tokyo and Berlin-Tokyo circuits was more succesful in Australia than at G.C.& C.S and its other out-stations).

Yours sincerely,

David S.

(D.C.S.Sissons)

P.S. Recently I wrote to Ralph Thomson asking if, as their former O.C., he could explain to me the techniques whereby 52 Section found the stations transmitting Japanese diplomatic traffic, watched them, and isolated that from the mass of other encoded traffic transmitted by them. I received a prompt and courteous lettter from his wife to the effect that he had died a year ago.

Annex 15. David Sissons to Kenneth McKay, 9 November 2004

22 Savige St
Campbell
A.C.T., 2612
<d.sissons@tpg.com.au>

9 November 2004

Mr K L McKay

Dear Ken,

Another request for help and guidance. Once again please pardon my importunity.

Mr Hibi's Request

At the suggestion of the Military Attaché, Mr Hibi eventually approached me. I was able to give him some help, but unfortunately was not able to produce the items he sought—sound recordings of Japanese news broadcasts on the day of the Emperor's surrender announcement.

Mr Hibi was under the reasonable misapprehension that the monitoring of Japanese civil transmissions was one of the tasks allotted to our cryptographic organisations. In fact it was the task of the Short-Wave Division of the Department of External Affairs. Their monitors had an office somewhere in the city—in Temple Court, I think—with landlines to their receiving station at Ballan. Mr Graves and his successor Mr Whittall were part of that organisation. You may remember that their secretary, Mary Stewart, used to come over to our eyrie for afternoon tea. On the day of the Surrender she brought us a copy of the English translation of the Emperor's broadcast, which Whittall's organisation had monitored.

For Mr Hibi I was able to locate the hard-copy transcriptions of the broadcasts that were monitored. It was, however, the recording disks/cylinders that he required. Unfortunately, these appear to have been destroyed.

GEAM

Since I wrote to you in May I have devoted a good deal of time and effort to the History; but I have to report that, alas, I have made little progress. Please cast your eye over the updated version of *The Breaking of GEAM I* (**Enclosure A**) and you will see why. (That document, of course, is merely my thoughts to date and bears little resemblance to what will be the final text).

Essentially the thesis that emerges in *The Breaking of GEAM I* is that, according to his cables to TANTRUM:

(i) Trendall on August 9th had since August 5th sent London about thirteen keys (some of which we now know to be wrong) but had established no 'good' bigrams (although he had noted some frequently occurring short concatenations — of row length or less);

(ii) On August 10th he received the Hanoi to GEAM statistical list that gave him the bigrams for comma (UF) and the ten numerals;

(iii) He remembered that UF represented comma in LA also and analysed his accumulated GEAM traffic on the hypothesis that some other bigrams represented the same plaintext in both LA and GEAM. He was in luck; for this was the case for 48 out of the 60 kana syllables and for an additional 30 syllables and 4 punctuation marks.

(iv) Thus armed, he was able within twenty-four hours to establish, by anagramming, the correct column order and to establish the bigrams common to LA and GEAM and the values of another nine bigrams where GEAM and LA differed (including the bigrams for the very common syllables *wa* (UR), *no* (GO), *o* (BO) and *to* (FO).

Underlying my thesis are the following considerations:

(i) In all the examples of columnar transposition that I have seen — namely Sinkov, Friedman, ADFGX and FUJI (**Enclosure B**) — solution of the column order has depended on prior identification of 'good' bigrams and/or the presence of some short columns among the long (and in GEAM I there are no short columns).

(ii) GEAM's code is cunningly devised to prevent this — e.g. GI represents *ni* but IG represents *nin*; AC/CA which represent *kan* and *ki* respectively appear more frequently than GO/OG which represent *no* (the most common kana syllable) and *Begin English* respectively.

2

My problem is that my thesis is inconsistent with the account given by Eric in his *Report*:

> It merely remained to put these groups together on repeats. This part of the job did actually present a few stumbling-blocks, as the presence of a row-order was not at first suspected and we were unfortunate enough to have constructed all the repeats backwards. The code-breakers were therefore somewhat baffled when these texts were presented to them—although it was later found that the main difficulty was the fact that the early messages were encoded from an English text. The first guide to the real solution was given by the incomplete blocks in which an incomplete line of five letters appeared at the end of the line instead of at the beginning. Thus we saw that we had our keys backwards; this was remedied and then long repeats were found going from one line to another, the second line not necessarily being the next in order. From then on the breaking of the code and row order was a relatively simple matter and the complete code and cypher system were known within a fortnight.

Eric's account is of unassailable authority—he was a very gifted and experienced cryptanalyst, he was present at the time, and in 1946 when he wrote the *Report* the comprehensive and well organised records of every message received and decrypted were still intact and at his disposal. The *Report* suggests that, before the first code group was known, Trendall had established column orders, in several keys, that were in each case correct except that they were in reverse. We know that this was not done by the usual method of anagramming on the basis of known 'good' bigrams. Perhaps the clue lies in the sentence: 'We were unfortunate enough to have constructed all the repeats backwards'. Perhaps these 'repeats' are the single-row concatenations enumerated in Trendall's August 10th cable? In the absence of any known bigrams did he attempt to anagram on the basis of these? But how can this be done unless the code values of these bigrams were known? Was this not doomed from the outset—as evidenced by the fact that in most of these repeats he got it wrong way about? But here I must be mistaken; for Trendall and Eric, of all people, were highly skilled and understood completely what they were doing.

The basic question, I suppose, is how is it that Trendall managed without identifying a single bigram, to produce solutions for a dozen keys in which he was fairly confident.

It appeared to me that in the absence of any identified bigrams the only technique available to Trendall was Friedman's 'Solution of Messages Containing the Same Long Plaintext Phrase'. I accordingly, as an exercise, tried to apply this technique to a couple of GEAM messages that I concocted (**Enclosure C**). But as you can see, this proved to be a task beyond my ability.

It was foolish and presumptuous of me to imagine that, totally devoid of mathematical aptitude or cryptographic experience, I could reconstruct Trendall's solution.

I hate to impose on you yet again; but I'd be greatly indebted to you if you would cast your eye over what I have written and, with your experience with transpositions, perhaps put me back on the rails.

THE BIBULOUS SIG

Over the years, I've tried to find some documentation for the case of our bibulous Sig, who over a cup of tea in the Cathedral recreation hut palled up with a young rookie, explained the GEAM system to him and urged him to contact Col Little for a job in the outfit — which the rookie promptly did. It was Ian Smith who told me the story:

> His name was Cpl Budge, a heavily built man, with a fleshy pock-marked face, sallow complexion. He got sozzled one day (late 44 or early 45) in a city bar and began narrating to all and sundry details of our operation... He was arrested, never to be seen again... I saw him again in the early fifties on an Essendon tram (I.H.S. to D.C.S.S. 18/9/90)I

If he were court-martialled, his name would appear in the comprehensive alphabetical index to court-martials available at the Australian Archives. If the case was disposed of summarily by his CO (or if, instead, he was merely posted elsewhere) this would be noted in **Routine Orders Part II** of his unit. But to search these records I need to know the Sig's name. I think that Ian may have got it wrong. A couple of years ago the Department of Veterans Affairs published on the internet their roll of AMF personnel who served in World War II. I have worked through all the Budges in it and there are none in the Aust Corps of Sigs whose postings fit our chap. I remember, however, that one of the AWAS who operated our cipher machines was named Budge; and the Veterans Affairs roll confirms this (W45806, Sgt BUDGE Helen Lindsay, b. 5/8/23, 1 Aust Cipher Sect, disch. 13/3/46). The odds against two people with the rather uncommon name, Budge, serving in the same small unit must be fairly high. I wonder if Ian may have got the names mixed up. Do you happen to remember the chap's surname and Christian name?

4

Annex 15

ARTEMIS

I wonder how ARTEMIS came to be chosen as the Section's cable address. I doubt that Bletchley or Cable & Wireless Ltd dealt it out at random from some previously prepared list. It has nothing in common with the cable addresses of kindred organisations e.g. MOUSETRAP, TANTRUM, AMBITION, etc. Was it chosen by some wag in M.I. with a classical background who saw Trendall as the virgin huntress and the rest of you as his attendant nymphs? Or did Trendall himself choose it in some play on words obvious to any classicist but not to me? Trendall appears to have enjoyed jesting with cable addresses — Treweek told me that he once despatched the following signal to Kilindini (whose cable address was AMBITION): 'Your proposed solution indicates grievous lack of serendipity. Ambition should be made of sterner stuff'.

Once again, my apologies for burdening you with these requests.

Yours sincerely,

(D.C.S.Sissons)

Annex 16. Notes on the Breaking of GEAM Using the 'Winds – Set-Up' Message

David Sissons

Greater East Asia Ministry (GEAM) was introduced on 21 July 1943. The *Report on Japanese Diplomatic Cyphers* describes it as follows:

> It was a transposition cypher with a bigram and tetragram code, the bigrams being consonant-vowel or vowel-consonant and the tetragrams made up of a double consonant and a bigram. All letters of the alphabet were used and Y was regarded as both consonant and vowel. The code was patterned after the manner of LA. Messages were transposed in blocks of ten by ten without blanks. There were 26 indicators each providing a column and a row order, the row order containing only nine figures as the bottom row of the cage was composed of dummies, namely the first letter of the indicator repeated ten times. The 26 keys were designated by the letters A through Z and each key was indicated by its letter and the following letter of the alphabet in the form ABABA. The indicator was located at the head of the cypher text.

In the race to break GEAM, Trendall had his solution completed by August 12th, beating his rivals from both London and Washington. From the account given in the report, and from the box-copies of Trendall's daily cables to London for that period (which miraculously survived among the office files of the Captain I(x) at Victoria Barracks), it is possible to piece together how he did it.

As the cyphertext of only one of the many thousands of messages intercepted by 52 Special Wireless Section has found its way to the National Archives of Australia (NAA), and that was encyphered in BA not GEAM, I have for the purposes of illustration selected a typical Japanese Foreign Ministry message[1] and encoded it using the copy of GEAM's code and encyphering instructions for GEAM Mark 1 that are held by the US National Archives.[2]

---

1 Circular 2353 of 11 November 1941, the famous 'Winds – Set-up' message, reproduced in D. Kahn, 'Pearl Harbor and the Inadequacy of Cryptanalysis', *Cryptologia*, October 1991, at pp 288–92.
2 US National Archives, Record Group 457, Box1328, File 190/37/34/3, 'US/UK Technical Exchanges and Information on Solution of JBB' (19 pp).

Breaking Japanese Diplomatic Codes

Specimen Message — Encoded

Kanchō fugō atsukai.
AC YK HU LY WA UF

Kokusai jōkyō no hippaku no kekka itsu saiaku no jitai ni
TU YU YH YC GO HI FU QA CU GO SU CA BI FU YU BA CU GO MI WY GI

tachiitaru ka mo hakararezaru tokoro kakaru baai waga hō to aite koku no
FA FI BI FA KU CA JO HA CA KA KE MA KU UQ CA CA KU PA TA ZZLO FO TA FE TU GO

tsūshin wa tadachi ni teishi serarubeki o motte waga hō no gaikō kankei kiken ni hinsuru
IR ID UR XXOH AW DI DE KA KU PE CI VVQI ZZLO GO RRAD AC ZI CI EC GI IH DU KU

baai ni wa waga kaigai hōsō no kakuchi muke nihongo news no chūkan oyobi saigo
PA TA GI UR UR LA YA VI HY DY GO ZA FI JU CE GI OH LO YQ DU GO YJ AC YE YU LO

ni oite tenki yohō to shite (1) Nichibei kankei no baai ni wa "higashi no kaze ame"
VVEL EF KI RO HY ZZBI CCVY WI UW AC ZI GO PA TA GI UR IN HI LA DI GO CA ME BA JE

(2) Nichiso kankei no baai ni wa "kita no kaze kumori" (3) Nichiei
UN CCWE WI DO AC ZI GO PA TA GI UR IN RI FA GO CA ME CU JO KI UN CCWY WI XA

kankei no baai (tai shinchū mare Netherlands East Indies kōryaku o fukumu) "nishi no
AC ZI GO PA TA NI WY ID YJ JA OT AK IB CY YX BO IZ JU NU IN GI DI GO UN BO

kaze hare" o 2 do zutsu kurikaeshi hōsō seshimeru koto to seru o motte
CA ME HA KE UN BO VU NO MU FU CU KI CA BE DI HY DY WWKU KU CO FO DE KU VVQI

migi ni yori angō shorui to tekitō shobun aritashi. Nao migi wa gen ni gokuhi
IW VVIK KI AB LY SO KU BI FO FE CI FY SO UP BA KI FA DI UK UX IW UR EL GI RREN

atsukai to seraretashi.
WA YA FO WWIK FA DI UK

In this example the Japanese cypher clerk would have selected the appropriate encyphering key (in this case FGFGE) and proceeded to enter the encoded text into a series of transposition blocks of 10 cells x 10 cells dimensions, row by row, in the row-order prescribed by the key FGFGE (which is: 1 2 3 4 5 9 8 7 6)

On completion, the first block would look like this:

6	W	Y	G	I	F	A	F	I	B	I
7	F	A	K	U	C	A	J	O	H	A
8	C	A	K	A	K	E	M	A	K	U
9	U	Q	C	A	C	A	K	U	P	A
5	Y	U	B	A	C	U	G	O	M	I
4	G	O	S	U	C	A	B	I	F	U
3	G	O	H	I	F	U	Q	A	C	U
2	U	F	T	U	Y	U	Y	H	Y	C
1	A	C	Y	K	H	U	L	Y	W	A
	F	F	F	F	F	F	F	F	F	F

He would then write out the message for transmission, column by column, in the column order prescribed by the key FGFGE (which is: 10 2 6 9 7 4 3 1 5 8).

176

Annex 16

Thus it would appear on his message pad, and on the message of the Australian telegraphist receiving it, as follows:

[Originator, Addressee, Number, Date, each encoded]   FGFGF

IOAUO	IAHYF	YAAQU	OOFCF	FJMKG	BQYLF	AAEAU	AUUUF	BHKPM	FCYWF
GKKCB	SHTYF	FCKCC	CFYHF	IAUAI	UUCAF	IUAAA	UIUKF	WFCUY	GGUAF
IURYO	EWROF	RCAAV	EREAF	ZDUHL	PAIFF	CHIIZ	UHOOF	CKUDG	CDITF
AGTYQ	KXTZF	AIGVZ	KOGLF	IURYO	IIDAF	DIAAI	AXUZF	REPLV	DUFTF
CIIEI	FEQUF	YONAO	OOIOF	AGDJB	EYYJF	WAAAZ	LCOIF	ZUGUC	KYDCF
WPHMH	VYOZF	UTLBZ	EALFF	IRONC	IUUEF	IAIEY	VJHAF	VGICR	LGGGF
AJYUI	OAAOF	CITON	ARICF	PYCNW	JFTDF	ODBUY	UIAIF	TJYIX	KGGAF
ZWAIC	MIGWF	GIIJW	CRPWF	AAXNA	IOICF	IYKZC	ENOEF	ANOBU	CUZCF
UKUYU	EUENF	OIBOY	UOAIF	KIKFK	BMKUF	EVOIW	AOAOF	VKBSK	DFUBF
FILFD	KVMDF	DVSCW	CNHGF	VIIOU	IUNOF	OWYEY	IUEIF	CQAFH	CBCGF
RAAXA	FKIOX	PFUWF	XFFWN	KXIFE	YDUDF	URWXB	FIEIX	KFLAI	KIFXR
WXAFU	GFXUF								

Trendall's technique of solution was the application of a sequence of processes, the first of which is is described in the report as follows

> A frequency count of a few messages showed that consonants and vowels were used in almost equal numbers. As we already had an example of a vowel-consonant, consonant-vowel code (LA), the theory was straightway suggested that GEAM was such a code transposed. The regular occurrence of the dummy letter at intervals of ten gave the probable length of the lines as ten. Moreover, as the dummies appeared at shorter intervals at the end of a message (when the final transposition form was incomplete) and these final dummies always began after a multiple of 100 letters, it was obvious that the size of the block was ten by ten.

Applying this technique to our specimen message, an examination of the incoming message for periodicity reveals the Indicator (FGFGE) followed by the cryptogram in which the letter F appears at intervals of ten up to the 500th letter and thereafter at intervals of six. The latter suggests that the encoded message has been encyphered by transposing it in blocks of ten cells x ten cells until the concluding block (in which the columns are only six cells, instead of ten cells, high). If so, Block 1 consists of ten columns, each ten cells high, which for convenience we may identify by the letters a to j, thus:

a	b	c	d	e	f	g	h	i	j
I	Y	F	A	B	G	F	I	I	W
O	A	J	A	H	K	C	A	U	F
A	A	M	E	K	K	K	U	A	C
U	Q	K	A	P	C	C	A	A	U
O	U	G	U	M	B	C	I	A	Y
I	O	B	A	F	S	C	U	U	G
A	O	Q	U	C	H	F	U	I	G
H	F	Y	U	Y	T	Y	C	U	U
Y	C	L	U	W	Y	H	A	K	A
F	F	F	F	F	F	F	F	F	F

a	b	c	d	e	f	g	h	i	j
I	Y	F	A	B	G	F	I	I	W
O	A	J	A	H	K	C	A	U	F
A	A	M	E	K	K	K	U	A	C
U	Q	K	A	P	C	C	A	A	U
O	U	G	U	M	B	C	I	A	Y
I	O	B	A	F	S	C	U	U	G
A	O	Q	U	C	H	F	U	I	G
H	F	Y	U	Y	T	Y	C	U	U
Y	C	L	U	W	Y	H	A	K	A
F	F	F	F	F	F	F	F	F	F

The next task is to arrange these columns in their correct sequence. If in the GEAM code the bigrams were restricted to vowel followed by consonant and consonant followed by vowel it may be possible to fit the columns into their correct pairs on that basis. This Trendall proceeded to do. Let us apply this technique to our example, omitting of course, the terminal F dummies. Take Column *a* and put it beside each of the other columns in turn to see whether in any case it produces only bigrams of this restricted pattern. The result is that it will not pair with either Column *b* (that would produce adjoining vowels OA AU OU IO AO and adjoining vowels HF), Column *d* (adjoining vowels IA OA AA UA OU IA AU), Column *f* (adjoining consonants HT), Column *h* (adjoining vowels II OA AU UA IU AU, and adjoining consonants HC), Column *i* (adjoining vowels II OU AA UA OA IU AI), or Column *j* (adjoining vowels UU). It pairs, however, with Columns *c*, *e*, or *g*.

Continue this process with each column in turn. Column *b* pairs with Column *j*. Column *c* pairs with Column *a*. Column *d* pairs with Column *g*. Column *e* pairs with Column *h*. Column *f* pairs with Column *i*. Thus we have all five pairs:

Annex 16

ac		ca		bj		jb		dg		gd		eh		he		fi		if
IF		FI		YW		WY		AF		FA		BI		IB		GI		IG
OJ		JO		AF		FA		AC		CA		HA		AH		KU		UK
AM		MA		AC		CA		EK		KE		KU		UK		KA		AK
UK	or	KU	or	QU	or	UQ	or	AC	or	CA	or	PA	or	AP	or	CA	or	AC
OG		GO		UY		YU		UC		CU		MI		IM		BA		AB
IB		BI		OG		GO		AC		CA		FU		UF		SU		US
AQ		QA		OG		GO		UF		FU		CU		UC		HI		IH
HY		YH		FU		UF		UY		YU		YC		CY		TU		UT
YL		LY		CA		CA		UH		HU		WA		AW		YK		KY
		3 1				*10 2*				*7 4*				*5 8*				*6 9*

From here, the report continues:

> It merely remained to put these groups together on repeats. This part of the job did actually present a few stumbling-blocks, as the presence of a row-order was not at first suspected and we were unfortunate enough to have constructed all the repeats backwards. The code-breakers were therefore somewhat baffled when these texts were presented to them— although it was later found that the main difficulty was the fact that the early messages were encoded from an English text. The first guide to the real solution was given by the incomplete blocks in which an incomplete line of five letters appeared at the end of the line instead of at the beginning. Thus we saw that we had our keys backwards; this was remedied and then long repeats were found going from one line to another, the second line not necessarily being the next in order. From then on the breaking of the code and row order was a relatively simple matter and the complete code and cypher system were known within a fortnight.

The next task is to discover which five of these ten possible bigram columns are the correct ones and their correct sequence. (The answer is indicated by the italicized figures that we have inserted beneath the bigram columns above). How on earth Trendall managed to do this beats me.

Where a cryptogram is merely the plaintext transposed, the sequence of the columns can be be established by anagramming, taking advantage of the characteristics and idiosyncracies of the mother tongue in which it is sent. A good example of this method is the solution of the

following English language cryptogram of a military report:[3]

---

3   L. D. Callimahos & W. F. Friedman, *Military Cryptanalysis,* part 2, vol. 2 (Aegean Park Press reprint, 1985), p.p. 418–20.

Breaking Japanese Diplomatic Codes

1	2	3	4	5	6	7	8	9	10	11	12	13	14	15	16	17
N	R	E	O	U	N	M	P	L	E	T	C	A	O	N	Y	E
E	T	T	H	U	E	E	J	H	R	S	E	U	T	N	D	R
T	S	D	O	F	R	D	A	O	U	D	H	R	S	C	Y	E
E	S	R	E	I	O	S	O	E	V	D	N	A	S	G	R	S
F	T	H	E	R	T	H	E	P	A	S	T	E	O	E	R	T
L	F	X	A	R	C	A	G	M	A	O	L	E	S	M	N	H
T	M	S	D	R	F	R	E	W	I	E	H	N	Y	E	E	I
D	D	W	U	R	I	T	W	A	N	O	F	O	S	T	O	N
S	C	H	O	S	E	C	N	W	A	A	L	T	T	T	O	R

We note the J in column 8. In English, J is always followed only by a vowel, usually U. In this row columns 5 and 13 have a U. Let us provisionally postulate the latter and pair columns 8 and 13. In English the bigram JU must be followed by a consonant, usually N or S. These letters are present in columns 15 and 11. We now juxtapose columns 15 and 11 in turn against our 8–13 pair. This provides the alternatives

```
8   13   15          3   13   11
P    A    N          P    A    T
J    U    N          J    U    S
A    R    C          A    R    D
O    A    G          O    A    D
E    E    E          E    E    S
G    E    M          G    E    O
E    N    E          E    N    E
W    O    T          W    O    O
N    T    T          N    T    A
```

The English-language trigrams formed by columns 8–13–11 look more like plaintext trigrams than do those formed by columns 8–13–15. From here, the anagramming progresses rapidly, by expanding the trigrams into the words that have begun to manifest themselves, such as PATROL, JUST, ROAD, etc. The complete plaintext together transposition key emerges as below.

Annex 16

E	N	E	M	Y	P	A	T	R	O	L	E	N	C	O	U	N
T	E	R	E	D	J	U	S	T	T	H	R	E	E	H	U	N
D	R	E	D	Y	A	R	D	S	S	O	U	T	H	O	F	C
R	O	S	S	R	O	A	D	S	S	E	V	E	N	E	I	G
H	T	T	H	R	E	E	S	T	O	P	A	F	T	E	R	E
X	C	H	A	N	G	E	O	F	S	M	A	L	L	A	R	M
S	F	I	R	E	E	N	E	M	Y	W	I	T	H	D	R	E
W	I	N	T	O	W	O	O	D	S	A	N	D	F	U	R	T
H	E	R	C	O	N	T	A	C	T	W	A	S	L	O	S	T

It was just in order to prevent anagramming of this nature that in the GEAM sytem the plaintext is *encoded* before transpositon. How is anagramming to be conducted when all one knows about the code is that it consists of vowel-consonant and consonant-vowel bigrams and tetragrams each representing a *kana* syllable or common word or phrase?

Trendall must have gone about identifying the code groups of particular syllables by the frequency of their appearance. Let us attempt to apply this method to our specimen message. Here the report's list of the most commonly appearing syllables in the Japanese language is of assistance: *no, ni, wa, o, shi, mo, to*. These six, presumably, are listed in their order of frequency in a large collection of diplomatic messages. In a message of 833 syllables that I selected from the *Pearl Harbor Hearings*,[4] the number of times each of these appeared was as follows: *no* 37, *ni* 15, *wa* 20, *o* 28, *shi* 12, *mo* 8, *to* 16.

The report says: 'It merely remained to put these groups together on repeats'. Which are 'these groups'? What is here meant by a 'repeat'? Does it mean the reappearance of a commonly occurring sequence of bigrams (e.g. VVSY AS ** LY VVDY = 'Reference my telegram No.**'). If so, it would not appear to be a technique applicable at this stage; for we do not yet know a single code group, or in which row the message starts. I'm afraid I've no alternative but to seek your [i.e., Kenneth McKay] assistance.

GEAM was introduced on July 21st. By a rare stroke of luck a complete file of your *outward* signals to London from August 5th (until the following April) has survived. Perhaps these cast some light on how it was done?

On August 5th and succeeding days you sent London the column order for about 5 keys each day.

---

4   United States Congress (79th Congress), Joint Committee on the Investigation of the Pearl Harbor Attack, *Pearl Harbor Attack; Hearings*, part 37, p. 988, Ambassador, Washington to Consul-General Honolulu N. 384 of 27 November 1941.

The following are some of your signals. I have inserted in square brackets the actual values taken from the code charts in Appendix L.

August 10th

Following bigram sequences have been established as frequent in more than one key: (a) BO [o] DI [shi] often preceded by KI [ri] or KU [ru]; (b) CU [ku] MU [zu] FU [tsu]; (c) FA [ta] KE [re] often preceded by CI [ki] and followed by UR [wa] BI [i]; (d) FO [to] CO [ko] KU [ru] (two of this group ususally occur in very close proximity; (e) FU [tsu] MI [ji]; (f) JO [mo] KU [ru] often preceded by GO [no] or FO [to] and followed by DU [su]; (g) KU [ru] DU [su] often preceded by JO [mo] RY [yu] and/or folllowed by FO [to] or CU [ku]; (h) KU (ru] GA [na] often preceded by LA [ga] and/or followed by AS [dai]; (i) TI [1] AS [dai]; (j) BO [o] KU [ru]; (k) KU [ru] MA [za] BE [e].

My comment is that, except for the fact that all of these are back-to-front, many of them make sense; for example, in (b) tsuzuku is a common word in such messages, meaning 'to continue'; in (k) ezaru is the negative potential inflexion meaning 'cannot'.

August 11th

1. GEAM cypher is based on bigram table similar in general arrangement to LA with which many groups are identical. Individual sentences are read backwards but present evidence suggests that successive sentences, as separated by full stops UF, should be taken forwrards.

2. Following groups are different from LA: SA zero, TI 1, VU 2, WE 3, XO 4, AR 5, IS 6, UT 7, EV 8, OW 9, UR wa, BO o, CO ko, DO so, FO to, GO no, LO go, RY yō, YE oyobi, CA kan, VI gai, ZASS kiden [your telegram], SYVV ōden [my telegram], DYVV ni kanshi, FUQQ aritashi.

3. LA Spelling Table is used apparently with OG and QU.

My comments are that these values are correct except for 'end spelling', which should be YY not QU, and for the tetragrams, which are back-to-front and should read SSZA, VVSY, VVDY, and QQFU.

August 12th

1. Further research shows that instruction to read backwards by sentences is incorrect and following should be substituted. Keep message in originl blocks consisting of 9 rows of 5 bigrams each. On keys so far supplied, each of these lines should be read backwards, but order of reading horizontal rows inside block varies according to key, which

Annex 16

accordingly consists of two sets of figures, one for vertical columns and one for horizontal rows. Rows so far established are: ABABA 1 to 9 in serial order; XYXYX and FGFGF 6 7 8 9 5 4 3 2 1; OPOPO and QRQRQ 4 3 2 1 5 6 7 8 9. Blocks are read successively in natural order downwards.

2. In order to avoid nuisance of reading backwards we shall in future transpose column order in pairs. Thus ASASA column order will be 5 2 8 6 4 9 1 10 7 3 instead of present 7 3 1 10 4 9 8 6 5 2. Same bigrams will then read naturally forwards, but tetragrams will appear with double consonants first, thus VVFY instead of FYVV and we shall in future quote them in this form.

3. LA bigrams in series BA to PA, BI to PI, BU to PU, BY to PY, UB to UP, EB to EP, and OB to OP seem to remain unchanged. . .

In each of the days that followed you sent London large packets of bigrams and tetragrams that you had established.

From the above it would appear that: (i) You had the whole game completely sewn up by August 12th; (ii) You had worked out how to establish column orders by August 5th without knowing any code groups; (iii) Without knowing row orders you were, by August 10th, working out indicative frequent bigram strings merely on the basis of individual rows of 5-bigrams length and from this you were able confidently to establish the correct values of some bigrams and tetragrams by that date; (iv) Armed with this information you were then able to establish row orders. Have I got this right?

Annex 17. David Sissons to Kenneth McKay, 28 November 2004

22 SAVIGE ST
CAMPBELL
A.C.T., 2612
<d.sissons@tpg.com.au>

28 November 2004

Mr K.L.McKay

Dear Ken,

Many thanks for your very prompt and effective response of November 18th and November 23rd to my request for assistance. It is very kind of you to help me in this way. I am very much in your debt.

Please excuse my delay in replying. Because of my ignorance of such techniques it has taken me several attempts to absorb your suggestions.

You may remember in 1945 my passing around John Buchan's short story *The Loathly Opposite*. It purports to be the tale told by the Director-General of G.C.&C.S. when it was his turn to address the dining club of V.I.Ps of which he was a member. It was Buchan at his most dramatic and the characters were writ large. Some of the dialogue promoted considerable merriment among you and your colleagues. Here are a few typical pieces.

> 'I had besides a metallurgical chemist, a golf champion, a leader-writer, a popular dramatist, several actuaries, and an East-end curate. None of them thought of anything but his job, and at the end of the war, when some ass proposed to make them OBEs, there was a very fair imitation of a riot...

> 'Once you have written out the letters of a message numerals there are many means by which you can lock it and double-lock it. The two main devices, as you know, are transposition and substitution, and there is no limit to the ways one or other or both can be used.... By way of an extra complication,

too, the message, when decyphered, may turn out to be itself in a difficult code. *I can tell you our job wasn't exactly a rest cure'*.

Burminster cried out like one in pain 'It can't be done. Don't tell me that any human brain could solve such an acrostic'.

'It was frequently done'...

'*Give me the trenches*' said Burminster in a hollow voice. '*Give me the trenches any day*'...

'We called this particular cypher 'PY', and we hated it poisonously. *We felt like pygmies battering at the base of a high stone tower'*.

For the next few days, whenever confronted with a troublesome passage, Ron or Eric would come out with one or other of the exclamations italicised above.

I'm afraid that, devoid of both experience and aptitude, I feel very like one of the aforementioned pygmies. So, please continue to be patient with me in your explanations

UK versus KU

In the third paragraph of your letter of November 18th you write: 'From my UK/KU example you could guess that if b-j is right then h-e is to be preferred to e-h, or vice versa'. Could you spell out the logic of this in more detail for me, please. If KU in j-b and not UK in b-j is right, why is it then more likely that e-h and not h-e is right. In fact in each of these cases KU=*ru* is correct. But why does this follow? In the whole message KU/UK occurs 11 times — on seven of these occasions it is KU=*ru*, on the other four occasions it is UK=*comma/period*; but until the code-values are known, had the cryptanalyst any grounds for suspecting a preponderance of KU over UK?

You return to this problem in the 3rd-last paragraph of your letter of November 23rd — in the context of all seven blocks of our specimen message. In the whole message GO/OG appears 11 times, of which GO=*no* accounts for 7 and OG=*begin English* for only 4; but I can't see what grounds the cryptanalyst would have for considering OG the more likely.

2

Annex 17

Sinkov's Chaining

I'm much encouraged by your suggestion that Sinkov's chaining technique may be the answer to our problem. (Incidentally, why is it that in Sinkov's example he can chain all 8 columns in a single operation but in our's we arrive back at 1 after only 1-4-9-2-8?). You suggest that chaining may limit us to only two possibilities — 10-2 6-9 7-4 3-1 5-8 or its exact reverse 8-5 1-3 4-7 9-6 2-10. This is exciting; for it seems to be exactly the situation that Trendall had reached — he was, before he knew any code values, providing keys correct in every particular except that they were reversed. I'd be most grateful for any subsequent thoughts you may have on this.

Budge

I think I may be able to reduce my search for bibulous Budge in the Dept of Veterans Affairs roll to manageable proportions if I can narrow down his age group. In the 'pep talk' that Ron gave me on my arrival, he described him as 'an older man who is unlikely to last long in jungle conditions'. Can you narrow that down a bit further — e.g ten years older than yourself? Twenty years older than yourself? In my day there were two or three Sigs, who used to alternate. The one who was there most days was Cpl Power (who participated in our *sezumba* conspiracy at Ian's expense). According to the Veterans roll Power was born on 28/11/07 and served with 4 Aust Special Wrls Coy in Greece and Crete in 1941. Hence he would have been 37 in 1944. Do you remember Budge as the older of the two. One of Power's reliefs that I remember (Finlay?) was much older — he told me that he was a telegraphist on *H.M.A.S. Sydney* when she engaged the *Emden*. (I suspect that Finlay had a gambling or a drinking problem; for at our first meeting he tried to borrow money off me).

The Emperor's Codes

I found this one of the best books on the subject. The author makes very enterprising use of extensive British documentation until very recently withheld from public access. It provides chapter and verse for the decision in late 1942 to disband Nave's organization. Apparently it was a decision taken at the highest level (in which Bletchley participated) and not, as Archer believed, unilateral action by Cdr Fabian and his American superiors.

Once again, many thanks for your expert and patient assistance. it seems to me that you have solved the thorny problem. My hearty congratulations.

Best wishes,

(D.C.S.Sissons)

Annex 18. David Sissons to Kenneth McKay, 19 December 2004

22 SAVIGE ST
CAMPBELL
A.C.T., 2612
<d.sissons@tpg.com.au>

19 December 2004

Mr K.L.McKay

Dear Ken,

Many thanks for your very helpful letter of December 2nd in response to my queries of November 28th.

I'm not sure that I fully understand your explanation of how far the cryptanalyist could establish the correct sequence within each bigram pair from the occurrences of OG/GO bigrams throughout the whole *Takasago Maru* message.

It seems to me that all he could say is that they are probably a mixture of a frequently occurring code-group and another less common group. Suppose he arbitrarily opted for one throughout, settling on GO. This would provide him, in the page of alternatives attached to your letter of November 21st, the following pairings: in Block 1 j-b, in Block 3 c-a, in Block 4 g-d and either f-i or i-f (alerting him to the fact that in this message both code-groups GO and OG are present), and in Block 5 h-e. In the case of j-b, c-a, and g-d he would have been correct; in the case of h-e would have been wrong. Thus, because GO represents *no* (the possessive suffix and the adjectival suffix), one of the most commonly occurring syllables in the Japanese language, and because OG, 'English spell' is a rarely occurring group, he would have achieved a limited success, securing the correct sequence in three out of five of the bigram pairs. But is this limited success of any use to him? Can he make use of it as a first step towards the correct pairing of the other two bigram columns?

In the hope that another long message might help, I encoded in GEAM using the same key (FGFGF) the famous *'Winds' Code Set-Up* message of 18 Nov 1941 (Attached). My hopes, however, were disappointed. I'm afraid that I can get nothing out of it.

One interesting thing, however, emerged. Unlike the *Takasago Maru* message, this *'Winds'* message does not contain the code-group OG (=Spell English). Furthermore, it appears to me likely that only a small proportion of messages would contain 'Spell English'. Therefore, if the cryptanalyst had believed that the GEAM code contained only the one code-group GO/OG, he would on the basis of the *Winds* message have paired all five of the bigram columns correctly; for as luck would have it GO is present in each of the five. Trendall, however, was aware that the Japanese diplomatic code vocabulary was so large that every bigram <u>and its reverse</u> had to exist as code-values. Similarly he had no means of knowing that of the two possibilities, GO and OG, one was relatively little used. It is therefore to me inconceivable that Trendall would have resorted to such a dangerous procedure to solve the pairing problem.

In the blocks I have underlined some long repeats. These, however, did not show up on the message-pad. I don't know whether they can be of any help towards a solution.

And so it looks as if I must, at last, admit defeat and throw in the towel. You went to a great deal of trouble to help me. I do apologise for wasting your time.

Many thanks for your great help.

With very best wishes to you and yours for a Merry Christmas and a Happy 2005,

Yours sincerely

(D.C.S.Sissons)

Encl: 1

www.ingramcontent.com/pod-product-compliance
Lightning Source LLC
Chambersburg PA
CBHW061138230426
43662CB00023B/2462